Collected Richert Papers

The Justice Letters

Volume II

Written by

William Richert

ALSO BY WILLIAM RICHERT:

Collected Richert Papers: The Movie Stories – Memory Snapshots Letters

Collected Richert Papers - The Justice Letters, Vol I.

Collected Richert Papers: The River Phoenix Letters

A Night in the Life of Jimmy Reardon Screenplay

Executive Privilege (with Mike Watt)

THE JUSTICE LETTERS, VOL II, written by William Richert.

ISBN: 978-1-951036-52-2

Contents

Foreword

There is no coincidence that William Richert wrote, directed, acted in and produced his own independent feature film version of *The Man In The Iron Mask—The Face of Dumas*. Respect, honesty, honor, courage, the pursuit of justice.

These are just some of the many virtues of character of The Three Musketeers. William Richert possessed these virtues in abundance, which enabled and emboldened him to act always to defend justice. Bill lived his deep understanding and commitment to the reality that we are all one, equal and eternal. His thoughts and actions originated from a deep wellspring of truth and respect and the simple demand for fairness. This rare philosophy and these unwavering qualities led to many conflicts with the ignorant, greedy and shortsighted.

"While there is suffering, is there time to spare?"
The Phillipe,
The Man In The Iron Mask - The Face of Dumas

These are the words that Bill put into the mouth of the Good twin king in his independent feature film *The Man In The Iron Mask—The Face of Dumas*, words he wrote for his friend River Phoenix to say. This philosophy reflects Bills urgency that justice must be served immediately and justice delayed is intolerable!

Bill was a courageous defender of the good from a very early age. Bill was a natural protector of his siblings beginning in childhood as the oldest of 4 children in a family that moved around the country frequently because of his father's work in the government. As he grew up every year he would find himself at a new school with a new batch of bullies to contend with. Far more challenging were the occasions when the four children did time at Catholic orphanages. One such orphanage was run by Italian nuns that did not speak English and believed the Earth was the center of the universe.

Worse things happened at these orphanages, and Bill was always protecting his sibling in these horrid institutions. Bill said that he felt "lucky" that he and his siblings had parents because he witnessed boys who did not have parents that would just "disappear." In stark contrast to these horrific Catholic orphanages at one time Bill was interred at an orphanage on an Indian Reservation in Anadarko, Oklahoma, where he lived with the Indians. He remembers the Indian children for their kindness, respect and peacefulness.

Bill was not just some loud, angry guy—difficult and contrary—as some of his opponents might try to claim in their weak, disrespectful defense of their wrongdoing. What is true is that Bill embodied an enormous stage presence, was extraordinarily charismatic, and possessed a powerful, commanding rich voice the volume of which always had to rise above the horrible hissing, ringing curse of tinnitus, an injury incurred by gunshots during the filming of *My Own Private Idaho*.

There is a distinct difference between the anger of enmity, wrath, sullenness —which will get you hell-and the righteous anger that releases the powerful force of good to fight injustice. Bill felt it a solemn duty, a responsibility, to act to abolish injustice in its many forms of fraud, treachery, theft, bullies, liars, cowards, phonies, the cruel and the like.

Bill's many courageous battles against injustice emerged from a unique combination of qualities of Bill's character. Bill was enormously talented and produced many scripts and ideas of great value. Bill possessed the amazing quality and diligent choice to maintain trust. These two qualities of character in combination with his steadfast commitment to justice and truth led to many conflicts in his lifetime.

Two of the biggest thefts and betrayals occurred in the middle of Bill's life during the upwardly successful trajectory of his movie making career. One was the theft by the Writers Guild of America of the "Written By" credit for Bill's script *The President Elopes* AKA T*he American President*, and it's enormously lucrative and popular spin-off The West Wing, AKA The Executive Wing. The other devastatingly tragic theft in Bill's life-and in the life of innumerable others-was the theft of the LIFE of River Phoenix and the outrageous injustice of the uninvestigated cause of River's DEATH!

Bill dedicated his remaining years of life to getting truth and justice for these two tremendous injustices. There are two separate volume of *Collected Richert Papers* dedicated to these two events; *CRP - The Presidents Daughters* and *The President Elopes Letters* and *CRP - The River Phoenix Letters.*" Additionally, the excellent book by Mike Watt, *Executive Privilege*, painstakingly reveals through letters, contracts and annotated documents, how step by step, the Writers Guild of America and accomplices stole Bills "written by" credit and gave the writing credit to the lying crack addict plagiarist Aaron Sorkin, and then how the Writers Guild of America Blacklisted Bill, effectively ending his filmmaking career in the Hollywood film industry.

In *Collected Richert Papers—The Justice Letters: Volume I and II* are just some of the many, many letters Bill wrote for the good, truth and justice. Even with the blacklisting by the WGA in 1995 Bill continued to produce valuable scripts and products.

Collected Richert Papers—The Justice Letters: Volume I contains the chapter about Bill's experienced insights regarding the Writers Guild of America, Directors Guild of America, Screen Actors Guild, Hollywood Unions Strikes. The second chapter involves the destruction of Bill artist vision when his novel, "*Aren't You Even Gonna Kiss Me Goodbye?,*was made into the feature film *A Night In The Life Of Jimmy Reardon* by greedy, talentless Hollywood executives.

Collected Richert Papers—The Justice Letters—Volume II contains the chapters regarding the theft of William Richert's independent feature film *The Man In The Iron Mask—The Face of Dumas* by an unscrupulous, despicable foreign sales distributor and the chapter concerning the attempted theft of Bill's invention INCOGNITO: THE ORIGINAL SOY COFFEE ALTERNATIVE by a stupid and greedy chiropractor.

In the chapter called "Sampler" are selected letters from the aforementioned *Collected Richert Papers* concerning River Phoenix and *The President Elopes.* For the collection of letters Bill wrote with his lightening fast, razor-sharp often scathing wit delivered with precision and attention to the onslaught of daily events, please read *Collected Richert Papers—The Political, Religious, Reply Letters*, Chapter IV "Reply."

The biggest, high profile battle that Bill was involved with is the class action lawsuit Richert VS. Writers Guild of America in which Bill was the Class Action Champion for all American writers, union and non-union alike. This lawsuit involves monies generated by the sales of U.S. movies overseas, collected by the major Hollywood Studios and the Writers Guild of America (and the Directors Guild of America and Screen Actors Guild too!) in secret for decades which is owed to the writers and filmmakers. Bill represented the writers and filmmakers for over sixteen years to demand enforcement of the settlement and never sold out to the Hollywood Unions or the Major Studios. The magnitude and courage of this heroic effort is revealed in "*Collected Richert Papers—The Richert VS.* WGA *Letters, Volume I* and *II* containing hundreds of letters to Judges, lawyers, the class, the press, contracts, and annotated documents. A few select letters will be included in the Sampler chapter. The lawsuit remains unenforced and is looking for a lawyer to represent the class.

William's silent, sacred, solemn oath, his deep conviction to doing good, grew stronger and more impassioned over the years even as the deceptions and corruption of injustice continued. Bill never stop his noble and heroic efforts for truth and justice, especially for his friend River Phoenix. Sadly, many did not receive the justice they deserved in their lifetime. The publication of Bill's letters is a continuation of Bill's quest for truth and justice.

What Would I Fight For?

I am not sure I would always fight for my life.
Life might not be worth fighting for.

I am not sure I would always fight for my wife. A
wife isn't always worth fighting for.

Nor my children, nor my country, nor my fellow-
men. It all depends whether I found them worth
fighting for.

The only thing men invariably fight for is their
money. But I doubt if I'd fight for mine, anyhow,
not to shed a lot of blood over it.

Yet one thing I do fight for, tooth and nail, all the time. And that is my
bit of inward peace,
where I am at one with myself.

- D. H. Lawrence

Justice is having and doing what is one's own.

- Plato

If fighting for one's own inward peace and for having and doing what is ones own, then Bill was victorious and received justice daily and eternally by living his earthly life always on the right side of goodness and living everyday on the truthful side of history.

Crucial to his eternal success in justice was his remarkable capacity-even through the most painful, unhappy events-to maintain his diligent choice and generosity of spirit to forgive.

"Looking out from eyes clouded by deep sorrow and pain of loss it is almost impossible to see the truth of things through the fog of despair. So perhaps it is better to wait a while to look at certain people and places until the hurt clears and better vision is restored. You can always forgive yourself for trusting the wrong people. Your trust itself must be preserved and honored. It is trust alone that builds the hope that keeps us going when no other person is around. We got to be careful not to break our own hearts."

—William Richert

Bill did not leave this earth bitter or resentful because of the injustices he endured, fought against and, in many cases, saw unresolved. Rather Bill departed peacefully and gracefully with his truthful integrity and loving, forgiving heart and soul intact, holding eternally dear trust and hope. Bill would inspire his friends and fellow humans through encouraging each to take heart by, every day in some small way, making "energetic progress in the good!" Bill's greater vision and his magnanimous warrior spirit guided him through this life and delivered him love unto death and beyond.

— Gretchen Richert 2026

Collected Richert Papers

The Justice Letters

Volume II

I. The Man In The Iron Mask/ The Face Of Dumas
VS
Hannibal/ Rionda Del Castro

The
Face of
Dumas
The Man In The Iron Mask

NEGRO HERITAGE OF ALEXANDER DUMAS EXPLORED IN NEW FEATURE FILM

AUTHOR OF 'THE THREE MUSKETEERS' REVEALS SLAVE ANCESTRY IN NEW ADVENTURE DRAMA

"THE MASK OF ALEXANDER DUMAS" TELLS THE STORY BEHIND THE STORY OF THE MAN IN THE IRON MASK

HOLLYWOOD, CALIFORNIA

CONTACT: The Indivisible Studio
310.394.7308
FAX 310.394.6028

FOR IMMEDIATE RELEASE

The black heritage of Alexander Dumas may have been the hidden basis for his masterpiece "The Man in The Iron Mask" and other novels, according to a new film by William Richert.

Dumas, creator of the first great literary "franchise" with his tales of swashbuckling musketeers, was known to his 19th Century generation as a duelist, a womanizer, and spendthrift as well as a hit playwright and the author of more than 1,200 plays, books and travelogues, including "The Three Musketeers," the source of countless versions and imitations.

He was also the grandson of a black West Indian slave and a French General, and it is thought that his racial background may account for his comparative lack of official prizes and honors in his lifetime.

While his contemporary Victor Hugo and others won numerous awards, Dumas' French colleagues mainly regarded him as an entertainer and showman, even though George Bernard Shaw called him "the Shakespeare of France."

"THE MASK OF ALEXANDER DUMAS" is a romantic account of the night Alexander Dumas goes bankrupt while finishing his manuscript about

The Three Musketeers last adventure, the rescue of the legendary Man In The Iron Mask.

As he recounts the famous tale, Dumas reveals to his mistress that he is the grandson of a Haitian Slave, and he describes the mask he wears in Parisian society as being akin to the mask worn by the imprisoned brother of King Louis XIV.

"A Night In The Life of Alexander Dumas" stars (in alphabetical order) Edward Albert, Dana Barron, Timothy Bottoms, Fannie Brett, Meg Foster, James Gammon, Dennis Hayden, Nicholas Richert, William Richert and Rex Ryon.

William Richert ("My Own Private Idaho, The Client") plays Alexander Dumas. He also wrote and directed the film.

Best known for his beloved series of books about "The Three Musketeers," and "The Count Of Monte Cristo" Dumas' most powerful creations were stories of powerful men who were locked away or locked out from society.

"His novels about a man locked away in an Iron Mask and the imprisoned Count of Monte Cristo, two dramatic examples of the wronged and isolated, offer clues to Dumas own character," asserts William Richert.

"Our movie draws a parallel between the story of the man in the iron mask and Alexander [Alexandre] Dumas own relationship with the white Parisian society of his time," says Richert.

"In fact, this movie grew out of my work on an independent new version of THE MAN IN THE IRON MASK. As I was editing and re-cutting that movie, I began to be haunted by a feeling there was something missing in the story. Over time, I realized that it was the author who was missing.

"Once, when I was re-reading the Voltaire references to the famous man in the velvet mask, looking for clues to the actual existence of such a character, I heard a voice in my head which said: 'But you are missing the point, Monsieur!' It was the ghost of Dumas, or so I remain convinced.

"That's when I suddenly realized that Dumas might have worn a mask of his own in French society. Politically exiled, Dumas was certainly no friend to the King. Among his fellow writers and playwrights, he suffered a kind of ridicule laced with innuendo about his 'character' – a character shaped by the ancestry of slaves."

"THE MASK OF ALEXANDER DUMAS" grew from this new insight as a film showing Dumas own life and character as a counterpoint to the myth of a twin brother to Louis XIV, a brother who is locked in a dungeon as a boy, then rescued and brought to the throne of France by those famous fighters, The Three Musketeers.

"THE MASK OF ALEXANDER DUMAS" features Robert Littman, Roger Callard, Bridgid Brannaugh, Louis "Reeko" Meserole, Jeremy West, Russell Gannon, William Hayden, Jerry Trimble, Rick Smith, Joe Garcia and Paul Monte.

Costumes were designed by Academy Award nominee Salvador Perez, Production Designer is Jacques Hebert and William Barber is Director of Photography. Additional Photography by Jeff Greene. Larry D. Webster and Gloria Pryor are co-producers. Executive producers are Dennis Hayden and Mark Terry. William Richert wrote the screenplay, produced and directed. He is also writer-director of such cult favorites as "Winter Kills," "American Success Company" and "A Night in the Life of Jimmy Reardon."

Production was filmed in Panavision at Universal Studios, the Paramount Ranch and the fabled Mission Inn in Riverside, Calfornia. Color is by Deluxe.

CONTACT:
The Indivisible Studio
310 394 7308 Fax 310 394 6028

THE INVISIBLE STUDIO & F.C.B. FILM CORPORATION
16027 Ventura Boulevard, Suite 420
Encino, California 91436
Ph. 818 501 5743 Fax 818 783 9530

FOR IMMEDIATE RELEASE:

"THE FACE OF DUMAS" UNMASKED IN NEW FILM

The eccentric life and loves of legendary author Alexandre Dumas are given a new twist in writer-director William Richert's fictional cinematic memoir, "The Face of Dumas."

The original tale takes place in Paris, 1843, on the night Dumas completes his masterpiece, "The Man in the Iron Mask."

"It is a film about a writer and his characters, who on the creative level are inseparable," says William Richert, who plays Dumas with the same abandon as he portrayed his critically-acclaimed Falstaff character in Gus Van Sant's "My Own Private Idaho."

Dumas' fictional mistress is played by Fanny Brett, one of the young discoveries in James Cameron's "Titanic."

"The Face of Dumas," a story-within-a-story, also stars Timothy Bottoms, Edward Albert, Dana Barron, Meg Foster, and James Gammon. The Three Musketeers are played by Dennis Hayden as D'Artagnan, Rex Ryon as Porthos and William Richert in a dual role as Dumas/Aramis. The Man in the Mask and the young Louis XIV are played by newcomer Nick Richert.

"In the film we are witness to the bittersweet romance between the aging Dumas and the youthful Sylvie, and can see the source of the fictional General Athos' love for the fictional Valliere, who are characters in the book Dumas is writing."

Alexandre Dumas is rarely mentioned in the pantheon of great black writers, partly because he was of mixed race, partly because he wrote to the predominantly white audience of its time – mainly the readers in France and England, where he was hailed by George Bernard Shaw as the Shakespeare of France – and partly because, like the Russian poet Puskin, he himself seldom made an issue of his heritage. Instead he was famous for his drinking, carousing, dueling, womanizing, and fantastic literary output, even keeping a stable of other writers to flesh out his fabulous and multitudinous plots.

Richert's unique approach to his material evolved over a period of several years, when he directed short scenes from various drafts of his screenplay in order to raise money. These efforts led to financial turmoil in his own life which duplicated some of the hardships Dumas faced. Instead of forcing him to abandon his goal, these difficulties instead led him closer to the subject of his work – the author himself.

"In writing this story about the parallels between Dumas' real and imagined universe, I've used the same methods Dumas himself used when he re-wrote Voltaire's original 16th Century story of a man in a velvet mask which Voltaire wrote to satirize the tyrants of his time.

"In a way, this is a movie about the writing of books," says screenwriter Richert, who began his career as a novelist with the literary success of "Aren't You Even Gonna Kiss Me Good-by," which he filmed in 1987 as "A Night In The Life Of Jimmy Reardon," starring River Phoenix, Matthew Perry and Ione Skye.

"Dumas made up his stories about the musketeers the way I made up this story about Dumas – tales partly true, partly imagined, but thoroughly heroic in nature. Alexandre Dumas wrote about a pattern for living as a way of warning his materialistic countrymen about the folly of greed. These lessons can be heard also in modern times, and in the most modern mediums of communication," says Richert.

"This is information on a grand scale, a kind of fictional biography in a long tradition."

"When Alexandre Dumas reveals his slave ancestry to the alluring Sylvie, at the same time he is world famous as the "King of Paris," it becomes a metaphor for the very act of creation itself, which is always a union of the invisible and the known, a joining of opposites – like the film's fictional pairing of Alexandre and Sylvie.

"The Face of Dumas" offers filmgoers a completely original new version of the daring last exploits of the Three Musketeers, as well as their intimate love stories. This provides a modernistic insight into Dumas, his culture, and his reasons for choosing heroic tales.

The story-within-a-story of "The Face of Dumas" is equally the story of the making of a movie within a movie.

Parts of the film were originally shown as a variation of "The Man in the Iron Mask."

When the filmmakers ran out of money, they cut together footage already shot into a version of "The Man in the Iron Mask" but without the central character of Dumas. The vastly different movie was sold to several foreign territories, and the money raised was used to make the new film.

"To sell a movie to make a movie is an unusual way to finance a picture," notes Richert.

"But when the average cost of a studio picture is eighty million dollars and rising, with few corporate studios inclined to take chances on controversial subjects, individual producers must find new ways to make their art.

"We devised a method whereby all the participants – from the actors and crew to post-production houses and labs – could contribute to elimininate the stranglehold of giant budgets, which force many moviemakers underground or out of the business altogether. We saved fifty million or more in production costs, which means that someday we may actually show a profit."

Executive Producers are Dennis Hayden, Louis Meserole and Jean Marc Felio. Co-producers are Gloria Pryor and H. Roy Matlen. Donald Slemp is Associate Producer. Cinematography is by William Barber and Jeff Greene. Casting by Aaron Griffith. Original Score is by Jeffrey R. Gund and Jim Ervin. Editor is Andre Villancourt. Costumes were designed by Sal Perez, Jacques Hebert is Production Designer.

Fastest Cheapest Best Film Corporation

LAST MUSKETEERS

FOUQUETS

UNMASKED

DR GUILLOTINE

THE IDIOT

QUEEN ANNE

.5 Matilija Ave,
Sherman Oaks,CA
91423-2918
Phone (818) 501 5. .
Fax (818)783 9530

PHILIPPE'S WEDDING

Aramis Athos D'Artagnan Porthos

Colbert and Williams

Starring
(In alphabetical order)

Edward Albert	James Gammon
R.G. Armstrong	Dennis Hayden
Dana Barron	Robert Littman
Timothy Bottoms	William Richert
Meg Foster	Nick Richert
	Rex Ryon

Philippe

"Funny and touching!"
"An eccentric romp through Dumas' most beloved classic. Director Richert (*Winter Kills, A Night In The Life Of Jimmy Reardon*) and his superb ensemble cast weave a 90's spell over the fifties - the 1650's!" --Robert C. Hardwick, *Sonoma Film Festival Viewer*

"A handsome production!... Edward Albert and Meg Foster are excellent... hearkens back to the... children's adventures Disney used to [produce.]" --Chris Garcia, *Santa Rosa Press Democrat*

Turnkey Commandant

DEATH OF ATHOS

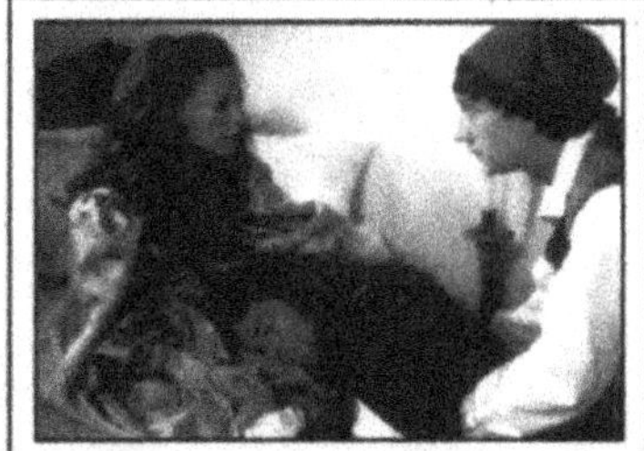

MOLLY LOUIS HENRIETTE

ABOUT THIS FILMMAKER'S COLLECTION OF LETTERS TO A FOREIGN SALES AGENT

As of this writing, it has been almost five years since I entered into a distribution agreement with a man named Richard Rionda Dell Castro. The whole idea behind the agreement was that he help with post production of THE MAN IN THE IRON MASK INDEPENDENT VERSION, and, when it was finished, he would sell foreign territories. Since then, Del Castro has built a one hundred millon dollar empire, while my movie has been shown around the world. Yet our company film remains unfinished, and neither I or my backers has received has gotten money from these sales.

Instead, our dealings with this French foreign sales agent and his accomplices around the world have left us almost destitute, and almost despairing. It is only because of the force of the work on the film itself, and its insistence to be complete and to be seen, that we continue to look for justice in a world where there is very little.

That is the reason I am placing these letters in a book form. Once the dealings with Del Castro left us unable to hire a lawyer (who wants, without a fee, to represent an unfinished film with unknown foregin sales.) During this time, I used the only means I knew for redress, the written word.

If this collection of letters written in frustration and anger, or delusional relief, will not solve the problems with foreign distributors/sales agents, it will at least show a path not to take.

There is information in the following pages which, if nothing more, can offer independent producers a visual aid in conjuring the future of their movie's representation. This long stealing of our movie and our resources happened to us the way Hemmingway said people go bankrupt: gradually, then suddenly. Readers will see the hope in the early contracts, then the fall, and then the fight back.

Although we have found ourselves today in the stance of an unwilling victim of a sociopathic thief, we do not think one has to live in the shit forever.

One can always write a book.

William Richert
Santa Monica, California
October, 2002

LETTER TO A PRODUCER IN SPAIN FROM A U.S. DIRECTOR/PRODUCER

I AM preparing a lengthy deposition on this matter, but the short answer to your question is: Hannibal Pictures and Richard Rionda Del Castro broke every contractual and verbal commitment to me and my film, caused irreparable harm to me and my actors and investors, sold country after country without my approval or consent as stated in our contract, paid out up to ten thousand dollars per "presentation" at film markets totaling tens out thousands of dollars, but accounting for none of it except a poster with photos of actors who are not even in our film. Richard Rionda Del Castro got control of the film rights by promising to fund a loan of $190,000 from the Imperial Bank of California to shoot some much needed additional scenes. But after I signed off various rights, and after Rionda disappeared to France (where later we discovered he was in jail), and only after all my rights were in escrow to the Imperial Bank was I told by Richard's production manager that no filming whatsoever was allowed from the loan, that it would violate the completion bond; and so we needed to use our own funds to film the completion in order for the German company Hermes to accept the film – otherwise the bank the completion bond company would have taken all rights and – in the end – Richard would have owned the movie completely. (I wonder how many banks/distributors acquire ownership of films in this manner.) In spite of everything, and using our own money, we managed to finish the movie, Hermes approved, and then we discovered Richard was selling the world rights my film THE MAN IN THE IRON MASK when he only had rights to the later version, THE FACE OF DUMAS. We have received dozens of email from fans who saw our film in Spain, but all refer to THE MAN IN THE IRON MASK, which Hannibal has no rights to sell. We have no idea which version is selling in your country. This year we were informed that Richard sold four South American countries for $125 US each, less than the cost of the digital elements. All my business dealings with Richard Del Castro began with the need to add additional scenes and a final mix to my picture. In 1999 Richard promised almost two hundred thousand for finishing costs to be backed by a German sale to Hermesfilm of Munich. When the full amount of the promised money did not appear, I renegotiated my deal with Hannibal to state that no sale would be made without my permission, that all expenses verified, etc., and that my unfinished movie called THE MAN IN THE IRON MASK would not be sold anywhere. But you can see what happened to that promise in the long-delayed accounting Hannibal provided which is on my website, www. Williamrichert.com, which shows that Richard was charging upwards of $10,000 US against my film, claiming he was screening it at various markets, when he was not; claiming he had made new posters etc., when he did not; and using the wrong title, which he agreed not to do by contract. In short, Enron-style bogus accounting was used through and through; even worse, while I was struggling with my partners to finish the final version of our film, he openly continued to sell territories with contracts he refused to allow me to approve. How could he be so bold and brazen? Once Richard realized that I had maxed out all my funds, that my investors had withdrawn from the project because they couldn't believe my promises any longer that foreign sales funds would be forthcoming; when Richard discovered my wife's credit has been ruined and with his knowledge that he could scuttle any new deals I might possibly make with a threat of lawsuit, Richard began to gloat about his abilities. This spring he told me he had made three sales of my film at the AFM, and was going to receive the short-form contracts at this year's CANNES. However, he explained, he wouldn't tell me about these sales because of my "attitude." Another time he confessed he'd used some of his sales money to pay off a famous agent under the table for his client, and even sent me a copy of the star's contract as proof of the good use he'd made of funds which ought to have been spent on the final 35mm print of the theatrical movie I was continuing to make, borrowing equipment and editing facilities and pleading for time at CGI computers. I do not need to relate to you, whatever level of achievement you have attained in your career, that trying to finance an unfinished film, when all production funds have been exhausted, is difficult at best. It is made impossible by the likes of Richard, who uses his small piece of control as a cudgel to intimidate, defraud, manipulate and depress anyone who cares truly about his work. This activity is only possible when one has no conscience. Without conscience, it is in fact quite easy to convince others – especially filmmakers – that you are acting in the best interest of the project. Richard's greatest misdeeds come from injury to the hopes of others. After signing the loan at IMPERIAL BANK LHO in California, Richard gave me a check to start production in the amount of $11,800. I immediately paid my production debts etc., and then the check bounced. That was the second time one of his large checks bounced, and I had to explain to my associates the almost inexplicable – but now I must hurry to conclude this first response to your question. Excuse me, I wanted to be brief but I have much to say on this issue, since it is clear to me that Richard doesn't act alone, that he sets up his "sales" at AFM and CANNES and MIFED and that these places must be notified they are abetting the likes of this man and his operations. I am presently writing a long and extremely detailed account of my relationship with Richard Rionda/Heaven Cinema/ Geronimo Pictures/Hannibal Pictures as part of a complaint in the Southern California United States District Court where I am preparing to file civil charges along with Racketeering charges, including RICCO. In addition, I will be putting up on my website every single piece of paper and correspondence with Richard and his associates. Under the Lantham Act, I intend to regain the original copyright granted under Hannibal's Loan, for, after getting me into the deal with a check he bounced, he included clauses making me an "employee." This was another of his mistakes. We will also review all contracts made by Hannibal when Hannibal was in breach of contract. These companies got rights to our film through illegal deals, or what the Latham Act describes as "fraud at inception."

IN CONCLUSION: Thanks for your inquiry. Though we are complete strangers, I wish nobody the events which have befallen me and those I care about since dealing with Richard Rionda Del Castro. I am hoping that my description of these months and years of frustration will save others in the future. I will be posting more on the website in the coming weeks and months. One day all of this information can become part of research into what really goes on inside those giant film-sales emporiums held around the world, which, for all the rightful profits the producer sees, might as well be floating crap houses. We need more investigations like the one being conducted by the FBI in Los Angeles on behalf of the U.S. and Intermedia, involving Elie Samaha's FRANCHISE PICTURES and banking officials. I am hoping we can participate in the process of this ongoing case. When the foreign sales game gets this kind of scrutiny around the world, there may come a day when producers will actually see the profits they are entitled to. This will mean a new source of films, since independents won't be forced out of business waiting for the checks which are never in the mail. In the meantime, Richard Rionda Del Castro and Hannibal Pictures have four or five major indie films in production – Richard laughed at me in our last conversation, saying he had "17 million in the bank, what can you do?!"– well, one suggestion being studied very closely is that my enterprise and investors should participate in those budgets and those credits, since we surely helped provide the seed money. Eh? One more thing: we don't know which version of our film is being sold in Spain, only that the company on the VHS cover we obtained is called "American Films." Any idea if there are scenes with Alexander Dumas himself in this film? (I play the character, as I was the only actor we could afford under the circumstances described above.) It would be of interest to know what they are selling in Spain of my work, information which Richard has denied us. The original deal with Spain was listed as Negro y Azul, but we have not been supplied other information, except that Hannibal is now producing with this company.

Soon there will be copies of all documents, scanned into the computer, onto the website, so future producers and investors will know what to look out for.

-- All Cheers and best of luck, William Richert, Producer, Writer, Director, Actor 'THE FACE OF DUMAS'

Ps: as they said in the last frames of INVASION OF THE BODY SNATCHERS: "Warn your friends!"

Hannibal Pictures

FCB FILM ENTERPRISES

September 13, 2002

TO: D B Esq.
1901 Avenue of the Stars
Suite
Los Angeles, California 90067

FR: William Richert
FCB Film Enterprises
1423 Euclid Street Suite 2
Santa Monica, California 90404
310.394.4641

Dear Mr. B

Enclosed you will find the first entries into our campaign to remove Richard Rionda Del Castro, CEO, and Patricia Rionda Del Castro, CFO, of Hannibal Pictures Inc., a California Corporation, from their ability to harm filmmakers and their investors.

We are contacting all distributors/agents/companies who engaged in fraudulent conveyance with Mr. Del Castro, and we once again ask you to return immediately the money illegally paid to you by Hannibal Pictures and which is listed on the Hannibal "registry."

As his chief legal advisor and business partner, I suggest you advise your client/partner to pay the 75% of the several million U.S. dollars his company has received in undeclared fees and commissions relative to the sale of THE FACE OF DUMAS/THE MAN IN THE IRON MASK and the other projects he has funded with our money, which he is currently using to produce motion pictures with Negro y Azul starring actors provided by J at ICM and others.

It seems to me it is time to look after your own reputation and ability to continue to practice law in the State of California.

It is time to come clean with the complete accounting of the loan granted to Hannibal Pictures and FCB Films, from LHO, a division of the Imperial Bank now under investigation by the United States Government.

It is time to come clean with the hidden contracts Rionda made with distributors around the world, which Rionda has admitted to me.

We hope that within the next 30 days you will be asked these questions by the L.A. Times and the New York Times and Premiere Magazine.

Tell Rionda: " 'fess up and pay, and get out of the film business."

Sincerely,

William Richert
Copyright owner, THE FACE OF DUMAS/THE MAN IN THE IRON MASK

DAVID: This tells most of story. Written to D B

Hannibal's lawyer

1.) ***A FILMMAKER CALLS A DISTRIBUTOR'S LAWYER A DISGRACE AND A PARTY TO FRAUD; SAYS RICHARD RIONDA DEL CASTRO AND HIS WIFE AND THEIR COMPANY HANNIBAL PICTURES OUGHT TO BE FOREVER BARRED FROM THE ENTERTAINMENT BUSINESS; CALLS THE PAIR 'PORTRAITS IN GREED'***

2.) **TO: D B Esq.**
3.) **FR: William Richert**

September 23, 2002

RE: Your specious Letter of September 18, and your attempt to silence and intimidate a writer/director.

RE: A continuing pattern of racketeering activity; of embezzlement, deceit and lies; of predatory practices and false accounting, possibly involving major banking institutions and bonding companies. Surely involving the $100,000,000 distribution entity now known as Hannibal Pictures, Inc.
4.)
5.) Dear Mr. B

As part of the therapy I have imposed on myself for the four years of my film has been held hostage at the hands of a sociopathic French citizen named Rionda, I am responding briefly to your letter of September 18, in which you pretend to forget all that has happened during the unfortunate time I have been involved with the lies and machinations of Richard Rionda Del Castro and – since his marriage – the blatant false and fraudulent accounting of his wife and CFO, Patricia Rionda Del Castro.

As I don't want the spore of your malignant note to linger in its waste long enough to ferment or forment any further mendacity in or from your mind, or the greed-addled brains of CEO Richard Rionda and his CFO wife Patricia, or the innocent others – perhaps a few at ICM – who might look to you for solace or comfort -- who are the true reason you wrote your little piece of pettifogging prose – I hastily pen this quick reply:

6.) You say in your letter of September 18 that someplace in time I actually agreed to Hannibal's undisclosed contracts for my film, and agreed to the tiny amounts he claims he was selling it for. Like selling four South American countries for $125 each? {As if anybody ever sold a feature film to a nation for the price of dinner} Shame on you! I have been held hostage and my film has been, in effect, kidnapped

since what were virtually the first dealings I had with Rionda, back when his company was called Geronimo and he was in business with the head of an insurance company called Liberty Mutual [owner's name to be supplied.] Yes I renegotiated the Dec. 5, 1999 agreement with Hannibal – but only because he never honored any part of it. And only because the only way I could find out what Rionda had sold and to whom was to stay somehow in business with him. Rionda and his associates – including you yourself – are guilty of what I understand is called "fraud at inception." Was I a willing victim and participant in this fraud? No, I continued in business with Rionda because it was the only way to save 7 years of work – a period which has grown to ten years. I had several pretty good reasons to make a new 2000 contract with Rionda -- as the U.S. had reasons not to depose Saddam in 1991 – [though now that all is questioned] and part of those reasons included Rionda promising one more time to honestly account for sales, promising $380,000 from France and $480,000 from Italy OR MORE. And this came when I and my fellow producers had spent all, exhausted all in money and energy, and were in dire need of finishing funds. So, in 200, when Rionda sent $10,000 in two payments over Christmas to prove he had changed, we believed him. In a sense, we had no choice. We had no way of really knowing what Rionda had done with our film, and I thought that to give him one more chance, we could find out, and perhaps press on. But then Richard Rionda Del Castro started back on his old ways. You say I myself drafted the 2000 contract; that's true, I drafted it. And then within a few months, Hannibal broke it just like he broke the earlier contract. Two years passed, it is only recently that I have gotten some kind of accounting showing sales I never authorized or even knew about. But no money was sent with these new sales and accountings. Again and again, I have asked Rionda to cease any sales until our film was finished and a theatrical print was struck. In August 2001 my investors and I wrote letters telling Hannibal they were in breach of contract, and to cease and desist from any sales. This year Hannibal informed me of three sales at AFM, but refused to say to whom, and what they were. On February 15 of this year we received a copy of a contract for $10,000 to Mr. Willem Prui of a company called SOURCE INVESTMENTS B.V. THE CONTRACT WAS SIGNED ON MAY 13, 2001. HANNIBAL SENT IT TO US ONE YEAR AFTER IT WAS SIGNED. Our company never got any actual register of sales and disbursements from Hannibal until this year, on February 7, 2002. It is clear that the accounting is a registry of venal and gratuitous theft. We have spent long years not knowing which countries had purchased our film – at a time when were receiving thousands of email fan letters from viewers throughout the world. During this period we were unable to function, as we had no way of knowing exactly who held rights to our picture. Even the underlying copyright to our film was held hostage by Rionda. Although the LEWIS HORWITZ ORGANIZATION of the Imperial Bank returned the copyright to our film on March 11, 1999, Richard Rionda Del Castro denied having received any such document until he finally sent us a copy of the report in 2002 – almost three years later. At almost every turn we have prevented from proceeding with our work by the anti-competitive business practices, sharp negotiating tactics, unethical and creative accounting and predatory practices of Hannibal Pictures, all of which have had adverse impact on our film, our investors, and other profit participants.

7.) MORE OF WHAT YOU ALREADY KNOW BY HEART – THOUGH, CAN IT BE? – YOU LIVE WITHOUT A HEART:

8.) TO VIGOROUSLY DISPUTE YOUR LAWYERLY ALLEGATIONS: Hannibal has not honored a single clause of the 2000 contract, as you state that he has over your licensed signature. No sales agreement was ever sent to FCB before signing, as the contract stipulated. No amount in excess of $1,000 was ever approved by FCB, as Rionda agreed in writing. No joint bank account was opened No 35mm print was ever struck. No money was spent on promotion or screenings of the film as promised. No accounting was provided until two years later, days before the 2002 AFM, and then only because I threatened Rionda and his wife by saying all the Musketeers would show up at the Santa Monica film market in full French Uniforms, and picket them and their booth. Evidence shows that none of the agreements Rionda purported to have made with foreign distributors – Rionda claims to be a "distributor" but distributes nothing but bogus and fraudulent contracts – has any merit or legal force, but are instead copyright violations and film pirating. I am presently contacting each and every one of the countries Rionda sold without telling me, and I will send them the "Musketeers Bad Contract Retribution Kit."

9.) AS Rionda's attorney, you will recall that I drew up a contract in 2000 after Hannibal breached all the agreements in the earlier contract, dated December, 1999. In the 2000 agreement I added the clause about no prosecution of earlier misfeasance or fraud or bank theft regarding Hannibal because Rionda said he didn't want to sign any new contract when I could sue him for telling us we were getting nearly $200,000 for finishing our film on a bank loan with Imperial Bank when instead he knew all along we would only receive $80,000. He was afraid I would charge him and Jean Marc Felio with embezzlement and maybe even involve David Hut[illegible] and others at Imperial Bank with investigations of all kinds of criminal acts. He knew that just after the loan had been granted, but filming not begun, I was informed that in actual fact, no filming was to be done at all with any of the money, even though the fundamental and overriding purpose – shall we say that the entire purpose of the loan was for post production, especially the filming of additional action and connecting scenes. I had Paul Winfield interested in playing the role of Alexander Dumas, and had assembled a production manager and budget for a five day shoot. This was not to be. After getting my signature on the loan agreement, Rionda fled the country. A producer named Jean Marc Felio arrived suddenly from Montreal, Canada, saying Rionda had hired him to oversee the payout of the bank loan, which was not to exceed $80,000. I protested that the loan was made for $195,000, and that Rionda and Hannibal had even said that they could provide additional funds by additional foreign sales if needed. I explained that the picture needed a noted actor like Paul Winfield, and that anyhow Dumas had been a descendent of African slaves. But Jean Marc Felio, hired by the completion bond company from Canada, said there was no money whatsoever for additional filming, and that if the completion bond company discovered that any filming was taking place, they would "seize the picture." This was a phrase used many times when again and I again I attempted to press for more money from the loan which my movie had actually funded. The loan, after all, was based entirely on the German sale of the film. The result of this was that instead of Paul Winfield, I had to play the part myself because no other SAG actor could be

hired without notifying the Guild that filming was taking place, thereby triggering a takeover of all our work and efforts by the bonding company. As a great favor, one of the actresses in the original unfinished version of the film agreed to work without additional credit or pay to help the movie. I had been working on this independent costume picture since 1992. It was made abundantly clear to me that our entire film would be lost forever in litigation -- Jean Marc Felio in fact *assured me the film would not ever be completed* – unless I found a way to shoot within the narrow confines of the new budget, which I discovered only one week before filming was scheduled. We had $120,000 less than Rionda had promised and the loan had promised, and we had only one third of the time to deliver the completed picture to Hermesfilm of Germany, who had guaranteed the loan by their purchase of the German rights. Thus I had to re-write my screenplay (the screenplay that Hannibal had based the loan upon and promised to shoot is available to be read by any jury.) Almost overnight, I had to re-write the part of Dumas for a white man to play. Luckily – in this very particular instance -- Alexandre Dumas was the grandson of an interracial couple. But this required a complete re-write of weeks of earlier work, a monumental new effort which required a round the clock effort of screenwriting, shooting and editing for a period of weeks instead of the months that we had been promised. All of this took a great toll on my health and my well being. Again and again, before he fled the country, Rionda had told my Malibu landlord, Barry McManus, about sales estimates in France and Italy and Spain which would bring in at least five or six hundred thousand dollars. In addition to being my landlord, Mr. McManus was an investor in the film. When the money never materialized, Mr. McManus had to put his house up for sale. I had to move out of my home, and sell my furniture to a cut rate company, antiques and heirlooms and all. I had already used up all my savings and acting/writing/directing residuals earlier. I was forced to declare bankruptcy. Even though Mr. McManus always knew “show business” was speculative, he had seen the early cuts of the movie and believed that foreign sales would pay back all his investment. He never thought Rionda would never pay a cent to the filmmakers or investors, or flee the U.S. It is clear to all that if I had not used my own limited funds, used up all my wife’s money and good credit, along with the help of friends for doing the work, our film would have been taken over by the bank and the completion bond company and by Richard Rionda. You remember all of this very well because you were Rionda’s lawyer. Miraculously I performed my duties to my film and finished on time to supply the contract with Hermesfilm of Germany. This entire loan was based on Rionda’s sale to Germany of $185,000.

10.) In 1998 When Rionda called me from Europe and said he had sold Germany, and was going to sell Italy and France and Spain for even more money when the film completed principal photography and post production, my investors and I were overjoyed. We were happier still when he said he would definitely exceed his original sales projections of $1,342,000. But once the contract for the loan was signed and my copyright in the hands of Lewis Horowitz Organization and the Imperial Bank, all of the sums in the loan were changed. Even as the loan was being made, Rionda gave me two checks totaling $25,000 – both of which bounced.

11.) TO RECAP: My Hobson’s choice was to file a civil lawsuit for fraud and switch-and-bait and coercion against Rionda, the bonding company and the Imperial

Bank – involving an incomplete production, which would remain incomplete until the lawsuit was settled – or finish the movie as best as possible under the circumstances, hoping the work would be acceptable to the German buyer, thereby keeping our film alive for a better day. Knowing the years of work at stake, and the care which dozens of artists and technicians had put into the project, including my own script and direction and acting, Rionda gambled that he could steal funds from the loan, disappear from the country, and still keep ownership in a project that the director and cast were determined to keep alive. It was a hard and miserable time for all concerned. We were like those folks you read about who lose homes to unscrupulous lenders, yet still keep making the payments. In spite of all, I renegotiated the early contract in 2000 with Rionda as you said, but only after Rionda made countless calls with apologies and protestations, saying he had been locked up and handcuffed by the INS, that he hadn't understood himself all the problems with Imperial Bank and the loan, that he had made upcoming sales in five or six countries, and that any moment was going to sell Italy and Spain. He said he was young, and had made mistakes. He said that Hermes of Germany was not going to release the movie under the title THE MAN IN THE IRON MASK, which was another early version that THE FACE OF DUMAS was intended to improve – it should be noted that this was a completely privately financed film up until Hannibal got the Imperial Bank involved, and it was an ongoing effort. When the funds were available, we made improvements in the picture. It is now 2002, and we have been moving scene by scene to complete a costume picture of the same kind that MGM spent $80,000,000 to make. We use our time instead of money. However, and sadly, because of Hannibal's repeated lies and half-truths, we have lost months and years on what should have been finished in 1999. Rionda has abused all our hopes and trust. It was my misfortune to enter what I thought would be a reformed agreement with him in 2000, after I had gone bankrupt still thinking somehow his promised would come true – after all, he had delivered on at least a part of his promises – and then he said he would prove his earnestness with an offer of $10,000 advance in good faith – which I used to continue working on the film. This $10,000 – he swore – was only a harbinger of an additional $600,000 in future sales. Within days of signing the 2000 document, Rionda was promising to send $20,000 from a sale to Brazil to help make a new answer print. I spoke to the lab and told them to prepare. My associates and I talked to marketers and public relations and distributors, believing that soon we would have the funds needed to finish and release our picture. Rionda called from markets saying he was showing the film and countries were interested. Then suddenly, he began telling me about the lull in the buying world. There were no sales he said. His calls stopped coming. It was not until months – even years later – that I began to receive an accounting of his sales. He never consulted me on any sale other than Germany, according to our contract, which stipulated clearly that I would have approval over each and every sale. Hannibal never opened the joint bank account Rionda swore and agreed to open. He never asked my approval of spending amounts more than $1,000 as provided by the January, 2000 contract. In short, he never intended to honor the contract at all. The evidence for that is that he did not honor it in any form at all, except for those small payments he made to keep us believing that perhaps, somehow, he would prove trustworthy; in fact, he left us with almost no other choice. He had promised in

writing that David Hut ˙ of the Lewis Horwitz Org. would provide us with complete and total accounting of every cent spent from the loan, so that I would see where all the money went. No such accounting arrived. He waited almost two years before sending me the Copyright return that Hutchins at Imperial Bank had given him in March, 2000. He only forwarded that document and the contract for a sale to Benelux when I told him I would make him famous by contacting VARIETY during the February 2002 AFM. Richard Rionda Del Castro and Hannibal Pictures have caused great distress and financial harm to a group of filmmakers whose only goal was to make a movie. Instead, he has used up our time and resources, sold our film at ridiculous prices – selling four South American countries for $125 each defies any explanation except payment under the table. With the exception of Germany, none of his contracts was enacted with our prior knowledge or approval. The February 7 he and his CFO, Patricia Rionda Del Castro, is a textbook example of fraudulent accounting. We were lied to by Rionda from the start. If I was fooled, this cannot mean that I must be fooled forever. It has taken me a long time to begin to understand the underlying "culture" of foreign sales, if you will. Even the pros can be misled when confronted by the complex morass of bank regulations, copyright laws, foreign sales advances and promises involved in overseas distribution. From what little I do know, Richard Rionda Del Castro ought to be put in jail for his illegal use of our movie to enrich himself and harm others. If I do not spend more of my efforts trying to get the FBI interested in this case – which I have done, only to be told the dollar amounts are not big enough – although that was before the Elie Samaha case – it is because I have been accomplishing digitally what the loan was to help do on film negative. I still have to free up the foreign market to promote the major distribution that a costume picture like ours requires. Rionda admits he destroys all our efforts by selling the movie as a made-for-tv film when the negative has been waiting all this time to be cut. If we have no theatrical print, how can we sell a theatrical picture? He has prevented our ability to function. His is a sin against free enterprise.

You say in your letter that I have previously been proved wrong in my accusations. Do you mean when I believed Rionda and Hermes of Germany that they were going to distribute the film with the correct title, THE FACE OF DUMAS? Are you joking? Hermes broke that promise for Rionda the minute he made it. It is only this year, after I wrote a letter to Hermes, that THE FACE OF DUMAS began to appear on the Internet Movie Data Base (Imdb.com). My offer to Rionda of criminal immunity or immunity to litigation was based on repeated promises that for once he would keep his word. Instead, he broke the contract at the first opportunity.

In the vernacular, there is a lot of bullshit going on between you and Rionda and Hannibal the LHO and the Imperial Bank and I just can't wait to get all of you in the good ole courthouse to discover/uncover the connections.

The settlement offer I made last week has not been accepted, and it is now withdrawn.

As soon as I finish my latest letter to Rionda and Mrs. Rionda and to the officers at Imperial Bank and that bonding company in Canada, along with the various buyers of my film Rionda claims in his recent "registry," I am going to pause in my "tirades" – as you call these heartfelt epistles -- and I am going to look for the right lawyer. Then, along with my fellow artists, I am going to sue Richard Rionda and Hannibal Pictures and we won't forget you, either.

You are going to the miss the generous and expansive tone of these letters. Unless, of course, you check out my website.

Sincerely,

William Richert
Bcc:

This is more info

William Richert

September 13, 2002

TO: J
INTERNATIONAL CREATIVE MANAGEMENT
8920 Wilshire Blvd.
Beverly Hills, California 90211

FR: Bill Richert
FCB FILM ENTERPRISES
1423 Euclid Street Suite 2
Santa Monica, Ca 9040
310.394.4641

BY HAND AND U.S. MAIL

RE: RACKETEERING CONDUCT OF RICHARD RIONDA DEL CASTRO, CEO, HANNIBAL PICTURES INC.

REQUEST FOR IMMEDIATE ATTENTION AND ASSISTANCE

Dear J

We last saw each other in '99 at the AFM in Santa Monica, in the company of Richard Rionda Del Castro and Phillipe Martinez. Since then, I have had business dealings with Rionda which have caused me and my actors and investors some pain and great financial loss. I am writing this letter because Rionda named you as person to whom he gave money, which he had promised to me. Now if some guy gave to me the sum $150,000 which was due to you, you might bellow about it and write about it as I am doing now. Rionda told me that he was entering into a contract with you and ICM for the services of Jean Claude . He said he gave you $150,000 as an advance, but that you were not giving him and that you refused to return the money, and that therefore he could not put up the funds he had promised for me to make a print of my film called THE FACE OF DUMAS. Now, there is nothing unusual about an agent taking an advance for the services of an actor; not only is it done all the time, it is obligatory when dealing with foreign sales agents or distributors, and Rionda would be

the first type any agent would demand front money from. However, it is unusual for an agent to be given money the giver admits belongs to a third party. Since Rionda lies as he breathes, he may also have been lying when he said he gave our money to you. When he made this revelation to me, I suggested to him that based on what he'd been telling me about his company's finances, I doubted he had enough money to secure a famous actor from ICM. To prove to me he did indeed have this arrangement, he sent me 's contract, which I enclose. A few weeks later, he told me that you had somehow arranged to place that same money, moved like chips at a gaming table, to Christopher or Gerard , I don't remember who. At that time, I just thought it was one more of Rionda's empty proclamations. Rionda is someone who carries a letter from the French Justice Ministry declaring him to be innocent of crimes he was formerly charged with. Rionda is someone who induced my company to do business with him on the basis of foreign sales estimates he swore to be true, and then proceeded to sell the film for a fraction of what he and I had discussed, and kept all the money. This year he told me he made three sales of my film THE FACE OF DUMAS at AFM, but refused to account for them. In violation of our contract, Rionda continues to make "sweetheart" deals with companies like Negro y Azul, who bought Spain for $15,000 when Rionda had promised me $50,000. Rionda's broken promises have caused great hardship to me and my investors, who had counted on foreign sales to finish production, as many other U.S. production companies use foreign sales to finish production. In the case of his partnership with Spain's Negro y Azul, I believe that our money was used to provide "seed" money to option properties and screenplays for Rionda's new productions. In South America, Rionda sold our film to five countries for $100 bucks apiece, less than the cost of a duplicate tape. This is a venal method of ripping off a film's copyright and investors, and takes all speculative profit out of the enterprise to the profit of the middleman. By signing name actors based on commitments to scripts or outlines – in some cases financed by money owed to my company -- Rionda continues his criminal operations by making loans from Imperial Bank guaranteed by completion bonds paid for by the money from loans based on the actors. All Rionda needs are willing agents and banks and someone else's money to start. In February of this year Rionda and his CFO, Patricia Rionda, presented me with an astounding document they call an "accounting." There is a glaring sum in the amount of $195,000 Rionda cannot account for. I have highlighted the number in my attorney's letter, which is attached. The amount and time period corresponds to money Rionda said he was spending for actors and screenplay rights. Then, recently, to my surprise, I read that Rionda and the "obscure" (quoting VARIETY) Negro y Azul are producing a slate of pictures with some of the actors Rionda told me my money was helping to acquire. Both the RICO ACT and the LANHAM ACT provide for the return of stolen property and copyrights, one court criminal and one court civil. RICO further provides that the profits from such theft be turned over to the U.S. and to the theft-ee, which means that one day Rionda's films may belong to my investors, who are the "true" original investors in all of Rionda's present productions commencing from 1999. I have plenty of evidence that in getting me to sign my film onto a loan for $195,000 from LHO of Imperial Bank, Rionda swindled my company and investors. He told us the money would be for filming. But once I had signed over my copyright to the bank, and all the elements of my film, the negative, sound track, screenplay, music et. al. were in the grip of Rionda and the LHO

Organization at the Imperial Bank and the Completion Bond Company, it was revealed to me by Rionda's henchman Jean Marc Felio in the square between Century City Towers that there would be no money for filming, that only $80,000 of the money Rionda promised could be used, and that if I protested or resisted, the bank and completion bond company would take all elements of the film and dispose of them to pay off the debt. My actors and investors and I were taken hostage. Rionda had fled the country. Now it is 2002. My many efforts to reach any kind of fair dealings with Hannibal and Rionda have come to naught. He tells me to sue him. He says my company is suspended, knowing his company never sent funds and he spent thousands illegally and with obvious, bogus accounting provided by his CFO, Patricia Rionda Del Castro. Some civil lawyers, seeing the extent of the case, and the difficulty of bringing Rionda to a true accounting, suggest that even if a court should decide against him and convict him on all counts, it means months and even years of litigation at a cost of hundreds of thousands of dollars. Hence I am looking for a short cut. I thought I would provide all parties "in advance" with the information that the scope of such a litigation would provide for each of them down the road. The names of those involved were given to me by Rionda, including your name and the clearly private and personal film contract of the ICM client Jean Claude he sent to me from Europe. If he would exploit an actor's personal reputation to convince a filmmaker to wait for his funding, it shows he would do anything for a buck. Greed has found its ultimate expression in the persona of Rionda. I have no desire to tabloidize a contract with an actor, and will not exploit 's unsigned agreement on my public website. You are receiving it only to show the extent of Rionda's need for self-aggrandizement at the expense of others. I hope that his $50,000,000 declared production funds, provided in part by the same Imperial Bank and other publicly-owned institutions, are actual and available. As much as the preceding, I am hopeful that someone associated with Rionda will see that he pays my company the $1,000,342 U.S. that he promised but failed to pay, and get from Rionda a written and notarized statement that he will no longer engage in the distribution of motion pictures in the U.S. or anywhere else. I believe that by simply informing THE IMPERIAL BANK, THE COMPLETION BOND COMPANY, THE LHO ORGANIZATION, NEGRO Y AZUL, HERMES OF GERMANY and the others who have dealt with Rionda, I will be able to find a person or entity who will, in effect, "sign off" for him. Richard Rionda Del Castro, an Elie Samaha wannabe, is part of a cult of dealmaking among foreign agents of U.S. independents which must be exposed, brought to justice, and eliminated. I have a strong hunch that he will soon be investiaged by the same F.B.I. agents looking into the Franchise case as part of an ongoing investigation involving all who do business with him. Rionda's banking activities must be unmasked and publicly exposed. There is no hope for emerging filmmakers if all their efforts are stolen, if they are lied to over long periods of time, using up their vital energies and resources. You are one of the top agents in a rough Hollywood landscape. I was a muckracking documentary maker, novelist and filmmaker before trying to sell films abroad, and I have lost none of my instincts. This is going to be one helluva story. In the final scene, law enforcement and angry investors will drive a financial stake right through the heart of the Draculan Rionda and his Hannibal creation. But Dracula, we know, sometimes lives on. And it is the future Rionda, the one who will sneak into the night, who needs a powerful agent to help him escape, and make sure he never comes back. He needs to sign a piece of paper with me

and my investors, giving us our money, and all rights to our film. It will require a special man to do the job. I would trust you with such a mission. You can take your standard commission. It will mean I can get on with other work. You can always say no, but I thought I would ask. At our age, who needs this shit?

Cheers, Bill Richert
cc D B Esq.

PS you can read more about all this on my world wide website at williamrichert.com. Click on "NEWS." My investors and actors and I are also meeting with reporters and editors in the interested press. This case will not disappear for Rionda; on the contrary: already several colleges are reviewing the material I placed on the Internet some months ago for their classrooms, and it is part of a book being written in Cook County, Ireland. I have promised Rionda that I will make him famous. Pretty soon it will be clear to all that Rionda cannot be trusted by anyone, especially his friends, and that a famous Rionda will even be worse for them. Imagine the reaction of actors like Jean Claude upon discovering a weasel like Rionda was using his confidential contracts to manipulate filmmakers. Imagine the result if Rionda used other contracts and personal information to defend his actions in a lawsuit, revealing the private financial concerns of actors at ICM, CAA, UTA as well as personal managers like Joan H along with banks, co-financers, co-distributors, completion bond companies and others who have entrusted Hannibal Pictures with their actors contracts or their deal memos.

"Now, this is not the end, or even the beginning of the end. It is, perhaps, the end of the beginning." Winston Churchill

williamrichert.com

May 25, 2004

Mr. J
ICM
By Email, Fax and US Mail

cc Jeff Berg, Nancy Josephson, Richard Levy, Timothy Bottoms, Edward Albert, Dana Barron, Dennis Hayden, Rex Ryon, Gloria Pryor, H. Roy Matlen

Dear J

There are ethical boundaries which ought not be breached. More than one year ago I wrote to you that my actors and I had been swindled by Richard Rionda Del Castro, Hannibal Pictures, and his wife, Patricia Del Castro.

I sent a document informing you that Rionda told me that he had given you $150,000 US for the guarantee of performance by Jean Clau in a Hannibal Picture. Rionda admitted to me that this money was taken from money he owed me.

You called and said that no deal had been made between you and Rionda and Jean Clau and told me that if I continued to include you in my demands for payment from Rionda, you would show my letter to ICM lawyers.

Now I ask that you do just that. Rionda has published on his web site the news that he is in a development deal with and that he has 14 million in the bank to make it. I have evidence sent to me by Rionda that our money helped bring into Rionda's picture, and, further, helped fund Rionda's entire slate of pictures.

It is commonly accepted as fact that Hollywood distributors cheat their producers, but very few Distributors have been jailed in two countries as Rionda has, or provided accounting statements as full as obvious falsehoods as Rionda has, or lied as blatantly.

It is my opinion that after being informed of the kind of sleazy thief Rionda is, and after being informed that Rionda was using stolen funds to pay for actors from ICM -- a payment known as "fraudulent conveyance" -- that due diligence on the part of your agency ought to prohibit a company like yours from doing business with known criminals like Richard Rionda Del Castro.

When a business like International Creative Managements deals with "bad guys,"there will eventually come a day of reckoning. A single sergeant Bishop, who abhorred the abuse he saw in Iraq, filed a report which eventually may lead to the downfall of the entire Bush administration. Richard Rionda Del Castro, in collusion with his wife Patricia, is equivalent to ICM as Amed Chabali was to the Pentagon. (And you know that I have a way with a conspiracy; you may be pleased to know that "Winter Kills" opened in New York in May, and once again I thank you for helping get Jeff for the role; they are having political discussions after the showing of the film in Brooklyn; I expect Rionda & wife to be a part of classes on film distribution one day.)

It is my duty as a writer and filmmaker to see that I am not abused by some unwritten complicity of back room greedy behavior, that my investors are not swindled and my credit destroyed by thieves like Richard and Patricia Rionda. Rionda is a public figure, and deserves public scrutiny of his thieving ways.

Please review the letter I sent to you; if you have lost it, I will fax you a copy. Please show it to your lawyers at ICM, unless your general counsel Richard Levy has time to review it. I am not ashamed that I was swindled by Hannibal Pictures, for I was unaware that he had been jailed in 2 countries for theft. Now that ICM is aware of his history, ICM should be ashamed to continue working with him, or promoting major actors to work with him.

Rionda wants me to pay for a lawyer, and to use the court system to delay payment to me and justice for him. Thanks to the Internet, I can shorten his payback time. If Rionda/Hannibal won't send me the money they owe, Jean 's name in the film started with my money will at least drive cineastes to the website controversy, and that won't hurt when our films reach the theaters.

You told me you "never had a problem" with Richard Rionda Del Castro. You were were wrong. You do have a problem. Jean Cla has a problem. Also, both you and he and ICM have a new partner on "Kumite": fcbfilms. Part of the 14 million dollar budget started with my funds, and those funds need to be paid immediately, in full. This at least I am addressing with legal counsel.

You can see some the letters I've written at williamrichert.com, where I an currently offering a select marquee of Hollywood bad guys, with blogs on all their houses.

Sincerely William Richert

for grand theft of

motion picture 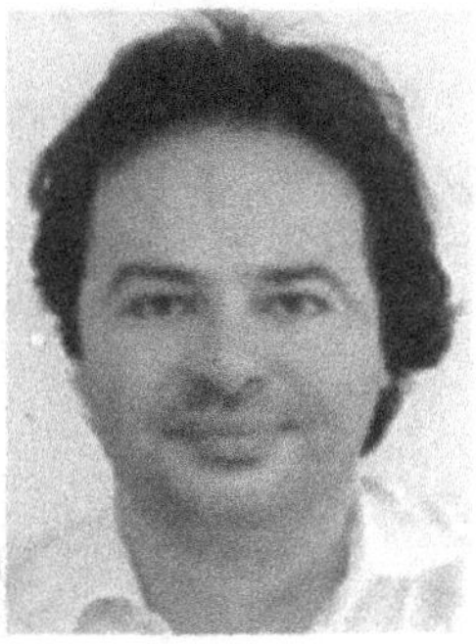
contact william@
williamrichert.com
HANNIBAL is
crooked!

THE INDIVISIBLE STUDIO

J

October 22, 2002

TO: Richard Rionda Del Castro
CEO Hannibal Pictures, Inc.
A California Corporation

THE CROOKS IN BOOTH BO9

HUSBAND/WIFE "RIP OFF TEAM" CHEAT THE INDIE PRODUCERS

RE: THE THREE MUSKETEERS VS HANNIBAL PICTURES
"The Company That Eats Movies"

FR: William Richert
FCB Film Enterprises
1423 Euclid Street
Santa Monica, Ca 90404
310.394.7308

Dear Richard,

Glad to see you are finally have your own Website, Hannibal Pictures.com. It will give the public chance to contact you directly. You may want to check out williamrichert.com, where you will find our past correspondence and upcoming events as I track down all your enterprises and film projects as they have originated with your sales of my picture THE MAN IN THE IRON MASK.

As you say: Your partner D. B who is also a lawyer, has informed you:

A.) It will take several years to sue you (in a civil court.)
B.) After we win, it will take a long time to collect.
C.) Should we collect anything, it may only be a percentage of what you have stolen, and you will have had the use of our money for a period of years, while we have endured hardship.

The better news is: All of the above will change radically if you wind up becoming extremely successful. Should Hannibal Pictures actually connive, bribe, swindle and lie its way into fame and fortune (upon that old well-trodden path) our chances of redress for your lies and thievery will rise side-by-side with your fame and opportunities and bulging accounts at LHO and Imperial Bank, among other banks.

Imagine, we have to wish you success so that we can get our due!

In the meantime, while awaiting U. S. Southern District Federal Court Relief, I will proceed to:

A.) Continue to place this and all of my letters on the williamrichert.com website, where I will shortly begin selling my new film, ALEXANDER'S MUSKETEERS, along with THE FACE OF DUMAS and THE MAN IN THE IRON MASK, my ballet documentary A DANCER'S LIFE and my director's cut of JIMMY REARDON. To help the Effort, Anchor Bay is re-releasing WINTER KILLS with a sensational new ad campaign. In view of this and other special previews (my home movies with Matt Perry and Martha Plimpton, for example) we hope the new website has many visitors, including members of the press and students of film and film culture worldwide. A young man in Mambia, India has written to me asking if I could send him the screenplay for AMERICAN SUCCESS, which he wants to place on the Internet. Imagine, India! for a movie rarely seen. I expect he will want as well to share the williamrichert.com website with those millions of Indians who perform such vital Internet functions. These people, who have suffered so much at colonial and other greedy hands, will surely recognize you and your company for the oppressor that it is.

B.) We are proceeding to discover and inform all actors, agents, partners, banks, etc. of your history with me and your history with the courts and police of U.S. and Europe, so they may arm themselves in advance against your mendacity.

C.) With all legal means, we shall enforce my demands for a complete accounting of the loan you took based on German sales of my film from the Lewis Horwitz Organization and the Imperial Bank. These lending institutions have obligations to the borrower according to law. We shall see what you did with the money you took from our loan.

D.) As each day we make some progress, we want to be remembered in the future for our efforts. We shall: Make sure that all information about your activities remains available through the coming months and years on my website and University websites, so that the name of Richard Rionda Del Castro, CEO, and Patricia Rionda Del Castro, CFO, will be linked forever to the crimes you have committed against me and the cast and investors of my film in the past and the ones you have told me you are committing this very day. You have told me that you will continue to sell my film worldwide at the artist's expense. The fact that your actions have caused my corporation to enter a state of financial suspension and near-collapse has made you giggle on the telephone when we speak. You may change the way you get your laughs in the coming years. The name Hannibal Pictures will become synonymous with Hannibal the Filmmaker's Cannibal. When a producer is ripped off, we can say he was "Hannibalized." The family name of Rionda Del Castro will be synonymous forever with rip off artists. At present, you may still find somebody to participate in your schemes, but the public will soon know you as the creep you are, and your relatives may not wish to be tainted by association you. In future letters, we will profile the actual artists and investors whose lives and livelihoods have been terribly injured by your fraudulent inducements and promises.

E.) Whether the Imperial Bank and Negro y Azul and ICM will want to stay in business with you and partners in your adventures, remains to be seen. Negro paid you $15,000 for my picture, but the deal was never approved. You promised us $50,000 from Spain. What happened to the rest of the money? With the exception of Germany, you have sold country after country without any authorization from me as provided by contract. You have charged us thousands of dollars for services and materials you never performed or provided. This is fraud on an international scale. Postal and banking regulations have been violated. You have explained to me in detail how you use two different contracts to take money for film sales, one being a tiny amount, the other being an actual amount. The accounting you gave me shows that our money was used for purposes other than promotion of THE FACE OF DUMAS. We will show that you entered agreements for actors and film properties which were funded by money due to us. We will show that your lawyer Γ B Esq. received funds from us in a fraudulent conveyance. We believe we can prove in court that our money was also used to pay for the up-front fees for actor Jean Cl based on the contract you provided to us. You must return our money and provide copies of all contracts you entered into while fraudulently claiming it was Hannibal Pictures paying out seed money, not FCB Films, as was the case.

The faxes I sent during the Cannes Film Festival to warn buyers/producers of your method of operations will become less costly and easier to send when all of the companies at MIPCOM, MIFED, CANNES, AFM, LONDON SCREENINGS etc. have email. We have composed letters to these festival markets asking them to refuse to rent you or HANNIBAL PICTURES any rooms from which to rip off filmmakers, offering evidence of your behavior with us.

By your efforts in publicity, you have made yourself a Public Figure. Your "fame" will increase further as film students study your bogus accounting and letters to see the dangers certain Foreign Sales Reps pose to Independent Producers. Already you are going to be part of the curriculum of at least two California Universities, as well as the University of North Carolina and a college in Ireland. I will be more specific later on, as we announce each college and teacher on my website with appropriate fanfare.

So far, only a producer from Spain has actually contacted me regarding a deal with Hannibal Pictures. But filmmakers in Ireland, England, France, Germany, India and others worldwide are also reading the letters we have posted on the Internet. My cast and crew, all professionals with a stake in the profits from this film, are meeting with editors of major newspapers and monthly magazines, and I am hoping that my old producers at 60 MINUTES will take a moment to check out the selling frenzies at AFM and other markets by you and your cronies to see what is really are being sold, and who actually benefits – if anybody at all -- among original investors and filmmakers.

We have just begun. As Hannibal releases each of the films we have initially funded, we Musketeers will sit side by side at the press table, sharing any profits or publicity rightfully due to us.

Sincerely,

Bill

William Richert
Aka Alexander Dumas/Count Aramis in "ALEXANDER'S MUSKETEERS."
CC the Universe

THE INDIVISIBLE STUDIO

Memo from: William Richert
williamrichert.com
Tel: 310.394.4641
Fax: 310.394.6028

To: D B Esq.
1901 Avenue of the Stars
Suite
Los Angeles, California 90067-6019
Fax 310.5

May 13, 2002

RE: 'FRAUD AT INCEPTION' & RICO

ATTENTION!!!: AFM/CANNES PARTICIPANT: HANNIBAL PICTURES AND RICHARD RIONDA DEL CASTRO LOCATED AT NOGA HILTON SUITE 356 DO NOT HAVE ANY RIGHTS TO THE FACE OF DUMAS OR THE MAN IN THE IRON MASK. PLEASE IGNORE IF THIS MESSAGE DOES NOT APPLY OTHERWISE IMMEDIATELY CALL U.S. 310.394.4641 FAX 310 394 6028 OR VISIT OUR WEBSITE WILLIAMRICHERT.COM AT THE AMERICAN PAVILION IN CANNES OR EMAIL US AT WILLIAMRICHERT.COM@WILLIAMRICHERT.COM

Dear Mr. B

Anyone can see from the photo-registry on my Internet website that Hannibal Pictures has paid you thousands of dollars from foreign sales of THE FACE OF DUMAS, THE MAN IN THE IRON MASK even though the agreements you worked out for Rionda specifically said that Rionda would pay his own legal fees. Since there was virtually no legal work required on the contracts – such as they are – we have received from Hannibal, it is clear to me that your work included such films as ABSOLON,

CRIME SPREE, THE FLYING DUTCHMAN etc. and was not limited to our movies.

Under the RICO act, congress has provided for the injured and the United States to claim ownership of what may have been produced or instigated with embezzled funds. I believe that when a complete audit is performed on Hannibal Pictures, it will become clear where Rionda's "development" funds actually originated.

You are not alone in your involvement with Richard Rionda Del Castro and Hannibal Pictures, but as a lawyer whose ethics must remain untainted by the kind of illegal activity engaged in by Rionda et.al. over a period of five years – with Rionda stonewalling me and my investors with alternate periods of lies and payments which never arrive – you are the man who should know above all the wrongs perpetrated by this "Distributor" and his cohorts.

As you know, since Rionda constantly asserts that he swears by all your advice and counsel, Rionda presently owes me and my investors $112, 672 in addition to the directorial work and production work I have done, and my associates have done, and which has not been paid for.

Rionda says you told him FCB is "suspended" and that therefore he no longer has any legal obligation to me or my investors. If this is true, I am surprised, since even a cursory review of the "United States Racketeer Influence & Corrupt Organizations Act" will reveal that the U.S. laws were written by Congress to protect "any individual, partnership, corporation, or any union or group of individuals associated in fact though not a legal entity…" from a whole range of illegal activities, including Creative Accounting and Predatory Practices, to name just two.

I urge you to renounce the work you do for Hannibal Pictures, Richard Rionda Del Castro and Patricia Rionda, President of Hannibal Pictures, and to send me all documents in your possession relating to the true accounting of our film THE FACE OF DUMAS-- THE MAN IN THE IRON MASK at your soonest convenience.

Rionda will have to live with his actions against our enterprise for the length of his earthly existence, so loud will be the clamor and shouts against him and his kind, even if the shouts are loudest from me alone. Surely all the partners who benefited from his illegal activity will hear the uproar – even if it is only whispered at the outset.

I inform you herewith: All voicemail and correspondence from you and others in business with Rionda/Hannibal Pictures will be placed on my website at williamrichert.com/.

The website already contains a few pertinent letters even though it is under construction. Most notably at present: it contains photocopies of what we believe to be the first Internet-published foreign sales "accounting" in history.

For years I had been hearing about the "creative accounting" of foreign (and domestic) distributors, but this is the first one I have actually witnessed. This may be of particular interest to the many filmmakers who sell at AFM and then never hear a word again from their foreign sales reps.

You can see from the 'registry' that Rionda & Co. live pretty well, off the labor of others. During our humble production, we could never afford the kind of expenditures he endows himself and his accomplices for hotels, cars, food etc. He ignored all our agreements which provided for my approval on his expenditures, as he ignored the agreements in total.

There are several hundred pages remaining to put up, including letters you wrote on Rionda's behalf. In the end, this website can be *de rigueur* among students of cinema economics. Rionda's behavior is another of those things they forgot to teach us in school.

In addition to the website, some of the early letters I have written to Rionda over the years have literary flourishes that will be read by actors from our film studio at liveradio.org in the U.S. We are also adding the history of the Rionda debacle to the DVDs of our latest productions.

Rionda acts as if I am a sore loser, having lost a large sum of money to him. That I am sore about the robbery is a certainty. However, In the End (finis) he will lose much more than I. It's not revenge I'm after here, or only the money, though both can be served cold and sweet. I want more than that.

I want Richard Rionda Del Castro removed forever from any kind of influence over any kind of true artist or personality. His kind of sociopathic abuse is pandemic, some say almost Darwinian, in our capitalist society. We, each and every one of us, have to press on against this sort of fellow/fellowess, lest they spread beyond recall. Nobody wants to ruin the gaping barrel of capitalism with the stench of a bad apple.

You might say that mine is a theatrical demand, but you cannot deny that it is equal to the situation.

You see, Mr. B we have decided to channel all the wrongs perpetrated against us into showbiz, which, like the poet says about poetry, is a "mistress who always receives."

You may email me at williamrichert.com@williamrichert.com. (If you email, it will enable us to post your letters more easily than if we have to scan them. Thanks.)

Sincerely,

William Richert

ILLUSTRATION by Riv Sauts

F.C.B. Film Corporation

Phone 310 456 3251 Fax 818 783 9530

19836 Pacific Coast Highway Malibu, California 90265

William Richert President

Mr. David Hutkin
Vice President
The Lewis Horwitz Organization
Fax 310.275.8055

Mr. Jean Louis Pommier
The Completion Guarantors
Fax 310.860.2115

Mr. Christian Michel
Vice President
Hermes Filmstudio
Fax 01 089 649 834 55

RE: THE FACE OF ALEXANDRE DUMAS, THE MAN IN THE IRON MASK – MOTION PICTURE

Gentlemen:

This letter is to serve notice that F.C.B. film corp. has not recieved funds sufficient to meet its contractual obligations regarding the above referenced motion picture. To date we have received less than fifteen percent of the funds promised by Richard Rionda Del Castro, Hannibal Pictures and his associate Jean Marc Felio, of Milagro Films Montreal, needed to complete the picture. We cannot proceed unless Hannibal Pictures and Jean Marc Felio release the approximately $102,000 U.S. which was provided for in our agreement with Hannibal Pictures and Del Castro.

Further, Hannibal Pictures and Del Castro have vanished from the United States, leaving no forwarding address. Hannibal's telephone number is disconnected.

send 5.17.02

MAJESTIC PICTURES

FAX TO: Aziz Alaoui DATE: MAY 17 2002
LOCATION: NOGA HILTON

~~[crossed out]~~ FCB FILM ENTERPRISES

FROM: Fastest Cheapest Best Film Enterprises
TEL 310.394.4641
FAX 310.394.6028
Santa Monica, Ca USA

HOLLYWOOD/CANNES
For Immediate Release: ALERT!! FRENCHMEN AND ALL HONORABLE FANS OF THE THREE MUSKETEERS!

AMERICAN FILMMAKER SAYS FRENCHMAN RICHARD RIONDA DEL CASTRO IS STEALING ALEXANDRE DUMAS & THE THREE MUSKETEERS AT CANNES MARKET 2002.

WILLIAM RICHERT, CO-STAR OF 'MY OWN PRIVATE IDAHO' AND WRITER/DIRECTOR OF "WINTER KILLS," "AMERICAN SUCCESS" AND "JIMMY REARDON" DECRYS CONTINUING BLATANT "RIP-OFF" ADMITTED BY FOREIGN SALES PERSONNEL RICHARD RIONDA DEL CASTRO AND PATRICIA RIONDA

ACCUSES HANNIBAL PICTURES OF SELLING UNFINISHED FILM TO UNSUSPECTING BUYERS

PLACES ENTIRE FOREIGN SALES ACCOUNTING ON THE INTERNET TO ILLUSTRATE OUTRAGEOUS CHARGES TO INDEPENDENT PRODUCERS BY THEIR OVERSEAS SELLERS

VOWS CAMPAIGN TO REMOVE THIS DISTRIBUTOR FROM SALES COMMUNITY TO PREVENT FURTHER INJURY TO FILMMAKERS. SAYS FULL PUBLIC ACCOUNTING NEEDED THROUGHOUT FOREIGN SALES RANKS AS ONLY MEANS TO GIVE FAIR SHARE TO INDEPENDENTS WORLD-WIDE

FOR MORE INFORMATION GO TO: williamrichert.com AT THE AMERICAN PAVILION or email williamrichert.com@williamrichert.com.

FCB FILM ENTERPRISES

May 20, 2002

FAX TO: Mr. Jorg Hermes
Mr. Christian Michael
HERMES FILM FAX (49-89) 6425 4632

Fr: WILLIAM RICHERT FAX 310.394.6028
www.williamrichert.com

RE: German sales of the motion picture THE FACE OF DUMAS- THE MAN IN THE IRON MASK

RE: Contract breaches by Hannibal Pictures & Richard Rionda Del Castro

Dear Mr. Hermes and Mr. Michael:

In December, 1999, we engaged in heated correspondence over whether HERMES would distribute the correct version of my film THE FACE OF DUMAS. I wrote to you and to the foreign salesperson Richard Rionda Del Castro saying that only THE FACE OF DUMAS was authorized for sale because Del Castro was not given the rights to sell the other film, and more importantly, the other film titled THE MAN IN THE IRON MASK was lacking narration, crucial action sequences, and the final ending. These are essential elements to any film, and the right to show the correct version of his work is essential to any artist.

The Directors Guild of America has set legal precedent and standards for the rights of a director of a theatrical motion picture. Richard Rionda Del Castro's company, Hannibal Pictures, and Hermes in Munich assured me that only the finished picture

THE FACE OF DUMAS would be shown in Germany. This was stated in a letter reflecting our agreement sent on December 20, 1999 (see attached.)

However, in the case of HERMES, Del Castro apparently supplied a digital master of the wrong movie and Hermes is distributing under the title "The Man In The Iron Mask."

WHAT IS REMARKABLE IS:

THE MAN IN THE IRON MASK, HERMES INCOMPLETE AND UNFINISHED VERSION, is becoming a world wide underground hit. We are receiving thousands of fan letters for the movie in places as remote as China and the Ukraine and Malaysia and Bulgaria and the Flores Islands, along with Indonesia and the Phillipines and Sweden, Austria, Holland, Finland, England, Ireland, etc.

A few weeks ago, it was brought to our attention that a film titled THE MAN IN THE IRON MASK is available in Germany on DVD. On AMAZON.COM we were not able to establish whether or not the film is the Incomplete version, and not THE FACE OF DUMAS, but it appears to be the "wrong" version.

In reading the publicity supplied with the DVD, it nowhere mentions the characters of the Author and Sylvie who appear in THE FACE OF DUMAS. It is apparent that you ignored our agreement of December 20, 1999.

The purpose of this letter is not to threaten you with lawsuits for showing a movie you agreed not to show. Perhaps HANNIBAL PICTURES convinced you this was legal and appropriate.

We have an announcement to make to Hermes: Without receiving any of the funds from sales of our film that Hannibal has made during the past two years, we nonetheless have worked with dedicated cinema artists and technicians to finally create a new film, "DUMAS 1842:" A NIGHT IN THE LIFE OF ALEXANDER DUMAS – The Story Behind the Story of The Man In The Iron Mask.

This is the movie HERMES should be offering its audience and buyers in Germany. This is the film intended by its director and its actors, and it is the one which will finally be released theatrically in the U.S. and offered for sale throughout the world.

3

We would like to offer you this movie.

This June, our Executive Producer, Dennis Hayden, will arrive in Europe to promote the "cameo" of his starring role in the new "Action Jackson." Mr. Hayden, who plays D'Artagnan in "DUMAS 1842," will be telephoning you to discuss our new film, and talk about the thousands of letters from German fans of THE MAN IN THE IRON MASK. In addition to doing publicity for "Action Jackson" and the new DVDs of "DIE HARD," Mr. Hayden will be tracking down just who is selling our film and where, as well as linking up "strategic partners" for future European distribution.

We have informed, and will continue forever to inform Hannibal Pictures that they may no longer represent our film, that they are in material breach of contract, that we trust none of their accounting, and are requesting an audit dating back to what we believe was "Fraud At Inception."

We have yet to receive the Hermesfilm "long form" agreement Hannibal promised, or a full, accurate and meaningful accounting of the money Hannibal Pictures received from the L.H.O. division of Imperial Bank of California.

The investors in this enterprise will not rest until Richard Rionda Del Castro fulfills each and every promise he made, and until he no longer is able to harm any group of artists from any country.

We will have a DVD of the new "DUMAS 1842" within two weeks. In the meantime, I will be sending you samples of thousands of e-mail fan letters for the movie Hermes is distributing in Germany.

This mail from Germany and dozens of other countries around the world is astounding because the film was never properly mixed, the music was not final, the narration essential to the story is missing and the ending is sad, not uplifting, as it is now. We can only imagine what kind of response and sales Hermes would make with the new film.

Based on this ongoing audience response, HERMES must have done an excellent job in Germany, even if accomplished with the wrong movie. This very day we received two more fan emails from German fans of the film. Musketeer films, and movies based on the characters of Alexandre Dumas, are rising in worldwide appeal these days, as audiences seek out the ethics and romance of old heroes.

4

In our new film, the Musketeers are rescued by thousands of angels pouring down from heaven. We were able to obtain software exceeding that used in CLOSE ENCOUNTERS OF THE THIRD KIND to produce spectacular special effects, unlike any ever seen before in a film about the Three Musketeers.

We think the story of making this picture, along with the movie itself, will become an underground hit around the world and will be one of the more interesting independent film stories of 2002-2003.

As soon as our DVD is complete, we will send you a copy. We hope you will offer German audiences and film buyers a movie that they will enjoy 10 times more than the incomplete one Rionda Del Castro sold to you, and the one you are selling to others.

Also, I would appreciate any accounting you may have given to Hannibal Pictures, as we have not received a credible accounting from them.

We are attempting to contact each and every buyer/seller at CANNES 2002 with our fury over Hannibal's activities, but the email and electronic systems are not fully in place. In a few years, it will be a vastly changed system, this buying and selling of international films, and Rionda et.al. will not be able to operate with impunity, without oversight and scrutiny, while filmmakers like me will have websites along with actual representatives to assure fair treatment.

For two years we have asked for a VHS copy of what you are selling, as well as any publicity for our film. Many of us have German ancestry, and it is surely only fair that we are allowed insight into what has become of our work in one of the most developed and cultured nations, and the source of much of America's heritage. It is an outrage to be treated so disdainfully by agents of our film. Perhaps you can send a copy of the VHS.

Working together, we may be able to accomplish something with this new film that could benefit us both financially and artistically.

Dennis Hayden will be calling soon to offer his help in achieving this goal.

Sincerely,

William Richert
1423 Euclid Street Santa Monica, California 90404 USA Tel 310.394.4641

HOLLYWOOD, CALIFORNIA
April 20 – May 20, 2002

CANNES, FRANCE MAY, 2002

FOR IMMEDIATE RELEASE: Commencement of INTERNET PUBLISHED Letters to Richard Rionda Del Castro of Hannibal Pictures.

A Filmmaker Speaks out Against A Rotten Thieving Foreign Distributor.

William Richert claims Richard Rionda sabotaged production of indie THE MAN IN THE IRON MASK and then sold his foreign clients copies of unfinished productions without informing them.

UNDER THE CLOAK OF INTERNATIONAL LAW:

Dear Richard,

As you break all the rules of decency and fair play, I shall adhere to the fundamental rule: Thou shall not allow oneself to be injured by inferior men.

You little shit (may I call you a little shit? Michael Eisner called Katzenberg a midget, and Katzenberg got 205 million from Michael Eisner. But maybe you can get more when I call you a "little shit" – or less. Is a piece of shit less than a midget or more than a midget? Katzenberg is no longer a midget, he is a giant. But you remain a little shit.)

NOTICE:

My attorney Max S Esq. is no longer involved with this case, and does not represent me or my film regarding my actions against you and your bullshit tactics, though I hope he will review the coming documents and help in my legal cause. Any legal documents or letters you wish to send to me you may send to:

William Richert
THE INDIVISIBLE STUDIO
1423 Euclid Street Suite
Santa Monica, California 90404

I shall begin this day by sending the letter I was going to send you earlier, but did not send, as you promised (You? Promised?) once again that you would sign off on all rights you claim to have in my film. In return, I agreed not to file civil and criminal charges against you in the U.S., France, Germany, Brazil, Australia, South America, Russia, Hong Kong, Norway, Denmark, Ireland or the Phillipines, etc.

You have disappeared once again.

We may or may not find you. Until we do, I will continue my work on the new and different films THE THREE MUSKETEERS & THE MAN IN THE IRON MASK as well as the historical version, A NIGHT IN THE LIFE OF ALEXANDRE DUMAS.

It is my intention to let these films stand as the final evidence of your illegal behavior, since these films would have been available to International buyers four years ago, had you kept your agreements.

When viewing these films in a courtroom setting, the buyers of the early, unfinished productions will perhaps realize at last that you have monumentally defrauded them by not revealing our previous agreements, or honoring them yourself.

You have received dozens of pages of letters from me telling you that you were selling a movie which was unfinished. It is almost May, 2002. If we are able to finish editing in time, and if the judges like it, and if there is still a screening available, we hope our picture will be opening this year at the SEATTLE FILM FESTIVAL, where I will be passing out a book containing copies of all of our letters, which now total almost 200 pages and growing.

Next year, we will offer our new films to festivals throughout Europe. By then film buffs and independents on the Internet will have been exposed to the dialogue in this letter, as well as your prior and future letters to me, and this may promote further interest in finally making foreign sales people of your kind accountable.

You little prick (may I say that in print? The French do. Hmm. Let's find out just how far the 1st Amendment takes us. Will somebody measure your little prick? How will we determine this question: (?) is Richard Rionda Del Castro a "little prick" a "little shit" or just a "plain old liar" and "con artist...?")

As little shits & little pricks often threaten violence against the truthtellers, as you did once or twice before, I should like to remind you that you have already been deported once from the U.S., and that entering into a conspiracy to harm (are you still in business with Phillipe? I remember he lied to me when he said you'd had a "heart attack" during our negotiations, but then it turned out you were in jail in France for the first time, I thought) is punishable by prison. You say you want to raise a family here. How will you do that? From a cell phone in a jailhouse up near Fresno?

Your acts towards those like me who do business with you are the acts of a devious and sociopathic mind, and therefore you suffer no guilt. The self-torment and pain in your voice is the pain of pure vanity being shown a mirror on itself.

As for my doing business with you to begin with: A grizzly caught in a steel trap is not dumb, only unaware of the snares of the uncaring and the greedy. I am no less noble or intelligent because I went into business with you. On the contrary, it is noble to explore and intelligent to learn: In these dealings, I have explored the limits of nobility and the

darkening of intelligence when faced with true mendacity. Evil succeeds because it never shows itself until it is too late. It is not too late in this case. You have been spotted.

The Faustian myth is that the Devil identifies himself when he makes his Hellish Bargains -- as if Mephistopheles is a man who keeps his word! -- Instead of the primeval Breaker of the Word, and a Liar. On the contrary, the Devil is a liar start to finish, backwards and forwards, and he only pretends to run from the Cross. We know, in fact, that he uses same to bring the Cloistered to Unholy Orgasm.

But no such luck with the likes of you, Rionda. You bring only loss of hope and dismal dissertations. Your hell is without fire, only ashes. You burn on the fuel of others, a contagion to be warned against.

People like you have got to be identified and filmmakers have got to know about the traps you set, traps that even the smartest among us fall into, because the breadth and scope of the con is so legitimized as it has been around for so long. Prostitution without gratification.

I look forward to receiving all the money that you owe me, which I calculate at $110,000 US, plus damages for pain and mental suffering. Even if my back is stronger, as the Arabs say, I still bear the scars along with my fellow Artists and Investors. The amount mentioned does not include any recent sales, which are not legitimate in any case.

This money must be paid in full. You are not getting off the book on this one, Richard. Not ever.

IN ADDITION: You **had better send me copies of the three sales you told me you made at this year's AFM. You had been informed in writing that you were in Breach of Contract before you attended AFM in 2002. Each of those buyers must be notified, for I will not be complicit in your swindle. All film buyers have the right to know when a producer says the seller is in violation of contract and has been told to Cease and Desist. The legal fees of the buyers, in this case, will be paid by you.**

When those buyers, Hermes and others, read this and other letters on the email I am **sending to EACH AND EVERY BUYER/SELLER at the Upcoming Cannes grocery market, they will surely look at your round face with a somewhat sharper eye. Is Phillipe still in Florida? What was the plot of MUSKETEERS FOREVER?**

You are going to repay in free publicity what you took in time and money from me. **I have spent ten years now on this film. I do not deny that the effort has been worth it. Do you really think you can abscond with such a long and difficult labor without a fight, like some bad postman stealing old folk's pension checks?**

In the future, I will sign no document from you or Hannibal Pictures, since you spurn all agreements once they are signed.

I am told that it's going to cost you and your company at least one to two hundred thousand to sue me for any kind of slander, possibly even more, but again, I think a trial in open court would reveal only more damages from you to those who entrust their work to your care. We'll let the judge & jury see the films, and then decide. This is all about a movie, and a movie has a right to be well seen and well sold, not hidden under the waistband like a counterfeit watch.

You may think you can ignore all our written and verbal agreements, but there is one deep fact: at issue here is a motion picture hundreds of people worked on for millions of hours, and it will not be stolen by you or anybody else, and since it was created to be a work of art, it will not be maligned either, or corrupted by being presented in an unfinished form, without informing the audience as they deserve. Our movie now has fans around the world. This mystifies you. Maybe you will begin to hear from some of them, and the mystery will be solved.

You have deprived us of our right to the entrepreneurial reward. Nobody worked on this movie to be paid the minimum wage, but to reap the rewards of a risk investment. Selling it for a penny on the dollar, as you have done, is a violation of the basic tenant of show business: to make a hit. You are anti-show-business, and sell goods like a baker, by the pound. This has cost us all much money and much time.

The crappy "registry" you gave me is available today on the Internet, as it has been since the day we put it up. The foregoing will be put up during the coming week, as will all correspondence between us, and my Once and Future lawyers, friends, fellow writers actors and producers, especially all of those who worked on our film.

Sincerely,

William Richert
AKA Alexander Dumas in A NIGHT IN THE LIFE OF ALEXANDER DUMAS

SENT TO:
RICHARD RIONDA AKA RICHARD DEL CASTRO
HANNIBAL PICTURES, INC.
1361 North Laurel Avenue
West Hollywood, California 90046
TEL: 323 848 2945 FAX: 323 848 2946 CELL PHONE 213 479 8375
Email: hannibalpictures@mindspring.com
FRENCH OFFICE:
No 380 La Garduere
Bandol, France 83150
Phone 33.49.432.2542
FAX 33.49.432.5011

7

[THE FOLLOWING LETTER WAS SENT TO RIONDA'S LONGTIME PARTNER, PHILLIPE MARTINEZ, WHO IS CURRENTLY PROCUCING AT LEAST TWO PICTURES WITH RIONDA. IN THIS LETTER, RICHERT ASKS THAT MARTINEZ SIGN OFF FOR RIONDA ON THE DISTRIBUTION DEAL, AS RIONDA CANNOT BE TRUSTED. RICHERT HOPES THAT MARTINEZ CAN BE TRUSTED IN THIS INSTANCE, SINCE THE PAIR HAVE AN ESTIMATED 40 MILLION U.S. IN THE BANK, AND THIS COULD BE VULNERABLE IN A LAWSUIT]

RE: THE THREE MUSKETEERS & ALEXANDRE DUMAS VS HANNIBAL PICTURES AND RICHARD RIONDA AKA RICHARD DEL CASTRO

A LURID TALE OF PARTNERSHIPS, PROMISES AND LIES

DEAR PHILLIPPE:

It is my understanding that you and Richard Rionda are presently financial, producing and distribution partners in at least two major motion pictures and other activities.

Richard Rionda Del Castro has further informed me he has 17 million in the bank. You and BAUER MARTINEZ STUDIOS may also be a party to this new loan, as you played a key role in his negotiations with the Imperial Bank on his loan for THE FACE OF DUMAS, from which Rionda has only recently informed me that he took $50,000., in addition to the other amounts.

Rionda knew that all funds from the LHO loan were to be used solely to finish principal photography on THE FACE OF DUMAS. It only becomes apparent in 2002 that LHO and the Imperial Bank and the Montreal completion bond company and the German financier were told something different and contradictory, or engaged in actions which had the same effect.

I do not know how much you and BETAR participated in this, only that you were a constant presence, and that Rionda told me you were his advisor in acquiring the loan.

Anyhow, I don't want this note to be too lengthy: suffice it to say that if you were/are involved in any financial dealings with Hannibal Pictures, and if you are receiving money from the sales of my copyrighted film THE FACE OF DUMAS, or if you or your company had any role in showing it, I am asking you at once to return all funds and to reveal all documents relating to you and Hannibal, especially those relating to "shared" hotel suites.
This is not merely a "fishing" expedition; it is the beginning of an investigation I am conducting on behalf of all the actors, artists, technicians and investors in my film.

2

Although I may not yet have all the facts before me, I know this: You were in the offices at Imperial Bank on that very night when Rionda was finally granted the loan of $190,000 because, he told me, you said you would withdraw your business from Imperial Bank and the Lewis. Horwitz Organization if the loan was not made to Hannibal Pictures, Inc. based on the sale of my copyrighted film; a sale which was made one month prior to the loan and prior to my signing the loan agreement.

You are also listed as partner/co-producer with Rionda in the rosters AFM, Cannes, MIFED etc. Rionda tells us all that you are his "mentor." I truly hope it is not your advice he is following.

I have recently been advised that your film "Musketeers Forever," which was made during the time I was doing business with you and Rionda on THE LAST MUSKETEERS, has similar themes, characterizations and plot situations to THE LAST MUSKETEERS.

You were aware that THE LAST MUSKETEERS was copyrighted, and that even though the Musketeers themselves are certainly public domain, the use of their characters in new formats is intellectual property, and subject to copyright laws in the U.S., Canada and France.

Please let us clear these issues up immediately. I will be happy to screen any copy of "Musketeers Forever" to assure myself that you and your investors have not engaged in any form of copyright infringement. I cannot find "Musketeers Forever" on the imdb, or at Blockbusters. Is it only available in Europe?

You are among the first five partners of Rionda that I am writing.

I begin with you because you did all you could to keep me in business with you and Rionda five years ago, first by telling me that he had a heart attack in France instead of revealing, as you did, that Rionda was actually in jail, and later on, in 1999, as I've stated, by helping Rionda in the offices of the Imperial Bank, where he obtained a loan under what I now believe were fraudulent circumstances. Rionda claims that I must prove that he is guilty. He forgets that there is no statute of limitations on fraud, so I have plenty of time, even without his 17 million dollar law firms.

Rionda thinks that perhaps, by having 17 million in the bank, and at least 3 other films in production with you and others, he will be able, via his business associate and lawyer D B to find a way to forever avoid "paying the piper."

Rionda has always proudly claimed you to be his 'mentor' and 'teacher' in the Distribution business. In that case, I urge you to remove him from any future contact with filmmakers, as the Catholic Church is now removing abusive Priests, with Zero tolerance, at whatever cost, to save itself if not those already wronged.

Rionda tells me that he is continuing to sell my film no matter what I do, that he will continue to take all the money, and continue to be in breach of contract, since FCB Films is now a "suspended" company due to his refusal to honor his word, his contract and his duty.

Part of the reason he gives for continuing his crooked enterprise is that he has 17 million in "The Bank." I do not know if he is once again using The Imperial Bank, but I cannot imagine any bank that would enjoy this kind of complicity.

If Rionda is conducting this loan the way he conducted the loan for my tiny production, then at least 12 million of the 17 million is going into his account, his lawyer's account, and the accounts of executives at the bank.

Rionda's twisted, self-centered logic in all matters is astonishing. He told me he sold three (3) territories at his year's AFM, but refuses to divulge them as long as I dispute his accounting. In fact, he refers to FCB's 'legal status' as a reason for his non-compliance. This is especially odious, since it is a condition he is personally responsible for, since I – like many independent filmmakers – put costs on my personal credit card when the money he promised was not forthcoming.

I am placing all correspondence, as well as tapes of all conversations between him and anybody I can think of who is a participant in this with him, on the Internet. If you call me, and I welcome any conversation with you, I will first click on my Sony TR900, as this may later be evidence. In addition, this will be part of our "electronic" press kit.

There is a very large body of Law to protect victims of schemes such as Rionda, but laws require honest and decent men to obey them.

Rionda has said that for 20 Grand he has lawyers who could "shut me up."

I can bring 200 witnesses, all professionals in the motion picture industry, all owed money, who can testify to the suffering caused by Rionda and his broken promises to me personally, both verbal and written.

At the very least, I, along with all the others who worked so hard on our film, intend to see that Richard Rionda and Hannibal Pictures Inc., a California Corporation, are removed from any further capacity, contact or ability to harm the faithful hopes of filmmakers and those brave investors who support them.

I do not know if you are one of the producer/distributors of ABSALON. I know that you are presently Rionda's partner on CRIME SPREE, along with Hermesfilm, and THE PIANO PLAYER. I have started research into the various entities you and Rionda have induced to conduct business with you.

4

It is well known in the foreign sales community tha you and Rionda share space at film sales markets, and that you raise large sums of money together. The budgets of Rionda's current films are estimated at north of 50 million +.

I do know that Rionda has kept none of our agreements, and that he scoffs at my demands for a fair accounting and payment, and at my placing all our writings on the Internet. Rionda thinks I lack the fortitude and the resources to contact every single organization at CANNES, as well as all future festivals. He thinks these are impotent gestures, designed only to annoy, but without bite or enforcement. He thinks he can hire more lawyers because he has more money from the productions he has funded via bank loans.

He has always underestimated me.

Refusing to pay my company from the Hermes sale, and refusing to honor his Jan 14, 2000 agreement – an agreement made without honest disclosure on his part -- has cost my company tremendously in time, money and mental anguish.

In fact, Rionda swore to me in January 2000 that the only money he received from LHO/Hermosa of Germany was out-of-pocket expense money. He swore that before taking any sort of "commission" he would fund the making of a 35mmprint – a print which mean theatrical sales could commence – that he failed to make.

I have pages and pages of documents showing all this.

Rionda Del Castro and Hannibal Pictures, Inc. used funds due and promised to William Richert and FCB Films as "seed money" to pay for script options and to hire rooms at sales conventions where financing was obtained for movies like ABSALON, THE PIANO PLAYER and, of course CRIME SPREE – a movie in which he was a partner with Hermes of Germany, the very folks who backed-up his loan from LHO with my feature.

As Rionda Del Castro used my money to seed his current productions, he must provide me with an audit of his producing fees, percentage rights and payback from the production and budgets and future sales of these films.

Rionda Del Castro and Hannibal Pictures Inc. spent upwards of $10,000 of verified FCB funds at Film Markets like MIFED and CANNES to publish lists of available rights to films other than THE FACE OF DUMAS.

It was only one month ago that Rionda Del Castro disclosed to me that he'd taken a $50,000 "commission" from the $190,000 completion budget negotiated by D
P and LHO instead of fulfilling his contractual obligations in 1999.

Rionda Del Castro felt able to reveal these new facts in 2002 because, as he informed me, FCB Films was in "suspension" and had no legal standing. It was strange to hear from Rionda facts about my company which I myself was not yet aware of. It was an outrage for him to gloat over the damage to my company, when this was the direct result of his double-dealing and lies. It was even more despicable for him to say that now that FCB was suspended, he would continue to sell my movie at whatever price he could get, regardless of our contracts.

FCB was not in suspension when Rionda Del Castro paid his lawyer D B thousands of dollars of FCB funds at a time when there was nothing for his lawyer to do regarding FCB, but plenty for D B to do as Riondas attorney on CRIME SPREE and THE PIANO PLAYER and ABSOLON and THE FLYING DUTCHMAN.

Each and every one of these films was sold at film markets using money from FCB and money promised to me, William Richert, by Richard Rionda Del Castro as CEO of Hannibal Pictures, Inc., a California Corporation.

It remains to be "Discovered" how much I am due from FCB's forced investment in these productions at a time when FCB was solvent and attempting to do business with Rionda.

Since no document with Rionda's signature is acceptable, as he ignores them, I am asking that you "sign off" for Rinoda as his current partner and partner of the past seven years. This is the same method being used today by Colin Powell, in asking the Saudis to sign for Arafat, and agreeing that the U.S. will back up Israel's declarations.

I am demanding the following from Rionda and ask that you sign as his mentor and legal guardian:

1.) Immediate payment in the amount of $112,672 U.S. as requested by my attorney.
2.) A complete audit of all of Richard Rionda Del Castro's transactions relating to sales made with FCB funds and disbursment of FCB funds to other entities and productions.
3.) A document signed by you stating Rionda will no longer represent any of my Musketeer productions at any place or any time.
4.) A document signed by you and D B Esq. stating that Richard Rionda will no longer acquire, finance, produce or distributed the completed work of any American filmmaker with a budget of less than 10 million USD. (I figure if an individual can part with 10 million for a movie, he can afford to deal with the likes of Rionda.)
5.) A document signed by you stating that no person involved with MUSKETEERS FOREVER, whether from Canada, France or Germany, employed as writer or director or producer, ever read or was told the plot of my screenplay for THE MAN IN THE IRON MASK.
6.) Copies of all agreements for ABSOLON, THE PIANO PLAYER, THE FLYING DUTCHMAN and the Hermesfilm CRIME SPREE: EACH OF WHICH USED FACILITIES PAID FOR BY FCB FILMS TO PROMOTE INVESTMENT AND FINANCING.

6

Unless and until these 6 conditions are met, I will continue my lifelong fight against liars and cheats, with Rionda and Hannibal Pictures, Inc. as Exhibit #1.

I can envision the day when I will see your faces in a courtroom, in front of a judge, with all the facts "discovered" from Hermesfilm, the Completion Bond Company, BETAR, Hannibal, Liberty Mutual and all the others I am investigating and will discover.

Until that day, we will let the whole world watch as this case evolves on the Internet, where fans of our marvelous film, and all those who wish success for a non-corporate cinema, will be able to share the moment.

Sincerely,

William Richert
AKA Alexander Dumas in A NIGHT IN THE LIFE OF ALEXANDER DUMAS
Cc D B Esq.
J. Hermes, C. Michael Hermesfilm
A-List

Ps. I have tried to explain to Richard Rionda Del Castro provisions of the RACKETEER INFLUENCE AND CORRUPT ORGANIZATIONS ACT ("RICO") AS APPLIED TO RIONDA'S FILM PRODUCTIONS WHICH WERE STARTED/ADVANCED THROUGH IMPROPER USE OF FCB FUNDS. Actionable is Rionda's "directly or indirectly investing income derived from a pattern of racketeering activity or through collection of unlawful debt in any enterprise affecting trade or commerce." – This means a court may find that as an investor I have a claim against Rionda's current productions as they are part of his illegal enterprise. Rionda, saying Fcb is no longer "viable," ignores the major portion of the Federal ruling, which defines the term "enterprise" in the federal act to include "any INDIVIDUAL, PARTNERSHIP, CORPORATION OR ANY UNION OR GROUP OF INDIVIDUALS ASSOCIATED IN FACT THOUGH NOT A LEGAL ENTITY..."* Italics mine.

"a pattern of racketeering" requires engaging in at least TWO INCIDENTS of racketeering conduct within TEN years of each other.

*RACKETEERING CONDUCT: Embezzlement from pension and welfare funds (read: SAG) – Mail Fraud – Wire Fraud – Interference with commerce and fraud in the sale of securities.

FRAUD: Intentional deception resulting in injury to another. Examples: Misrepresentation, Creative Accounting, Overreaching, Predatory Practices, Scam and White Collar Crime.

6 PAGE REPORT ON TELEPHONE CONVERSATION WITH RICHARD RIONDA, HANNIBAL PICTURES, FRIDAY MARCH 8 2002

Dear Max,

You were 12 hours off about Rionda calling the next day after he received your letter. He must have called within one half hour or so, since at 7 PM Friday night he was ringing up here. When I answered, he said with a voice agonized and put-upon that he got a nasty letter from my lawyer.

During the fifteen-minute conversation I said as little as possible, per your directions. Of course, if I said absolutely nothing, he would have said absolutely nothing and we wouldn't know much about his attitude or plans. Hence this longish letter which I hope will save us time later on.

Rionda was quite voluble and offended, even shocked. His first words were "I have money now! I am making big pictures with big stars. I don't need this kind of shit."

Next he played the wounded innocent. He said he had the greatest respect for me as a director and producer and that I had always been a gentleman with him and we always understood each other (sic). He flattered my directing and filmmaker ability. Then he turned righteous and angry about "the letter." He said he would no longer tolerate being called a fraud and a thief. He said he had been cleared of charges of being a thief and had written proof from the French Government (?).

Apparently he had completely forgotten that I had called him a liar and a thief less than a few weeks ago, before my last meeting with him, and that I'd written to others that he was a liar and a thief and that two years ago I quoted one of his former partners in saying he was a "con man thief and a liar" in a letter I widely circulated.

He said he was going to demand a written apology from you at once, on Monday morning, and if necessary he would go to court himself and demand damages double the 112,000 in asking damages for being called a fraud. He said he was going to the Imperial bank for the loan records to prove he'd stolen nothing. He said he signed off on the copyright issue two years ago. He asked why he was being harassed like this when we, that is he and I and his wife Patricia (who is President of his company) agreed that all was well on Feb 8 (or thereabouts.)

I told him our meeting was fine, and that it was fine that he gave me the check registry, but my obligation was to give this to experts like my accountant and lawyer. I said that there were very many items being questioned, like the costs of booths and material costs, etc.

Rionda said that all costs were justified, that our break-even point was $305,000, and that he hadn't reached that point yet.

Careful not to make him too defensive so that he'd clam up, I asked if spending $8,000 for a booth at a film festival was remotely reasonable for a film selling fractions of that amount. He said maybe not. I pointed out that if he had ten or twenty films, as he often said he did, the booth must have cost $160,000.

Then he changed tactics, stopped being quite so "sympatique." It is Rionda's technique to first ingratiate himself in an almost obsequious manner before he suddenly turns and then degrade his opponent with slurs and innuendoes.

His next tactic was an attempt to undermine my trust in Roy. Rionda said it was strange Roy M was working with me when Roy told him he wanted nothing to do with the Mask movie business, and refused to take Rionda's five hundred dollar check back in '99 if it tied him to me or the project.

Then Rionda said that FCB Films was no longer a California corporation, and that it had not paid its taxes, and had no legal standing to take action against him.

Then he reversed himself. He said that maybe he should just get out of the job of selling this movie, since he'd just secured a 17 Million dollar loan for one of his several pictures, with some already in production.

He said "I have money now, I will pay my lawyers whatever it costs. I have 17 million dollar in the bank. I want to meet this Max immediately with my lawyer and we will see what happens."

He said even if the accounting was "off," it was off maybe by twenty or thirty thousand dollars, hardly more. (?)
I said that was the price of a 35mm negative print I was promised.
He said he financed the finishing of the film.
I said we only got a small piece of the 190,000 and we weren't able to finish the film as he'd promised.
He said he never signed a single check from the LHO accounts.

(This was because he was in jail in France. I did not mention that, preferring to hear him out.)
He said he knew I should perhaps get some money soon, that they had sold a "few" territories at this year's AFM, and he was going to give me three thousand or so, but he'd been busy with the market and getting his financing in place.

(What territories? What three thousand? Our contract states I must be informed of such offers and such sales. His grandiosity as a "Distributor" does not entitle him to ignore the producer's contract. I tried not to enter any argument if possible, only to listen as you suggested.)

During the talk he said, more than once, that maybe he should just drop this and give it back to me. He said I could make a lot on American rights, and wondered why I had not sold the movie here. He said he was planning to sell more territories in the upcoming Cannes Film Festival, as there was some interest in "Musketeer" movies. But then he wasn't sure he would continue to sell the movie if it was giving such trouble, when he had so much money now. He said he had new offices and new staff and did not want faxes like this to hurt his business.

I didn't suggest that he quit or stay or anything. Any suggestion I made, I felt, he would spin against me. I said that many people worked on the movie without ever being paid, and that Max S and Roy M were going to make sure all accounting had back up, was truthful and complete according to our contract. He repeated he was not a liar or a thief and he was tired of being called a liar and a thief.

IN REVIEWING THIS CONVERSATION I had to wonder how, within one half an hour of getting your fax, on a Friday afternoon after six, he managed to find out California state and tax info about Fcbfilms. I wondered that he remembered and brought up Roy's talks with him two years ago.

It appears he was prepared for any actions we might take against him.

At the end of the conversation, when he said he was leaving town for the weekend to relax, I told him the situation was out of my hands, and that if he was completely in the right, he would have no problems, provided he had back up for each and every one of his claims.

It sounded like he had mixed feelings about signing off on the picture because he thinks there are sales in Cannes. Now I am wondering what territories he sold at this AFM, and how much he intends to bill FCB.

I decided not to ask why he could make any sales at AFM without consulting me first, as per contract. Why should I be forced to adhere to deals made without my consent? I decided not to ask about the dozens of figures above the $1,000 written approval required by contract. When he said he was still owed money (!?) I reminded him that according to all our agreements and contracts the first money had to go to making a 35mm print so the picture would not be perceived as a video release and hurt our investment. He got quiet.

I said categorically that I was no longer the one to discuss any of this with him, as my opinion was trumped by the questions you and Roy were investigating on behalf of the film.

When he said that he provided the production funds for the picture, I reminded him that FCB only got half of what it was promised from the 190,000 loan, and I said that I looked forward to his accounting for those funds. He was quiet again.

I might have added that the money he "invested" came from a loan based on a feature film he did not own. The film financed itself by its sale to Hermes, and Rionda was the sales-person. He fled the U.S. during the production and left us stranded with a fraction of our intended budget.

THE FOLLOWING WAS NOT INCLUDED IN THE CONVERSATION BUT I TAKE THIS MOMENT TO RECAP:

Hannibal Pictures has the rights to one film only: THE FACE OF DUMAS. That is the title and this picture is substantially different from THE MAN IN THE IRON MASK as well as the film we are presently making, "The Last Musketeers."

It is ironic that Rionda was able to say FCB could not pay its taxes when in fact it was Rionda's use of our foreign sales funds that prevented this. This is a speculative venture that needs all its components to work. Without a 35mm print and 35mm screenings, Rionda is only selling another straight-to-video movie among hundreds of titles with the limited sums that implies. This would hardly be worth the effort and investment any of us put into the movie.

It was Rionda's faliure to supply completing funds as promised, and to provide for the print and ads to promote the feature as a "feature" at film festivals and markets, and his "dumping" the picture for immediate gain without consulting me as part of our contract, which caused the financial hardship fcb and I have endured.

Not only were all marketing funds to be capped at 60 grand, and all costs to be accounted for, but the core of our agreement was that first money to come in to Hannibal was meant to promote the picture, as otherwise, in show business, without promotion and publicity, a film is almost valueless. In fact, at least one of the foreign sales listed by Rionda is very high for most low budget independent U.S. films. Even so, all sales would have quadrupled if we had been perceived as a theatrical feature, which was our attainable goal.

By selling our picture at the lowest cost without making a print, Rionda not only kept the money he was getting he disabled our ability to compete in the marketplace with a finished product, and stole not only money but the time and talents of many individuals.

By contract and verbal it was stated again and again that Hannibal was to open a joint bank account for the funds to be deposited in, and Hannibal and Rionda were to make no sales without FCB approval.

All of these contractual agreements were completely ignored. The contract stated that No amount more than $1,000 was to be spent without FCB approval. When I mentioned some of the amounts listed by Rionda to an expert in distribution, David S: · of the Cinemateque, he said the figures were outrageous and astronomical for an independent film.

AND FURTHERMORE I REFRAINED FROM TELLING RIONDA ONCE AGAIN: The picture was always to be called "THE FACE OF DUMAS" since that is the main title. "The Man In The Iron Mask" is not present on the film THE FACE OF DUMAS.

These are becoming important distinctions. THE FACE OF DUMAS is the first film to feature Alexander Dumas' black ancestry. "The Last Musketeers" is the story without the author, a straight narrative. They are separate films with separate scores and separate narration with separate storylines. And separate buyers.

Rionda seems to think that his contractual obligations no longer apply because FCB is no longer a valid corporation, if that is even true, as I have ownership rights and obligations no matter what the condition of FCB.

Next week MEDIA MAGIK will have finished our new DVD of THE LAST MUSKETEERS. I am working to complete THE FACE OF DUMAS in a TV Friendly mode for sales of the "story behind the writing of…The Man in the Iron Mask" and "The Count of Monte Cristo." This will be material for places like the History Channel and A&E – Not to mention world wide future sales.

Rionda's sales have not touched the actual value of these films. The vagaries at film markets do not vary with "costume" pictures because they are known to be expensive to make. Instead of being informed by right, by courtesy and by contract I am forced to speculate on what he actually got for "sales" at last week's AFM and why he didn't consult with us per contract, and why he didn't list the picture once again, and how much he intends to charge us for the shitty little poster he made, using the wrong title and depicting photos of actors not even in the film (we hope Robert Patrick of X-Files doesn't catch sight of himself.)

ALL OF THE RECENT MUSKETEER movies have made what would be astronomical amounts for an independent feature like ours, in many cases with names no "bigger" than ours. David S of the American Cinemateque is waiting for our DVD to show his publicist, the same guy who promoted THE FULL MONTY and other large indie grossers.

I mention this because we are only at the first stages of showing either of these films. While we have been struggling to complete our product, Rionda has been selling us out and overcharging as well. It is deplorable that something so many have worked on for so long is being fiscally fucked over by such a toad.

Rionda says you will hear from him and his lawyer first thing Monday.

When I said that with four films in pre production and De working for him and with $17,000,000 in the bank, these small amounts could hardly be worth his trouble. Yes, I agree with you, he said. It is maybe too much trouble.

Rionda is a dirty fighter, and I hope he gets his due. I further suspect that, over this weekend, he is going to wish he had not informed me of his 17 million in the bank,

Fax from fcb filmcorp. Inc.

January 3, 1999

TO: Richard Rionda Del Castro
Hannibal Pictures

FROM: William Richert
F.C.B. Film Corporation Inc.

SUBJECT: ACTORS UNION DECIDES IN SECRET INTERNAL REVIEW THAT A MOTION PICTURE HAS BEEN FINISHED, ALTHOUGH THE WRITER, DIRECTOR, PRODUCER AND INVESTORS SAY IT HAS NOT.

SAG LAWYERS ASSERT THAT 90% OF MOTION PICTURE REVENUE WORLD WIDE IS DERIVED SOLELY FROM FREE TELEVISON AND VIDEO.

SCREEN ACTORS GUILD STATES THAT IN 1999 THEATRICAL RELEASE ONLY ACCOUNTS FOR 10% OF FEATURE FILM REVENUE, IMPLIES MPAA DETERMINATIONS ARE NOT VALID.

SAG REFUSES TO ALLOW PRODUCER TO MAKE 35MM PRINT BEFORE COLLECTING RESIDUALS AND PENALTIES

SAG DENIES ACTORS THE RIGHT TO VIEW THEIR WORK ON MEDIUM OF FILM DESPITE INTENT OF INDEPENDENT PROUCER CONTRACT. INSISTS VIDEO AND TV BE SHOWN FIRST.

Dear Richard:

If the letter your company received from Julie J. Kleinberg of the Screen Actors Guild is correct, then all our agreements with SAG should have been made with AFTRA, since SAG has determined by its own internal review that THE FACE OF DUMAS (which SAG incorrectly calls "The Man In The Iron Mask") is a video film, not a theatrical film. If a production

derives 90% from television and video, it must certainly require an AFTRA contract.

However, we maintain that THE FACE OF DUMAS is a theatrical film which is still in the cutting room and which has the same right as every other film made by every director since D.W. Griffith: namely, the right to be shown to an audience, in a theater, in the medium used to create it, good old fashioned 35MM film. SAG is determined to deprive us of this right. Why?

The whole purpose of the SAG Modified Low Budget agreement our company signed in 1997 was to encourage independent filmmakers to make theatrical pictures using SAG actors. There are even built-in penalties for straight-to-video releases.

Yet just a week ago, on December 28, SAG allocated to television and video sales alone fully 90% of the money we acquired to produce and distribute our still-unfinished movie THE FACE OF DUMAS. SAG does this knowing we are still in production. SAG does knowing that if paid this amount we will not be able to complete and deliver the 35MM print, and without a theatrical release, foreign sales are meager.

SAG even refuses to call our movie by its rightful name, THE FACE OF DUMAS, even though our 1999 loan agreement with SAG was signed using that very title.

As you know, for the past eight years, beginning in 1992, our company has been in production on a mini-epic with a current working title of "THE FACE OF DUMAS". Lacking the funds of a studio, we made up with our own time and efforts what money could not provide. The film was shot entirely in 35MM film and the work print was cut on a 35MM moviola in a garage in Sherman Oaks, California.

Please allow a brief review:

In 1998, after unsuccessful test marketing of our early version of THE MAN IN THE IRON MASK, our company went back to work to improve our product.

After showing you a new budget with a new screenplay, you agreed to help us finish our picture and agreed to sell the new film abroad, and to arrange for foreign sales commitments to finance the new production.

After some months, you and Hannibal Pictures arranged a bank loan based on a sale of all German rights, including theatrical release, to a German distributor named Hermesfilmstudio. In return for obtaining this loan, and for undertaking to distribute the picture in foreign territories, you and Hannibal were granted certain distribution rights and sales commissions.

The money provided by Hermes for German theatrical rights and other German rights was to be used solely to make a new picture out of existing footage and added new footage. This money was not given to the producers or investors.

SAG was aware that money from Hermes was placed into an account at the Imperial Bank whose sole purpose was to fund a film production. All the agreements included clauses relating to the Screen Actors Guild which the Guild approved. No clause related to residuals being paid before the film was completed. And to be finished, according to all contracts which included SAG, requires a 35MM theatrical Release Print.

SAG was aware that this money was to be used solely for production, and that a 35MM PRINT was required to compete the loan and satisfy the deal with Hermesfilmstudio, who did not "advance" funds but placed them in escrow. SAG was part of the loan agreements and aware of all our efforts.

Since there would be no point whatsoever in any of this enterprise relating to the old film THE MAN IN THE IRON MASK, as neither the Hermes production money or the LHO Loan offered any rights whatsoever related to showing the old picture, which had been withdrawn from sales, SAG was aware that this new picture was different in focus and content and style and story telling and characterization – all elements which grant an intellectual property specific rights under copyright law throughout the world.

But now the Screen Actors Guild is demanding residuals on the money we spent for production. SAG knows we still haven't finished our 35MM print and have not yet the funds to accomplish this.

SAG knows that unless we make this print, we will be unable to meet our contractual obligations not only to those who have purchased the theatrical rights to our film, but our ability to meet the intent of SAG's own contracts will be destroyed.

SAG is knowingly and willfully penalizing us for not making a theatrical release of our picture at the same time it is refusing to allow us to do so. Where do funds for production come from if not from investors or from the sales of rights and territories? Ironically, the $11, 058. demanded by SAG is almost the exact amount needed to strike our answer print.

Under F.C.B. agreement with Hannibal, Hannibal shall receive the first 60,000 acquired in the selling of rights or territories in order to distribute the picture. We have agreed that part of that 60,000 must be used for an answer print. This is standard for a theatrical picture. SAG is demanding part of this money. We don't believe they have the right to claim it.

This was not a made-for-television and video production. It was shot and edited entirely on film and the elements – negative, sound track, etc. are all film elements. They were copied onto digital tape for sales and distribution purposes.

However: we do not have a print; ergo we have not finished the picture, as envisioned in the Hermes contract and by SAG's own Independent Producer contract.

We believe we have the same rights as other film studios, or auto manufacturers -- or any other commercial enterprise -- to create the best product in the best medium to eventually produce a well-earned return on all our efforts.

SAG's Residuals Determination, conducted by SAG alone, and ignoring all our pleas, has injured and nearly destroyed all our work. Thus far, this film has required 8 years of labor on the part of many artists, including wonderful actors whose work may never be seen on film.

If SAG can dictate when a film is be finished, dictate the percentage of amount of revenue from theaters before a theater is ever booked, even what "genre" it is -- then SAG must be in fact the author and producer, not to mention the main audience of the picture.

5

In fact, SAG is a union and its members were already paid in full at the time of work according to contract. SAG must certainly be held accountable to the same regulations as other members of the American Federation of Labor. For example, can any automakers union – in a secret, internal review -- decide for the banker, insurer, designer, manufacturer, promoter and sales force, when a Chevrolet is ready for market, or whether the auto must be a V8 or a straight 6 or stick shift only?

There is an endless list of movies which were previewed in one form and then trimmed or re-cut altogether. If SAG were to arbitrarily say a film was finished just because certain territories were sold to raise money, then scores of pictures would never see finished post-production, having sold territories to finance themselves.

F.C.B. and Hannibal must avail ourselves of the various legal precedents relating to these issues. SAG can't stop a director or producer from completing a picture without just cause and review. How can residuals be due before the movie is finished?

The DGA, which regulates the work of directors, provides for a theatrical screening of a Director's Cut. This screening has not occurred for THE FACE OF DUMAS. I am a retired member of both the DGA and WGA and they themselves have hard-fought rules relating to the rights of a motion picture director. Again, we didn't sign an AFTRA contract.

Regarding the earlier film which our company, under the trade name of THE INVISIBLE STUDO, released at the Aero Theater – we dispute the amount of residuals claimed by SAG again for the same reasons: the sums provided by video were spent on theatrical release and prints and ads.

If we have been forced by circumstance and lack of money to sell our film "as is" to certain countries and territories, this is a way of surviving in show business – like all other business seeking financing. This is not a reason to be penalized or threatened to be put out of business by union officials.

If GM sells China manufacturing rights so it can make and sell cars there, is the money China spends for buildings and equipment and metal sheeting considered food for residuals?

What are “residuals” ?

If SAG defines money acquired and spent solely for production and distribution as money subject to payment of residuals, then it must do so for all producers equally – Fox and Universal and Columbia and Lion’s Gate and Artisan and TNT et al. If those producers are allowed to obtain production money from the sale of rights and territories, why can’t we? Was the money spent by Artisan to improve the picture AFTER it acquired the world rights to Blair Witch Project – but BEFORE theatrical release -- subject to residuals? Was Artisan allowed to make prints and show the picture in theaters only AFTER paying residuals?

In addition to remedies provided by AFMA , both F.C. B. and Hannibal must explore all legal protection granted to small businesses under current interstate laws and SBA laws before succumbing to SAG’s unfair demands for money.

I insist, as our agreement provides, that Hannibal’s first money derived from sale of rights, after Hannibal’s basic functioning, be spent on completing THE FACE OF DUMAS so we can satisfy our contracts and so that we have the opportunity to be competitive with other films of our kind.

We will ask SAG how it arrived at a definition of our “genre” when SAG has not got the final screenplay and has not seen the print because it doesn’t exist yet.

The Wright brothers tried 600 times before finally getting their airplane off the ground. Under SAG’s Residual Determinations as applied to us, that first flight would’ve been declared the final result, the wings would’ve been sold for the value of the wood, and the Wright brothers would still be farmers.

Moreover, if SAG maintains that THE MAN IN THE IRON MASK (1998) is a finished film and subject to residuals, then what is THE FACE OF DUMAS (1999) but a new and different project, according to SAG’s own rules?

And if THE FACE OF DUMAS is a new and different project, why then the performances of the actors are in fact a “re-use”. This means that the payment of fees is differently apportioned, again according to SAG's own rules.

Indeed, if THE FACE OF DUMAS is the very same film, as defined by SAG, this contradicts and makes null and void Sag's own Buyers Assumption Agreements which SAG insisted we sign to obtain the LHO Bank Loan in 1999 – a full year after the test marketing of THE MAN IN THE IRON MASK.

And if it is the same film, how do we explain the fact that the story is completely different. The early reviews of THE FACE OF DUMAS are completely different from those received by of THE MAN IN THE IRON MASK. We are obtaining a new copyright.

(We are very interested in how SAG arrived at its 90/10 split of moneys on an unfinished production. We want to know why SAG determined our film wasn't under the jurisdiction of AFTRA if it knew this all along. We are very interested in what "genre" SAG has decided our film belongs. Once these decisions were reserved for the author, the director, the producer, even the critics. In the year 2000 it is SAG, apparently, who decides all by itself in a secret internal review what "genre" an author's work is, what audiences will respond to it and in what mediums. Who gave SAG all these rights? How did SAG obtain this power? Is it fair? Whatever happened to the right of a director and author and the actors to an "opening night"?)

In any event, THE FACE OF DUMAS is not finished, and we have the documentation, lab reports, editing bills etc., to show that we worked on the sound and picture for all of 1999 – in fact Hermes only recently completed the Digital track less than two months ago and we are presently looking at stock footage of swordplay. Also, we are awaiting funds to complete the mag track in order to strike a print.

If SAG wishes to force us out of the ability to satisfy the theatrical market and therefore reduce dramatically our chance to see any profit or return on all our work in order to enrich itself, SAG makes a pathetic case for the actors who will never see the fruits of their performances on the big screen, which is what the SCREEN Actor's Guild purports to be all about – and, most significantly, what the Modified Low Budget Film Contract is all about. Based on their own appraisal, SAG would have been wrong not to send us to AFTRA.

8

If SAG, by insisting on defaulting us while knowing this can put us out of business and in default on other contracts, then SAG should also take responsibility for paying me and my partners all our deferments since we aren't allowed to present our work in the marketplace, where audiences can decided the fate of a movie, as they were meant to, and where profits can be made for the millions of hours of effort.

In many telephone calls and long correspondence we have certainly advised SAG that by constantly calling and making demands for documents, etc., SAG is fatally undermining our ability to perform for ourselves and our investors, using their punishing legal maneuvers to exhaust and defeat us and bankrupt us.

Even now as we struggle for money to make our final answer print, SAG is demanding interest at 1% a month along with penalties.

No director can be said to be treated fairly until his or her film can be shown to an audience in the theater. This fundamental right , acknowledge by the Directors Guild of America and the Writers Guild of America, should not be denied to anyone without due process and grave consideration.

We ask that Hannibal send the funds required to complete our picture for theatrical release before sending any money whatsoever to SAG without arbitration, appeal, and judicial review.

Sincerely,

William Richert
SAG MEMBER (Current) , DGA AND WGA (Ret.)

President, F.C.B. Film Corp. Inc.

Cc Julie J. Kleinberg
Marla Singerman
Scott Whitehead

THE INVISIBLE STUDIO

DRAFT

FAX TO CHRIS R
General Counsel
Sightsound.com

FROM BILL RICHERT
The Invisible Studio

Dear Chris,

I saw on Peter Jennings' ABC NEWS that Metallica has six different versions of the same song on Netcaster. When I am done with the new endings on my two unfinished prints, I will have four original cinema versions of THE MAN IN THE IRON MASK. These versions, each with a different edit and soundtrack, are a journey in independent filmmaking as well as entertainment, and could constitute a crash course in how editing and music can make changes in a film, a subject of interest when the entire nation "wants to be a director." (They do not all have to be on the Internet. They can buy the DVD.)

Additionally, I am faxing you now, with hard copies to follow when I send the tape of the actual film, some interesting fan letters.

Only one of our actors is accessible via Internet. Dennis Hayden plays d'Artagnan in the picture. You can see from this sampling that he is getting fan letters from all over the world. Few of these territories have been sold, and the film cannot be downloaded until we're up on Sightsound.com, so we can only assume that bootleg copies are being passed around.

Since Mr. Hayden has never received letters like this in his career, and since not one dime has been spent promoting this picture, one can conclude that the movie has "legs" Internationally.

You may also note from the pages I'm faxing from Amazon and Tower Records that our film is not only on the same page as the $80,000 MGM Version starring Leo, but it appears to be gaining on it in sales (all of which sales are in breach of an earlier expired contract which I can make available to you. Until I began looking up our title on the *Internet, we had no idea any sales were being made. Now we discover the film is growing in popularity along with the genre – and without any promotion whatsoever. This is the power of a classic subject, and portends a terrific future for our movie.*

As soon as all our rights are clear, which we anticipate any day now, we will begin discussions with a manufacturing DVD/ home video company to commence sales of THE MAN IN THE IRON MASK & THE THREE MUSKETEERS as well as A DANCER'S LIFE featuring the greatest ballet stars in history in their classroom studies.

Both of these films have subject matter which are almost "required viewing" for ballet fans and Musketeer fans all over the world, and so have a waiting audience.

As an individual independent filmmaker linked to Sightsound.com, with a work-in-progress series of pictures with wide appeal, I believe I can benefit both my picture and your company, which is known for a fearless record of innovation and experimentation.

I read a lot about "stickiness" being a factor on websites. In fact, the popularity of Amazon.com is surely more for its gargantuan diversity than its single-mindedness. You can see in just one week our sales improved.

Our film brings "diversity" to the entire Dumas/Musketeer genre, which has been popular throughout the world for 150 years. Our association with Sightsound.com may also create new diversity on your masthead, with the introduction of new-age "period" dramas (the Bravo cable showing of THE COUNT OF MONTE CRISTO produced their highest-ever ratings.)

We have a trailer for this first version of THE MAN IN THE IRON MASK that is kind of sexy and hot, and only a minute or so long.

Tomorrow I will send you the new VHS so you can watch the picture yourself. The VHS selling world-wide is a bad copy of an unmixed track with no foley or sound effects. In an unprecedented action, we want to "recall" those tapes for a new, complete version, to sending this out in DVD at first, as an example of the speed new technology can display when competing with the standard, almost antiquated forms of distribution/exhibition/production.

When we raise the funds, we will add the ending you saw on the in-progress "Director's Cut."

All this can add up to a pleasant experiment in DVD-VHS promotion and theatrical exhibition, with an assisst from the news media, the fans of Alexander Dumas, and students and lovers of ballet across the globe.

We want to "reverse engineer" a hit, starting from the place major studios wind up, then moving forward (not backwards) towards the theater chains. Thus all mediums snap from the electricity of each other, and our films can reach their intended viewers at a fraction of a cost and multiplication of the promotion.

Our incomplete version of THE MAN IN THE IRON MASK is now selling on the world wide Internet on the same page $120 million MGM version based on original story. This is David seated at the same table as Goliath, sharing the same rewards. from the press and Dumas fans and ballet aficionados worldwide. Even China is watching our new version of THE MAN IN THE IRON MASK.

I look forward to speaking again with you.

Cheers,

Bill Richert, F.C.B. Films & The Invisible Studio

1423 Euclid St. Suite 200 Santa Monica Ca 90404 Tel 310.394.7308 Fax 310.394.6028

August 24, 2001

TO: HANNIBAL PICTURES AND RICHARD RIONDA, AKA RICHARD RIONDA DEL CASTRO

FROM: FCB FILMS INC
FAX 310 394 6028
And:

Dear Mr. Rionda, AKA Richard Del Castro:

We are each and together investors/creditors relative to the motion picture THE FACE OF DUMAS, which we have reason to believe you have been using to reap fraudulent financial sums in violation of contracts between yourself and FCB Films Inc.

Each of us has invested, or is owed, more than ten thousand ($10,000) U.S. in the motion picture, and each of us is a U.S. citizen currently residing in California.

You have stated that you and Hannibal Pictures Inc. have received $265,000 U.S. from sales of THE MAN IN THE IRON MASK, knowing that this is a film you are not authorized to sell.

Your contract with FCB Films stated that you would be entitled to $60,000 for the promotion, sales brochures, direct travel expenses and screening expenses for the film THE FACE OF DUMAS and no other film.

You and your company admit to netting more than $265,000 from the sales of the wrong title. You have misled or lied to foreign distributors stating they have the right to change the title. In return for selling them an inferior and incomplete film entitled THE MAN IN THE IRON MASK you collected the aforementioned $265,000 but have accounted for only a fraction of that amount.

Hannibal Pictures caused our company, FCB FILMS INC. a California Corporation, to enter into an agreement with you to promote and sell the THE FACE OF DUMAS in foreign territories in return for post-production funding.

Instead, you fled the U.S. during post-production, and then Hannibal Pictures took all of the money.

Hannibal Pictures has absolutely no right to engage in any U.S. sales. We have heard that you are attempting to do so. Demand is hereby made that you immediately cease and desist such activity.

The $60,000 dedicated to promotion and screenings exclusively for THE FACE OF DUMAS was fraudulently taken by you -- AKA Richard Del Castro. You continue to ignore our requests for a legal accounting.

It is clear that you -- AKA Richard Del Castro – did not use the $60,000 on the promotion of the film THE FACE OF DUMAS. In fact, not one item of promotional material has been demonstrated by Hannibal Pictures.

Instead of promoting the picture, we believe you used the funds to acquire real estate in France. This is a gross and fraudulent misuse of funds, which rightfully belong to investors.

It is well known that you -- AKA Richard Rionda Del Castro – were deported from the U.S. and jailed in France during the time you were supposed to be financing post-production and sales promotion of THE FACE OF DUMAS.

It is known that the sales listed by you are less than half of those promised in your earlier written estimates. According to expert witnesses in the field of foreign distribution and sales, the other amounts listed by Hannibal are less than 15% of standard payments from foreign distributors.

In the questionable accounting recently received from you after a request from Max Esq., you refer to income derived from sales of THE MAN IN THE IRON MASK, but list no sums received for THE FACE OF DUMAS, the only film Hannibal is actually supposed to be selling, and the only film Hannibal Pictures has the legal rights to.

THE FACE OF DUMAS was created by its owners to correct the flawed and inferior print of a picture called THE MAN IN THE IRON MASK, which FCB Films withdrew from distribution, as was known to you and Hannibal Pictures.

All foreign contracts re: THE FACE OF DUMAS, are required to be examined by FCB FIILMS INC. and its accountant. However, the final contracts have still been withheld, even the long-form contract with Hermes of Germany.

Only $80,000 of the $265,000 Hannibal admits to receiving for THE FACE OF DUMAS has been accounted for, and this was used for post-production expenses directly related to the finishing of THE FACE OF DUMAS.

It was astonishing for us to read your recent letter to Max S Esq. in which you admitted that you have allowed foreign distributors to use the false title THE MAN IN THE IRON MASK for our film THE FACE OF DUMAS in spite of contracts, agreements and volumes of correspondence stating you have no rights to any exploitation of that different film.

By your actions and admissions, you have made it almost impossible for the investors in THE FACE OF DUMAS to recoup our investment. It is apparent that you think your ability to flee the country at will can protect you from U.S. laws protecting investors and creditors from fraud and deception.

You have been informed many times in writing and by telephone that THE FACE OF DUMAS is part of a trilogy on the WORKS OF ALEXANDRE DUMAS by William Richert. You are aware, and Hannibal Pictures Inc. is aware, that releasing this film under the false title is not only an attempt to rip-off the public by misleading them to think that this is the DiCaprio film, but it destroys our ability to use THE FACE OF DUMAS as part of the promotion for our upcoming picture in the DUMAS TRILOGY.

We demand an immediate accounting of the $60,000 that Hannibal has taken to promote THE FACE OF DUMAS.

If, as we believe, THE FACE OF DUMAS was not promoted by Hannibal Pictures as required by contract, then we are doubly damaged: not only was $60,000 denied to rightful investors and owners, but sales of our pictures THE FACE OF DUMAS were rendered impossible in Foreign Markets because no promotion or screenings or advertising was done.

FCB Films was promised sales in the millions for THE FACE OF DUMAS, and it was your repeated assertions and written projections that these sums would be paid that caused us to enter into any contract with you and HANNIBAL PICTURES INC. at all.

You have breached the contracts with FCB Films time after time with impunity. Now that you are in the U.S., we can deal with the issue without concerns of foreign courts.

We are currently requesting that our attorney, Max . S examine the facts of this case and present this information to those authorities he deems appropriate.

We regret that you are continuing to play your old tricks within the U.S. borders, but we are grateful for the chance to prevail in this matter before you again flee the country.

Sincerely,

William Richert

RE: THE THREE MUSKETEERS VS HANNIBAL PICTURES: DO FOREIGN AGENTS RIP OFF INDEPENDENT PRODUCERS? A PRODUCER PUTS HIS PROFITS ON THE INTERNET

Dear Richard,

In our February 8 meeting, you said that the difference between U.S. law and French law is that in France you can be handcuffed into jail on mere suspicion. You said that is why they put you in jail in France. You showed me a notice given you by the French Government which allows you to travel. You said you were sick and tired of being called a liar and a thief, and you know that it's true I have myself called you a lair and a thief, and I have said that you managed to take $267,000 from our picture's proceeds without fair accounting, and that you sold foreign territories to my film in violation of our written contract and our verbal agreements.

Perhaps you believe that the sums involved are too small to attract much attention. However, Independent producers and filmmakers world-wide recognize a big smelly rip-off when they see one. According to a recent New York Times article, which I will forward shortly, the whole world hates a cheat; in every nation, among every culture. When unmasked, they are reviled and despised. I cannot imagine how companies currently doing productions with Hannibal would feel any different when they get to know you as I know you.

I have placed the outrageous "registry" you sent to our company on the Internet. It is my hope that in the vast world of fans of movies and believers in fair business dealings and common decency there will be a response to your deeds, which pollute the entire economic foundation of the independent cinema as an art form.

It is my hope that reporters of various news and electronic media, university students interested in film finance, producers and directors of all kinds, will pick up on this bogus "accounting", and see it for what it is: Rionda's transparent method of putting a film and a company out of business for short-term immediate – and a pitifully small – profits. That you are not the only foreign sales agent who behaves like this is no excuse.

It may happen overnight, or it might take years of court appearances to compel you to behave like a normal "human". Nevertheless, in the course of events it will become apparent to all that your "Hannibal" is no hero, and anybody who enters a contract with this "Hannibal" may find the specter of Lector, not the friend of the artist. Every single player with an email address in the distribution business throughout the world is going to be made aware of the harm you have done, by the same means that Alexandre Dumas, the subject of our film, fought repression in France so long ago. For me to remain silent would be tantamount to complicity in your wrongdoing.

You are aware that since you are selling our film without our permission, all your "sales" are detrimental to us. You not only keep our share, you make it impossible to sell that film to anybody else. Notwithstanding, this "bootlegging" does have an unexpected advantage: we know now that audiences of all ages love the picture. Experts in marketing are stunned by the thousands of email fan letters the movie has gotten. Perhaps we can make up for you lack of fair business dealings with wide publicity. In the greed and evil of our fictional King Louis, people may see the mirror of a non-noble person like Richard Rionda Del Castro, and hope for a similar comeuppance.

Now we will offer our new and different production, 'A NIGHT WITH ALEXANDRE DUMAS" for free, with only the cost of postage, to every country willing to accept it, to all citizens who want to see it, on any medium willing to show it, outside the United States. "A NIGHT WITH ALEXANDRE DUMAS" is a romance of swashbuckling honor and decency. You will soon know what Dumas knew: not only is the pen mightier than the sword, but word lasts long after swords have rusted into dust. Like I said, I'm going to make you famous. What you have refused to give us by right, we shall recoup in publicity. We are, after all, in show business.

You have laughed at our request that you honor your contracts, while attempting instead to lock me and my fellow artists into an Iron Mask of financial hardship, and put us out of business. I believe this will backfire, and you will reap unto you the rewards you justly deserve.

You will soon discover the power of what in the U.S.A. we call "The First Amendment."

Sincerely,

William Richert
Writer/Director/Producer "THE THREE MUSKETEERS AND THE MAN IN THE IRON MASK"

Fax TO RICHARD RIONDA DEL CASTRO
CEO HANNIBAL PICTURES 1.323.848.2946.
FR WILLIAM RICHERT
DIRECTOR 'THE FACE OF DUMAS' 'THE MAN IN THE IRON MASK (UNFINISHED VERSION)' 'THE THREE MUSKETEERS & THE MAN IN THE IRON MASK' AND 'A NIGHT WITH ALEXANDER DUMAS'

April 4, 2002

Dear Richard,
Whilst you may not immediately see the connection between yourself, Hannibal Pictures and the pollution of the California ground waters by MTBE, you will perhaps recognize the passion of an anti-polluter on a crusade. This is the first of my salvos into the toxic atmosphere of your pervasive mendacity, with many to come. Literature is replete with defining moments of artistic defiance, but the film business has a long way to go in righting the wrongs done by lying and thieving foreign agents of American filmmakers (though it may also be the same for foreign filmmakers sold in the U.S.) You and others like you rely on the legal process for the protection of your activities, since it takes a long, long time and much more money to

bring motions before a judge than most filmmakers can possibly afford. For this reason, I am proceeding against you in the worldwide court of common sense.

To begin, what we've done is establish a website devoted to the length and breadth of the transactions between you and me. For the first time in all of history, I believe, a producer has put his entire foreign sales accounting on the world wide web, and is forwarding this information to thousands of possible helpers in the fight against the costly legal hurdles you hide behind in a perversion of the use of the law, and the passage of time: laws which are, paradoxically, the very ones you depend on for safety. However, these hurdles can be overcome. Nothing moves quicker than a nasty rumor or a good idea. You and I are going to experiment with the use of mass communication, intellectual smart bombs, if you will. While we educate each other, we can share.

With millions of watching eyes and ears, who can hide? What publicity! Showbiz! And you know we independents have always depended upon word of mouth.

Onward!
William Richert

D'ARTAGNAN
(disappearing)
Aris -- come on!

ANOTHER AND ANOTHER SPIKE enter the giant's body.

BLACKSMITH
(eyes closing in death)
Be patient, sire. I am coming.

His head drops, but still his mighty weight blocks the thundering door.

CUT TO:

INT. GRAND COURT DOORS - NIGHT (uses interior + exterior)

The courtyard doors are closed and appear to be deserted. SUDDDENLY A CLATTER AT THE REAR. The Three Musketeers come running.

But just behind them, rounding the corner, A GARRISON OF ROYAL GUARDS, SPIKES HELD HIGH, chase after.

Suddenly they stop. In front of them are the dreaded, and beloved, Three Musketeers, backed up against the courtyard doors, swords ready.

D'ARTAGNAN
(shouts so all may hear)
LET'S TAKE SOME MORE WITH US, SHALL WE?

PORTHOS
HOW ABOUT THE ONE IN THE FRONT?

FRONT ROYAL GUARD: Shivers, steps back.

ARAMIS
(raising his blade; to D'Artagnan and Porthos)
Gentlemen, if we must part this night, I say let that portion of our souls which reach eternity never travel one without the other.

D'ARTAGNAN
So that if one laughs, we all shall laugh!

ARAMIS
(points his sword up)
We shall dwell in heaven with each other, and our kind.

PORTHOS
Let us be joyous until the moment we are dead!

ARAMIS
So be it!

He and the others lift their swords in a GREAT CLASH OF METAL.

THE THREE MUSKETEERS
(shout lustily)
ONE FOR ALL AND ALL FOR ONE!!

Then Pathos steps a mighty step backwards against the gothic doors behind them. With a CRACKING the doors part and the Three Musketeers rush into the courtyard, swords held high.

Just then, Gimbaud slips through the soldiers in the hallway, who are too startled to stop him.

GIMBAUD
(as The Three disappear)
Wait for me!

INT. CASTLE COURTYARD - NIGHT

The Three Musketeers, followed by Gimbaud, run into the courtyard, look around, momentarily astonished. It appears deserted. Then they all look up at a call from the castle walls above.

The Invisible Studio & F.C.B. Films present WILLIAM RICHERT'S THE MASK OF DUMAS

starring (In alphabetical order)

EDWARD ALBERT R.C. ARMSTRONG DANA BARRON TIMOTHY BOTTOMS

MEG FOSTER JAMES GAMMON DENNIS HAYDEN ROBERT LITTMAN NICK RICHERT WILLIAM RICHERT

and REX RYON Produced Written and Directed by WILLIAM RICHERT Executive producers DENNIS HAYDEN LOUIS MESEROLE JEAN MARK FELIO Co-Produced by GLORIA PRYOR and H. ROY MATLEN Associate Producer DONALD L. SLENP Production Desighner JACQUES HEBERT Costume Designer SALVADOR PEREZ Casting AARON GIFFITH Director Photography WILLIAM BARBER

Edited by ANDRE VAILLANCOURT Music by JEFFERY R. GUND and JIM ERVIN Sound Design FRANK SERIFINE

Additional Photography JULIUS METOYER and JEFF GREENE Music Editing CHRISTINE LUETHJE

Collected Richert Papers

The Justice Letters

Volume II

II. Incognito VS The Body Snatcher

N·E·W
The Coffee Alternative
INCOGNITO
100%
ROASTED
SOY BEANS

N·E·W
The Coffee Alternative
INCOGNITO
100%
ROASTED
SOY BEANS

N·E·W
The Coffee Alternative
INCOGNITO
100%
ROASTED
SOY BEANS

N·E·W
The Coffee Alternative
INCOGNITO
100%
ROASTED
SOY BEANS

Draft, December 5, 2001

BRIEF HISTORY RELATING TO THE EARLY ATTEMPTS TO CREATE A SOYBEAN COFFEE FOR THE WORLD

In 1986, after a long night's Malibu party, a friend gave me some soybean coffee which I had never tasted before. Almost instantly, my headache went away. Though the stuff tasted awful, it produced a quick jolt of energy. My friend said that Coca-Cola also began as a pharmacist's cure for a hangover.

Thus began my long interest in soy coffee and soybeans. In 1988 I started a company called CABINO, and invited a friend, Ellen Lee (now Ellen Tauscher, a California Congresswoman) to run the fledgling company. Though we tried for almost two years, we really could not produce more than a funky brew that turned more people off than on. Soon Ellen married our backer, who had founded Computerland, and moved North to San Francisco.

I continued to experiment with various combinations of beans and different roasters, however, and in 1991, while filming MY OWN PRIVATE IDAHO with River Phoenix and Keanu Reeves and the singer Flea in Portland, we all tested dozens of different kind of soybean blends until the best kind of beans were found. When roasted in a particular way, which had not been tried in the entire history of soy, the soybeans really did taste like coffee.

We called the new company INCOGNITO THE COFFEE ALTERNATIVE. After me, my main investor was River Phoenix, although a handful of friends put up additional funds. I also brought along my old investors from CABINO.

In 1991 we opened a store on Main Street and soon we were selling modest amounts of coffee in stores from Erewhon and Mrs. Gooches to coffee shops in New York. NBC TELEVISION did a profile on our company and another start-up, STARBUCKS. Michael Stipes wanted to invest, Dan Ackroyd did commercials in our blending room, Sting was drinking it at the White Lotus Foundation in Santa Barbara.

2

Then the unthinkable happened; River died. Though we were a rising company, the profits were small compared to my film work as a writer/director, and much of my enthusiasm for INCOGNITO was the vision I shared with River. It was true then and now that INCOGNITO, in addition to being a wildly popular hot drink, could be an inexpensive and complete diet for millions. It was portable, nutritious, and had a long shelf life. Without his encouragement and involvement, the "business" of manufacturing soybean coffee lost some of its allure. Further, we were being courted by Sugar Foods, makers of sweet n' low, and when that deal fell through, there seemed little reason to continue. With my store on Main Street in Santa Monica, with its overhead and employees, I was spending thousands a month with a fractional return. We shut the store, and I said we would wait until the timing was better to start again.

Soybeans had really been regarded as not much beyond cattle feed until very recently, but now that has changed. Millions are trying to get more soy into their diets.

I began to think anew about our INCOGNITO while being interviewed by Barry Lawrence for his book "IN SEARCH OF RIVER PHOENIX" in1999. I gave Barry a bag of our old stuff, he took it home to Petaluma, and soon I was heading back into the soybean coffee business with a presentation to Barry's father at a meeting in 1999. However, Barry's father decided to take a world tour and forgo an investment in INCOGNITO. I continued film work, making small amounts for me and my wife, awaiting the next right moment.

PARTNERSHIP WITH FAMOUS CHIROPRACTOR

In the spring of 2001 my wife and I undertook chiropractic treatment from noted sports doctor, Ron Marinaro D.C. of the Pain Relief Center in Studio City, California. Gretchen was in severe neck pain from an athletic injury.

During very first weeks of our treatment we became friends with "Doctor Ron," and during one of the treatments I spoke about the soybean coffee company I had founded almost sixteen years earlier, but which was presently in a state of suspension until the right funding could be found and right management could be put into place.

Dr. Marinaro said that many of his patients were desperately looking for an alternative to caffeine, and if the taste was right, he thought he had enough investors, which he called "pigeons, " among his friends and family to start the company back up again. He mentioned one woman in particular who had told him she had $250,000 she was looking to put into a speculative business, and that his best friend, Tony was being given $10,000,000 from his billionaire dad Merv to start up a new company.

Of course, Dr. Marinaro wanted to taste it first, as he'd never even heard of soybean coffee before, and was not even sure he knew what a soybean actually looked like.

Thus my wife and I made up some INCOGNITO, along with INCOGNITO 50/50, which combines soybean coffee with regular coffee, and we brought it along on our next chiropractic appointment. Our mini-roaster, of a kind which didn't exist before the coffee craze fueled by Starbucks, Peets and others, was purchased from the Gourmet Coffee Roasters, owned by Richard Karno. I had met with Richard Karno, the proprietary "Brand" roaster before my meeting with Barry Lawrence in Petaluma one year earlier. While Richard Karno had never seen a soybean either, roasted or not, he had agreed to roast a batch when the time came.

Dr. Marinaro accepted our bag of coffee, and on the next appointment brought us a nice bottle of Chardonnay from his personal cellar. He said that he and his wife Catherine had brewed the coffee and that they loved it, and he thought he could raise money from his family and friends, particularly Tony

Dr. Marinaro said that he himself, along with his brother and father, could put up $250,000 or more with no problem, as the start-up investment.

On April 23rd, in the treatment room in the office of the Pain Relief Center on Ventura Blvd. in Studio City, in the presence of Gretchen, Dr. Marinaro and I enthusiastically shook hands across the Chiropractic table: we agreed that we would become partners, with a 60/40 split. For his 40% share, Ron said that he would raise the start-up capital, that together we would hire a manager, and he and I would share the President's salary. As a fee for my work in rebuilding the company, I would receive $2,000 a month for the first three months, with an increase thereafter.

We also agreed that my trade secrets for INCOGNITO, along with all other proprietary information, would be kept secret. I know that Dr. Marinaro understood this because I explained that on other occasion where I had revealed information

4

about INCOGNITO, I had videotaped the occasion. He said, "I am your Doctor, your partner and your friend," a mantra he repeated many, many times afterward.

Dr. Marinaro was fastidious and thorough before making any kind of investment. He wanted to know everything about the business first hand. Almost immediately he wanted to put out $60,000 to set up a roasting facility, in order to bring the best beans to Merv with his friend Tony . I persuaded him to buy a cheaper roaster to experiment with roasting and with beans. I said our fastest best way to market would be using my "Brand" roaster Richard Karno, but we could certainly do the initial preparations ourselves.

To accomplish this I tracked down and ordered the purchase of a roaster from my contacts at AMBEX COFFEE ROASTERS in Florida for less than $5,000, the first expenditure in our agreement, while my wife and I bought organic soybeans from the local Co-Op and drove to his Malibu estate on B Drive, where we assembled the green roaster in his garage and made dozens of roasts until we found the right temperature and right time combination to correlate with the formula I had used with 2 ton roasters.

During these days I regaled Dr. Marinaro with stories of how It had taken me many years, and the experimentation with many different blends of soybeans, before I arrived at the only formula I knew which made INCOGNITO taste delicious, while his daughter Gabriella helped unload the beans from the bin to the bags. With his wife Catherine looking on, and the maids cooking and tasting the brew in the kitchen, it seemed to be the idyllic kind of partnership we had longed for.

Dr. Marinaro even gave Gretchen a chiropractic adjustment at the house, a sure sign of compassion and dedication.

Almost at once we were meeting on weekends at the Marinaros, where I was introduced to Tony and his wife and children. Gretchen had known Tony since they were in Darryl Hickman's acting class in 1994.

Dr. Marinaro said he'd given Tony some INCOGNITO and that Tony had fallen in love with it and felt this was finally the kind of business deal he could present to his father, Merv. Smoking some of Tony's fantastic Cuban cigars, I told the history of INCOGNITO to Tony. I told him the formula was a trade secret and never written down, and he swore himself to secrecy. Also present at these meetings were T.J.

5

Marinaro D.C., Ron's father, and Thomas Marinaro D.C., his brother, and his mother Rose, who we knew was the accountant at The Pain Relief Center.

In June we made two major presentations of INCOGNITO to Tony and the family of Dr. Ron, explaining in detail the history, the benefits and the enourmous financial potential of the product. Dr.Thomas Marinaro took digital photos, and said that he thought INCOGNITO would find its greatest success on the West Coast, while Catherine said it would go over just as well in New York.

Dr. Marinaro said Merv had had , and was using soy to help himself. He thought Merv would be the perfect backer, as Merv was a billionaire and into health, and he'd been disappointed by the other soybean coffees he had ordered from the Internet, especially one called Soyfee's Choice.

Thus began weeks of daily meetings and briefings at Dr. Ron Marinaro's house or at The Pain Relief Center, while my wife and I received chiropractic adjustments from him. I invited him to meet Richard Karno, my roaster, and showed him the equipment and bags and labeling process at the Gourmet Coffee Warehouse in Venice. Dr. Marinaro agreed that contracting Richard would be better than building an entire operation, and faster, too.

It was decided that Gretchen and I would make up at least a dozen bags of Incognito of both varieties which Dr. Ron Marinaro and Tony could present to Merv on his boat in the Mediterranean during the 4th of July weekend, 2001.

During the last week of June, just before his trip, Dr. Ron and Gretchen and I met in the garden at the Gourmet Coffee Roasters, where Richard Karno was preparing large quantity pricing and the pricing of his fantastic Kosher bird-friendly organic coffee.

When Dr. Ron arrived at the meeting, he revealed that without telling me had had new labels made for INCOGNITO by a designer named Elizabeth R, who owed money to Dr. Ron Marinaro as a patient, and who had agreed to make some samples to help pay off her debt.

In earlier meetings at Dr. Ron's house, on more than one occasion, generally loudly and in front of others, his wife Catherine Marinaro had said that she "absolutely

6

hated" my label, and the colors on my label. Once, when I had invited Barry Lawrence to the house of Dr. Ron to view his vineyard and perhaps offer some expert advice, Catherine had said the labels should be completely re-designed. I declared that since it was my company, I would run it, and that no new labels were needed at this point in time. Catherine continued to scream, out loud, that she had started and sold out seven major clothing lines, including Urban Outfitters, and that my methods were ten years out of date and would never succeed in the marketplace. Then she stormed out of the room, saying "I want nothing to do with this company!" Dr. Ron said she would "come around."

But on this day at the end of June, just before his presentation to Merv Dr. Ron revealed that he had been working with a label designer without telling me first. I told him that our best partnership would always include full disclosure in such portentious matters as the choosing of a label.
Dr. Ron said he understood, and would never make any further decisions without telling me first.

There were six labels designed by Ms. R (today, five months later, one of these labels bears the false name ROCAMOJO). But on inspection, we both agreed the labels were inferior and that we'd stick with our original.

This meeting was important because at this meeting, Dr. Ron made the first alteration in our Chiropractic office "deal." He said he did not want to take in stockholders or sell shares any longer, but wanted to finance the first money on his own, with his family, up to a quarter million dollars would be easy, he said. This way no stock would have to be sold, and we could keep our shares until a public offering, which was his ultimate goal.

I was reluctant to have him put up personal funds, I said, since that made me uncomfortable when asking for cash disbursements, and if he were to put up the money, I would want the entire amount in the bank as a regular investor would provide funds, with my fees as part of the budget. He asserted that he would, in effect, "pay as we went" since he was seeing me and Gretchen at least twice a week already. He had prophesied that Gretchen's neck injury would take a year or more to heal.

He asked me what the least amount I would accept in this case. I said that $2,000 per month would pay my expenses while we rebuilt the company for the first three months, but then I would like to earn fees commensurate to the work I was performing. He said he would provide $2,000 in consulting fees, as well as all other expenses relating to roasting, bagging, labeling, sales staff, office and overhead. Once we were in the stores and showing any kind of orders ("I'll be satisfied when we have our first reorder" was one of his favorite slogans) we could invite Tony and Merv and other large stockholders on board. This would give us much greater leverage and control.

I reminded him I was owed at least $250,000 from my own personal investment years ago. It was agreed that we would remain 60/40 partners until I was repaid, but that we would share control of the company equally. With mutual dilution of stock, we would include my prior shareholders

Since I'd already been working on re-starting INCOGNITO for several weeks, devoting many hours, I asked for the first consulting payment to be given before he left of the 4th of July meeting with Tony and Merv He asked if I would wait until Jeffrey Dash drew up the papers. He said it would take two or three days.

Thus Gretchen and I met with Jeffrey Dash in his Larchmont Offices to discuss the deal. Jeffrey said he and Ron were now part of the "team" and that the deal would be written up and that he would prepare an application for a Limited Liability Corp. with Ron and I as equal partners, subject to the payment to me of $250,000. Jeffrey Dash is a celebrity print agent and an authority on the subject of International currency. He had known Ron since they had both started their careers nearly twenty years ago.

On June 30 we held another of our meetings while being treated on the adjustment table at the Pain Relief Center. The meeting continued downstairs at the Aldente Restaurant, where Dr. Marinaro and I and Gretchen were joined by Jeffrey Dash. Earlier, I had gone over a long 4 page list of deal points with Dr. Ron, and given him a rough prospectus and history of INCOGNITO for his meeting with Tony and Merv I gave my new partner 6 bags of INCOGNITO.

Dr. Ron explained he was meeting Tony in London, where they would fly by Merv's private jet to Merv's yacht off the coast of France. There the bags would be presented to Merv and his actor friend, and their guests.

During the week that Dr. Marinaro and Tony and their wives were in Europe "pitching" our product, I spoke again with Jeffrey Dash several times on the telephone, and Gretchen and I met in his office, and I provided details of the cost of buying soybeans in large quantities, as well as various prices involving the cost of bags and labels, and the printing and design of labels.

8

Jeffrey Dash said he was making cost estimates and projections to go along with our presentation to Merv and future large investors. He said we should be "ahead of the game" when Merv got into the business, ready to take in funds and to spend them.

Dr. Marinaro and Tony returned from the meeting with Merv the second week of July.

Dr. Marinaro telephoned me the first morning of his return. He was excited, he said, and could not wait to get out of the business of "cracking backs," though he said he would keep a few patients, like Gretchen, my wife.

Naturally, I was pretty excited myself. When we met the next day for Chiropractic treatments and a business lunch, I asked how Merv liked the coffee, he said that in fact, even though they'd intended to give it to Merv to taste, he and Tony decided to wait until they'd left the ship for him to try it. He said that Merv had recently undergone , and had tried soy coffee as a medicine, but the coffee he'd tried he did not like. So, Dr. Ron explained, he and Tony decided to wait and have the chef offer the brew, and they had taken care that the Chef of Merv's yacht knew how to make it.

Although it didn't make any sense at the time that Ron Marinaro and his best friend Tony would fly thousands of miles to make a presentation and then not make it, Ron assured me that that was in the interest of "politics" and that all this was for the betterment of INCOGNITO.

At lunch Ron gave me $300 cash as part of our agreement. Jeffrey Dash was still making up the cost projections for the company, he said, so that we could take in investment. It was this reason, he explained, that our "deal memo," or the written document of our partnership, was delayed.

This delay was not entirely unknown to me, since I've made films where the negotiated deal memo took longer than the shooting schedule.

In July Ron and I and Gretchen and our food broker, Bob Krieger, who'd worked on INCOGNITO in 1992, arranged to meet at 9:40 at the Co-Op in Santa Monica. After our brief first presentation, the buyer for the chain was not sure about putting INCOGNITO on the shelves.

In the parking lot, Ron was incensed about the rejection from the Co-Op – though, as a salesman myself for INCOGNITO and its predecessors since 1986, I had experienced many rejections. He agreed that Bob Kreiger should make the Cosco, Whole Foods and Trader Joe's presentations without us present, since like a couple of jittery fathers, we weren't helping the birth.

All during July and through the third week in August, Gretchen and I worked daily with Ron and our broker and our roaster to get INCOGNITO ready for the stores. I helped supervise the making of new labels – although I disagreed that we needed to make new labels before testing the product in the stores – and I met with designers, and arranged shipping and purchase of soybeans.

Gretchen was excited that she could contribute to the future of a Chiropractor who, at that time, seemed to finally be curing her years of pain and sleepless nights. When my business relationship reached the breaking point with Dr. Ron, as stated below, Gretchen's pain was at its height. She could not lie down or sit down comfortably, and even though walking itself was painful, she forced herself to walk until she was too tired to remain awake. This part of the story is being written by Gretchen herself.

Ron continued to have many more conversations with our broker after the first retail presentation, until a few weeks later, he abruptly called me and said that his contact at COOKES MARKET in Malibu had suggested other food brokers to replace Bob Kreiger.

Ron asked if he could meet with these other brokers, and I said of course we should be meeting with every possible person to advance our product and get into the stores, but certainly I didn't think anyone could replace Bob Kreiger, especially in California, Kreiger's territory for decades.

The Doctor and I continued to meet three times a week during our treatments, either having lunch or coffee or long discussions in the treatment room.

I prepared more memos and projections, includng long range company goals, organic and company philosophy, cost vs profit statements, and various soybean blending estimates, along with all the other work that goes into starting up a corporation.

And each time I spoke to Jeffrey Dash, he said that our verbal agreement was in his "notes" which he was converting to a formal letter, and that he was still busy

working on financial projections along with the new LLC for INCOGNITO. I said that the agreement was taking an awfully long time.
When Dr. Ron kept saying it was Jeffrey Dash's job to write out the verbal agreement, I wrote a strong note to Jeffrey on August 8, quoting the famous dictum of Sam Goldwyn that a handshake agreement is only worth the paper it's written on. I could not figure out how Dash could make any financial projections at all without a firm underlying contract between Dr. Ron and me.

I received the additional $700, and then three more checks for $1,000 each, but each check required me to reassert our verbal agreement, which I continued to ask for almost daily in writing. Then the checks starting coming later and later, though Dr. Marinaro knew I was using my own limited funds for Incognito purposes. Dr. Marinaro became less accesssible accept when discusing direct company requirements; it was clear he was using my financial needs in some kind of insidious power trip: honoring one part of "The Deal" by doling out partial payments, at the same time still holding out putting our agreement on paper.

Jeffrey Dash was supposed to be drawing up our agreements and investment projections and memos, but it became impossible to get him on the telephone.

In the meantime, Dr. Ron was giving INCOGNITO to his patients, and getting rave reviews. I had meetings with an Internet designer and more meetings with Elizabeth R about new labels. Colors were chosen. Words had to be reviewed and re-written. We found our old lab reports on the nutritional content of INCOGNITO and had side labels printed.

We also contacted COSCO. Dr. Ron had been stopping by Cooke's Market in Malibu and meeting with the deli manager, Barry S a long-time friend of his wife Catherine. Barry gave Ron the names of two brokers, and Ron asked them to contact TRADER JOE'S AND WHOLE FOODS on his behalf. When I said that was Bob Kreiger's job, Dr. Ron said that these new men were more enthusiastic than Bob, and asked if I would at least meet with them. I agreed, but the meeting never occurred.

Dr. Ron told me he was also meeting with the President of Operations for Paramount Pictures and the President for Sony Marketing, Electronics, U.S., who were going to participate, he said, in our start up operations.

11

Memos from Jeffrey Dash began to stop arriving, even though Dr. Ron spoke to me about Dash sending copies to others. I protested that I should be privy to every memo and decision as partner.

One day Dr. Ron said he opened a bank account for INCOGNITO at Washington Mutual Bank, but I was not on the signature cards because they had required a credit application. He said I would be on the signature cards before checks were written. This didn't happen.

Around this time, Dr. Marinaro introduced me to Michael Moss, saying Moss was another patient whc money and needed a job because He said Moss would be a perfect manager because we could certainly afford him, and he was also a good salesman.

By now the new labels had been made in the thousands, we had contacted the special Vinton bean distributor and hundreds of pounds of soybeans were being roasted at our Proprietary Brand Roaster in Venice.

Yet, I still couldn't get a written contract from Jeffrey Dash. And even though I was bringing Gretchen to the Pain Relief Center on Mondays, Wednesday's and Fridays, and in the Incognito office, I was briefing Dr. Marinaro and Michael Moss on the history and methods and objectives of INCOGNITO soybean marketing and strategy. I continued to work on my company even though I was having difficulty getting Ron to pay me the $2,000 monthly consulting fee he was due to pay me according to our agreement.

When, in August, Dr. Ron said that Jeffrey Dash had arranged for the LLC, I refused to sign it until we had a signed written contract as well, describing our verbal agreement.

At a four-hour meeting on a certain Saturday in August, I told Dr. Marinaro that he needed to keep his agreements or get out of business with me. He said that he wanted to pay Michael Moss the money he was giving me. I replied that our deal was that he would put up to $250,000 of his money or his brother's money or his father's money, as we'd met and proposed INCOGNITO to each of them. Part of that money was to be paid to a manager, and part to me, as consultant, since I had put my company back together bit by bit and Jeffrey Dash's own projections showed a multi-million dollar grosser within six months.

12

On that Saturday Ron said I was right, and that he would continue on Monday, and pay me the $1,000 which was due. I asserted I still needed our agreement on paper.

Four days later, on August 15, with a check in hand, and with with Dr. Marinaro's firm assertion that our deal was in place, I said that I would go in good faith and trust and sign the LLC, which Jeffrey Dash had prepared, thus making our partnership official. However, I insisted I still needed the underlying agreement between us reflected in a written contract to be included within the LLS.

I continued company building while I awaited the final papers from Jeffrey Dash and more days went by, and more meetings about labels and business strategy and sources of large bean purchase were discussed. But still there was no contract on paper. And Dr. Marinaro continued to assure both Gretchen and me, "We are in business! We have a deal! We're partners!"

Central and still foremost in all of this was the trust in Dr. Marinaro, since he was my doctor and my wife's doctor.

But here were ominous developments on the medical front. Gretchen began to experience more and more pain on each adjustment. While I was growing increasingly agitated because Jeffrey was not writing out the deal, Gretchen needed greater amounts of painkillers to be able to sleep or even walk. I started to wonder if the doctor was making Gretchen worse so that he could pressure me with money and with my wife's illness both at the same time. One day I insisted that Gretchen see a MD, and drove her to Dr. Donna A: ι in Glendale on August 28

By now our Writer's Guild of America insurance had run out, and Dr. Ron was treating Gretchen in part for her daily work on INCOGNITO, as he was working Moss and R to p. to him.

In one of my conversations with Ron I appealed to him to continue his agreement with me since we were counting on it for medical reasons, if nothing else.

During lunch at a Ventura Blvd. Restaurant, I reminded him again that based on our agreement, I had used funds for my film projects I would never have spent. I suggested to him that he was using my dire needs to pressure me to change the deal. He said, "You're fuckin' with my head," but finally agreed to raise capital to continue our deal.

13

During the final days of August and early September, several things happened:

I stopped being treated at all by Dr. Ron, partly because my growing mistrust of him as a partner was poisoning our doctor/patient relationship, and partly because our INCOGNITO meetings, increasingly argumentative, were having a paradoxical effect on Gretchen's treatment. The more Ron worked on her neck, apparently, the worse it was getting. Her night-long pain, often excruciating, along with her worry that the long arguments with Dr. Ron were having a bad effect on her treatment, put a strain on our lives which could have led to a ruined marriage, but did not, for Gretchen knew her worst fears about her Chiropractor were gradually being realized.

I was told COSCO was being shipped INCOGNITO three-pound bags. But I was told this by our roaster, Richard Karno, not Dr. Marinaro and Michael Moss.

Then INCOGNITO appeared on the shelves of Cookes' market in Malibu, the celebrity supermarket, before I was told that the orders were being shipped.

When I asked Michael Moss (Dr. Marinaro was increasingly difficult to reach) how the sales were at Cookes, he said they'd sold out three times in three days, which was unprecedented.

When I called Ron and asked about the sales, the said the "vegans were circling" but said little else.

Then INCOGNITO appeared on the shelves at PACIFIC COAST GREENS, another trendy and very expensive Malibu grocery.

By the end of the second week in August, after I signed the LLC, Jeffrey Dash stopped returning my calls entirely

.

On the Sunday before my final meeting with Dr. Marinaro of the following week, Ron called me at home and said that he could no longer deal with me as actively involved in INCOGNITO because of my past credit ratings (!) and that the company was growing too fast for him to put up money an longer. He said he was signing for a $500,000 credit line, that he and Jeffrey were going to issue stock for $10,000,000.

On the one hand, I was surprised and even impressed that so much money was suddenly arriving in the INCOGNITO coffers.

14

On the other hand, I wondered how Ron and Jeffrey could make such deals, or any deals, without consulting their 60/40 partner: me.

When I asked Ron for the paperwork for all of this to bring to my business manager and accountant, H. Roy Matlen CPA, Ron said that he would meet with my "so called business manager" during the following week to work out a deal.

Work out a deal? What deal? Hadn't he been saying all these months that we HAD a deal? Hadn't Jeffrey been creating documents and projections and legal proposals for financing? Didn't we have product in the stores that was selling, and already generating capital, however small?

I said that definitely a deal had already been worked out, and I wanted copies of the agreements Jeffrey was working on these many weeks, as well as copies of the prospectus they'd been working on.

Ron said he was due at a barbecue and would call me the next day.

The following morning, on the way to his offices and the office of INCOGNITO AT THE PAIN RELIEF CENTER, Ron called at 7:15 from his cell phone. He said the company was a multi-million dollar business, not the smaller company I had started, and that he would have to give 80 percent to investors, leaving him and me with 20 percent to split. He said that from now on he would make all the decisions, and would explain to my business manager the new situation.

I said that we had "the" deal or we did not, the substance of our agreement remained, and I wanted it in writing before any further meetings could occur.

I also said that I wanted the money due me by him as investor. He said Jeffrey would take care of it, and hung up.

The meeting never took place because when my business manager H. Roy Matlen requested the documents Jeffrey Dash was to have prepared regarding our partnership, Jeffrey Dash denied having any such documents.
The following Friday, when I brought my wife in to the Pain Relief Center for treatment, I met with Ron and asked him for a copy of our agreement.

Dr. Ron said he did not have any such agreements, and that in any case our old agreements were no longer valid because "things have changed." He said that he

15

and Jeffrey Dash had discovered that my formula for Incognito was "common knowledge." I replied that if it were common knowledge, there would be no need to "discover" it, he would never have asked me to teach him the business, it would have been "common knowledge."

He said "Bill, I'm your only friend. Everybody's asking why I'm even keeping you in this deal!" He said that they were going to have millions in investment, and that I was not looking good in their conversations with banks, and that he was signing for a $500,000 loan, and that this wasn't part of our original agreement.

I replied that unless he and I were partners as originally agreed, then there would be no deal of any kind. I said the facts he was disclosing were troubling since we were partners, with a State LLC, and he had no right to withhold any documents or projections or loans from me. I said that until our contracts were signed and sealed, I still owned INCOGNITO, for he was breaching our verbal agreement by his one-sided actions.

I didn't realize it then, but this would be our last meeting. This final meeting took place, as had most of the others during the previous months, at his office in The Pain Relief Center. As we left the treatment section of the Pain Relief Center and walked towards the Incognito office on the same floor, Ron said that no matter what, he would always treat my wife.

Gretchen recalls in her statement that when he entered the treatment room, he smiled and said, "I'm giving Bill two more weeks to make up his mind."

Weeks earlier, when we opened our offices at The Pain Relief Center, I had placed a large nylon banner of River "Incognito" draped over the bookshelves in the office.

I took the INCOGNITO FLAG from the office of the Pain Relief Center.
I said that I would bring the flag back and we would be in business again when we had our agreement on paper and when he started keeping his promises. Ron said that we should meet the following week to resolve our issues.

I agreed to meet the following week.

While I waited in the parking lot, with a view of Suite 207 of the Pain Relief Center, the INCOGNITO office, Gretchen was treated by Dr. Marinaro just down the hall.

On the way home, as usual, Gretchen felt the pain – not only the chronic pain from the sports injury which led us to Dr. Marinaro so many months earlier, but the pain from the fear that her doctor was lying to her, and using her and her treatments to gain power over our company, INCOGNITO.

That same Friday afternoon, roughly five hours later, at around 3:30, I received a call from Richard Karno at our Roasters saying that Michael Moss had just telephoned from the Incognito Office at he Pain Relief Center and asked if Richard would roast for Moss and Dr. Marinaro under another brand name.

Richard Karno said that such a thing would be unethical, if not illegal, since his original agreement was with me and INCOGNITO, and that he was a roaster charged with the trust and confidentiality of his clients.

At 3:30, when Richard repeated this conversation with me, saying it was clear to him that they were trying to cut me out of my own company, I immediately sent him a letter telling him to roast for nobody but me and that I was out of business with Dr. Marinaro.

I wrote Michael Moss a detailed letter telling him I thought his actions were illegal and that he was breaking my confidential verbal agreement with him and that he was actively trying to steal my company in concert with Dr. Marinaro.

Michael Moss paid no attention.

The following week, Dr. Marinaro and Michael Moss telephoned again from the Incognito offices at the Pain Relief Center. This time they elaborated, and said that they had $2.2 MILLION which was being placed in the new company's accounts, and they were prepared to begin ordering by the train car load.
Again, Richard Karno said he only roasted soybeans for INCOGNITO.

I sent another letter to Ron Marinaro, and then more letters to him and his brother and father and mother, all of whom had met with my wife and me and said they would invest in INCOGNITO.

There came a 3 page letter from a New York attorney named [illegible] Godt who said that "soybean coffee is common knowledge."

17

Of course, INCOGNITO was not common knowledge at all, as it took Ron Marinaro, his family, and manager Michael Moss months to discover the secrets of making it, secrets I revealed to them with the trust of a partner and the trust of a patient towards his doctor.

CERTAIN REVELATIONS AND CONCLUSIONS

It is now clear to me that Dr. Marinaro and Jeffrey Dash were stalling the written agreement until INCOGNITO had proved itself in the stores and whatever financing they had in place was secure.

I believe that Merv did in fact come through on his promise of ten million to his son Tony . I believe that Dr. Ron used his power as a doctor, and his financial promises to me, to unfairly take my trade secrets, projections, company plans and methods to benefit himself alone, and his family alone, while hurting me and my family and my early investors by leading us on, giving us hope, in order to obtain maximum information about how to make and sell my coffee.

I believe that Dr. Marinaro has succeeded in putting INCOGNITO in Cosco, Trader Joe's and Whole Foods Markets along with all the other places he and Jeffrey Dash and I had brainstormed about.

Bob Kreiger long ago pointed out that a product like ours on the shelves of the 178 Trader Joe's stores could easily net $8 million PER YEAR, and the others could pay even more.

The prospect of a start up company in possession of $24 million in sales right out of the gate, backed by ten million dollars and the good will of a public Billionaire like Merv may have been too much of a temptation for the greedy Marinaro and his friends to resist. They probably felt a lawsuit from me would take years and be settled with a fractional piece of the value of what was stolen.

During various times in our last conversations, Dr. Marinaro said that articles were being written in local and regional papers due to the efforts of his wife, a former garment industry mogul (mogulette?). He told me that the Chief of Marketing for the Sony Corporation had asked for leave to work on INCOGNITO. He told me that top executives at KIRKLAND PAPER CORP. in Seattle were interested in forming some kind of partnership. He told me the Wall Street Journal was going to profile the company. He told me his friend and patient, the President of Operations at Paramount, was going to leave the studio and work with Moss at INCOGNITO. I

18

had asked him how all this could be happening without my knowledge or consent, and he replied that he was moving so fast, he could not tell me everything.

Apparently, what he was not telling me was that he was taking years and years of my efforts and labor and he was assembling them for huge investment, and keeping it all.

Today, if you call the former telephone number for INCOGNITO, the voice of Michael Moss answers saying the number belongs to "Rocamojo – Coffee, Only Better."

The name is different, but the slogan is the same and the product is the same INCOGNITO, which has been my company for many, many years.

AS OF THIS WRITING

Today, if you drive up Pacific Coast Highway to Malibu, you can find a product called ROCAMOJO on the shelves of Cooke's Market. Under the bags, in the same spot as the bags we put there earlier, the name INCOGNITO still appears. The name INCOGNITO appears also on the bar code at the checkout counter. No wonder. It is the same stuff.

On December 3 Gretchen and I drove to the Pain Relief Center and photographed our old office. Through the shutters it is clear that there are stacks of INCOGNITO boxes, while on the floor, other boxes hold empty INCOGNITO bags. Next to them are new bags of ROCAMOJO. The Marinaros and Michael are putting our product in their bags, bags which bear the exact labels Elizabeth R. had designed for us and INCOGNITO months before.

It is not without irony that ROCAMOJO and Dr. Marniaro & Company are all INCOGNITO.

On the www.rocamojo.com website, there is no mention that the President of Rocamojo is the same doctor who treated my wife and I from March 2001 until September, 2001.

There is no irony, either, that our treatment consisted of the days our INCOGNITO partnership was in effect, and both the agreement and the treatment were breached on the very same day.

19

I resent that my trust and faith in my doctor, for it is common knowledge that a doctor-patient relation is inviolate, was in this case abused and distorted into a method of deceit and, finally, theft.

Dr. Marinaro should pay for his deeds, pay for that part of my company he has sold, squandered or destroyed, and pay for the terrible physical pain I believe he has inflicted on my wife, who deserved nothing more than fair treatment from her doctor.

In the meantime, we are working daily on INCOGNITO as before.

NOTE: The facts behind the above are recorded in detail in the time-line of Gretchen Richert, substantiated by dozens of pages of memos, and require even more time to recount than the foregoing, which, I swear, is a short version.

William Richert
December 5, 2001

June 22, 2001 (1)

MEMO INCOGNITO

June 22, 2001

CONFIDENTIALLY SPEAKING

TO: Dr. Ron Marinaro
President
Incognito

TO: Mr. Jeff Dash

FR: William Richert
Founder-CEO
Incognito

Dear Ron,

As we discussed yesterday at the Roasters, here are some thoughts and statements about Incognito which may be useful on your Europen trip. Some of what's included in this memo could find its way into our business plan in greater detail, along with actual financial projections.

We may not need, for example, the early history of Incognito, although our early test marketing certainly proved beneficial and is part of our example of growth.

I'm dividing these sections alphabetically, but the order can be changed.

A: A brief history (just in time).

Incognito was started fifteen years ago, in the imagination of filmmaker William Richert, when he tasted a hot brew made from roasted soybeans as a cure for a hangover. Believing the roasted beverage could benefit others in different ways, he embarked on what has become a long campaign to vastly improve the taste of the product, and to find the right partners to introduce his new product to the world at large.

JUNE 22, 2001 

In 1992 the results of Mr. Richert's efforts were profiled on NBC Network Television along with another start up company from Seattle called Starbucks. At that time Incognito, the Coffee Alternative, was selling in selected stores up and down the coast of California, including Mrs. Gooches, Erewhon and Irvine Ranch Market. Nature's Best was introducing the product to it's several thousand stores, and pounds of the coffee were being shipped to New York and China.

Then, in 1993, Incognito went "incognito" for several reasons. One, the company's principal backer, River Phoenix, died. Two. Soybeans were a difficult sale to the mass market at the time, and even though sales were growing in multiples, the multiples were insufficient to keep the Founder and others away from the movie business.

All this changed towards Millenium. It was clear by then that no other company had the knowledge, means or interest to test and develop a competitor to coffee. The major coffee companys like the status quo, wherein they profit in billions per year. Why should they bring in an unkown contestant to their cartels, when the shape of an entire commodity might be affected.

As for the health food stores, and the health conscious sections of nearly every major supermarket: these sectors have grown exponentially since the time they were almost non-existant, one decade ago.

Thus Incognito became once again a solitary yet potentially unstoppable addition and alternative to the daily jolt of "joe" that hundreds of millions of adults swallowed daily, sometimes from morning till night.

In short, time time for INCOGNITO arrived. With its time, came a man with the interest and abilities to help bring the company to global attention.

Here, we will refer in this memo to you yourself, Dr. Ron Marinara, a highly successful and valued Chiropractor in studio city, with clients of all ages, with many different needs, as well as many different levels of activity and celebrity.

Dr. Marinaro began by thinking Incognito might help some of his patients, who needed to get off coffee because of health reasons. Some of them, unable to drink caffeine in any form, were having a hard time of it.

June 22, 2001 (3)

However, once Dr. Marinaro brewed some, and shared it with his family, he discovered something that not only tasted good, and was good for you, but an enterprise really worth persuing as a business and very lucrative hobby.

Now Dr. Marinaro includes his leadership in Incognito along with his work with hundreds of patients at his busy clinic on Ventura Blvd.

With Dr. Marinaro, Incognito is blessed with a truly health-conscious, professional and seasoned businessman and entreprenur, as well as a noted doctor. This is the combination of talent and acumen is rare and invaluable to a growing company.

It should be noted here that our Incognitocoffee, and our coffee roasters and our rich South American regular coffee, will all be strictly organic when sold under the Incognito label. Since the organic beans cannot satisfy the entire U.S. demand for coffee products, and until we are able to enlist more growers to produce organic beans, we will sell available coffee beans under an Off-Label, which Inconito will wholly-own and control.

We believe it is more important to introduce Incognito the vast and yet unknown markets of the world, than it is important for us to insist on oranic coffee at this time, when billions of mankind cannot afford it.

However, Incognito soybeans will remain organic.

We ought to list some of the markets.

Some of the buyers of Incognito are:

INCOGNITO STORES (WHEN THEY EXIST)
ALL HEALTH FOOD STORES
ALL SUPERMARKETS
ALL FRANCHISE COFFEE STORES HEEDING NEEDS OF AGEING BABY BOOMERS:
   Starbucks
   Peets Coffee
   Coffee Bean
   Etc. etc.
THE NAVY
THE ARMY
THE MARINES

JUNE 22, 2001 

THE FEDERAL EMPLOYEES
ALL HOSPITALS
ALL SPORTS STADIUMS
ALL HOTELS
ALL HUMANS OVER 55
ALL HUMANS UNDER 55
At this point, maybe some other specifics can be included, alphabetically:

A: A recent history of coffee houses which have grown by as much as 25 per cent per year, with no end in sight. Also, more reasons for a soy alternative/addition.

In 1996 a company called Coffee People in Portland, Oregon reported 13.6 million in sales from 23 stores.

Five years later, the growth of small companies like this have split the seams of old ideas about coffee and marketing. Even while the coffee bean costs have declined by almost 60%, lattes and espressos sold in the U.S. and world wide have reached prices of $3 to $5 per cup.

Incognito is a "coffee" too, but an entirely new and different kind. Made exclusively from soybeans, this new tasting brew is dark and satisfying like coffee, but it is not acid, contains no caffeine, and even provides nourishment in every cup.

With Incognito, the office coffeepot becomes a source of nourishment, flavor, and health.

In the past decade, soy products have come to the forefront in studies which combine interest in health with interest in nutrition.

Also in the past decade, high-octane coffee fueling stations have appeared on streetcorners and malls across America with profusion unknown in history, except perhaps the sudden appearance of gas stations with the advent of the car.

Coffee appeared suddenly and almost universally in the Sixteenth Century. Louis IV of France drank it, and sought to develop an unending source of supply.

In the 21st Century, coffee is ubiquitous and offered in as many varieties as a fine wine, along with the staple coffees sold in supermarkets.

JUNE 22, 2001 

B: Point of View Towards Growth
Incognito is not just an alternative to coffee, but a companion. Incognito's path is clear: follow the coffee lovers, and then make friends with all those interested in a daily nutritional drink that is also tasty.

The "specialty beverage" market, which includes popular drinks like Red Bull and Gatorade (which recently sold for fifteen + billion) is a 90 billion dollar yearly grosser.

The coffee industry is the second largest commodity in the world, and the dollar amounts, the yen, the franc, the pound, the peso – reach into the highest tier of billions.

Incognito's potential in the world marketplace is unlimited as well as presently unkown.

With no promotion and no paid advertising, the first test marketing of Incognito was done in the early 90's by its inventor, and within weeks found its way onto the shelves of almost every top health food store in the Los Angeles area.

This early R&D showed that a growing percentage of folks who tried Incognito continued to drink it, and give it to their friends.

Today, with 71 million adults hitting the 55 and plus age, with massive media information concerning the benefits found in Soy, both as digestible protein and the cardiac effects of Isoflavones, there is a built-in demand for Incognito among the "getting-older" the "I drink too much coffee" and those millions looking for an original and flavorful hot beverage.

If Incognito took only 2 percent of the coffee market within the next five years, it would become a major billion-dollar company.

One of the properties of Incognito is that the brew speaks for itself. One person tries it, gives it to a friend or relative, and it grows from there.

Therefore, the business of Incognito is to be in a position to grow as rapidly as the demand grows, not only in the U.S. but in Europe, Australia and South America – not to ignore Africa, Asia, and those few souls stationed at the international posts in Antarctica and the North Pole.

June 22 2001 

If Incognito took only 2 percent of the coffee market within the next five years, it would become a major billion-dollar company.

One of the properties of Incognito is that the brew speaks for itself. One person tries it, gives it to a friend or relative, and it grows from there.

Therefore, the business of Incognito is to be in a position to grow as rapidly as the demand grows, not only in the U.S. but in Europe, Australia and South America – not to ignore Africa, Asia, and those few souls stationed at the international posts in Antarctica and the North Pole.

We intend to facilitate our growth through our own manufacturing, marketing, sales and distribution teams. We will engage in partnerships, franchises, and we will encourage Ralph's, Safely, Vows, Awl Mart et al to put their labels on our product, thus going "incognito" ourselves.

At the same time we introduce our product to the public in health food stores across America, using existing, available coffee-roasters in central areas, we will expand abroad to licensee our methods and marketing to other manufacturers and distributors, using quick computer communications methods.

If, as we grow, we are able to supply incognito faster, better and cheaper than the competitors who will certainly emerge, we can become to soybean coffee what DeBeers is to diamonds.

C: What "Incognito" is presently doing.

Even as we formulate the current company funding and strategy, our product is being put on the shelves of coffeehouses and stores in the L.A. area. Without a single sales person or ad, Incognito is being passed from person to person, household to household.

We have contracted our first roasting operation, have designed and printed labels, and are interviewing brokers and sales people.

Within a few months we expect to be expanding into stores all across the state of California.

June 22, 2001 

To describe the profits which can be made from this enterprise only the words "no limits" appeal. As Bill Gates & Friends imprinted their windows onto the vast and empty DOS of computers in the 80s, Incognito can imprint its own roasting and blending "window" onto the crop and commodity known as soybeans, and be grown and sold in all places soybeans are grown and sold, as well as all places coffee is grown and sold.

The potential of the scope and penetration of this product offers an exhilarating prospect to investors and workers.

Our slogan "Try it for health…Drink it for Life"® can become a motto for present and future generations.

Incognito is a company worth joining, we think.

D: A WORD ABOUT THE MAN IN OUR LOGO

Actually, the man in our logo, who is Incognito, could also be a woman, or even a child. The idea is that in order to change, some transformation is required. Change requires an entry to a challenge yet to be discovered. And as our Forebears knew, it was always safest to travel "Incognito." And to recognize this ability to enter a state of transformation encourages use of our product by all thinking persons of every age: anybody at all who enjoys the thrill of being "Incognito."

Additiinally, our man in the White Hat, a deep symbol of the good guy, will enable us to bring celebrity support to our enterprise. After all, the celebrities will be appearing "Incognito."

D: ADDENDUM:

We at Incognito are in the early stages of what could become a kind of phenomenon, much as the way coffee itself was discovered, introduced, and quickly (for its time) grew into a world-wide habit and industry.

(213) 456-7594

36 29TH AVENUE
VENICE, CALIFORNIA
90291

June 26, 2001 (1)

MEMO INCOGNITO
June 26, 2001

To DR. RON MARINARO
FR Bill Richert
Incognito

Re: Investment agreement between William Richert and Ron Marinaro, D.C.

Dear Ron,

Here is an informal sketch of our agreement, divided numerically, based on our conversations and actions up to now.

1.) In your office, after tasting Incognito, you said you would be interested in helping find financing of the company, and seeing it grow. At that time you said you had a friend, a woman, who was interested in investing $250,000. You also had other friends in the entertainment/related industries with capital, as well as the heir to a food distribution giant with $10 million to "start" something.

2.) I said if you used your efforts to obtain financing to get Incognito off and running again, I would give you 40% of the company. I said that the corporation was dormant and only needed a start-up to begin sales and expansion. There was no discussion of using your money to begin operations, or of any duties you might assume in the running of the company. My focus was on your stated fund raising abilities, your interest and valuation of the product, and your intentions to promote various contacts to ensure continuing financing.

3.) Today you said that you needed more than 40% to enable you to secure investors. I said that I could not understand why. You also said you did not see a need to use your own money, as your money would not be enough to ignite the company in the size and scope which interests you.

4.) You said you thought 50-50 would be a more appropriate relationship, and you also seemed surprised to lean that if we issued stock, our ownership in the company would be diluted by the amount of stock we issued.

June 26, 2001 

5.) I made no specific demands on you as far as investment goes, that is, no specific monetary amount and no demands on your time. My idea was to create a partner relationship that would attract a certain "class" of investor, if you will, and also to find fellow entrepreneurs to join us as we cast a wide net over one of the largest consumer groups in the world: coffee drinkers.

6.) Also, it seemed that granting a per cent as large as this would create an incentive to succeed equal to the benefit.

7.) As this is an entirely new product, as you have had time to prove to yourself and others, the path to success is not marked.

8.) I said that the company foundered in 1992 not because of a lack of possibilities, but because I myself found the rewards too distant.

9.) However, the time has arrived for soybean coffee, and Incognito is in place to reap the benefits.

10.)I have articulated my plan for Incognito in a letter you, which will become a basis for a business plan. There is no greater authority in regard to this plan than me, as I invented the process and have identified the market. However, this is only part of the job. Getting the product in stores as quickly as we did before only shows how much work there is ahead.

11.)If you require a structure to bring money to the company, and I agree that one is required, a corporation can be drawn up to receive the money according to law and this company can issue stock. It is up to us to decide the valuation of the corporation, the number of shares, and who can own them at what price.

12.)I say it is up to you and me to decide this if we are in business together and it is clear that you are raising money and helping the business grow. It is to this end that you have purchased a roaster, equipment, and bags and beans. It is to this end that we have held meetings.

13.)Nothing has happened which need change the original proportions of our agreement.

14.)The agreement has not been consummated, however, in writing. Each day you have new plans for my company that I must consider. In that sense, each day the "deal" changes. You seem unwilling to give up what you call "your shares"

June 26th 2001 (3

to new money, while you are yet to establish what amounts this money will be, and where it will come from.

15.)I would like you to explain why 40% ownership of a corporation is insufficient, when you have no proscribed duties, no fixed amount of personal investment, and in fact nothing more asked of you than to honestly provide resources to enable Incognito to reach its true potential.

16.)I would like perhaps to explain to myself why I have offered you 40% of a company I have worked on for 15 years. Part of wisdom is patience and knowing when to act. The soldiers of George Washington performed very well without shoes. This enabled them to get much better shoes later on.

17.)You have said that a "mom and Pop" operation does not interest you. I have never proposed a mom and pop operation. It is not a phrase I normally use.

18.)Today you mentioned that you were arranging a meeting between ourselves and a major coffee producer or distributor. If, in arranging such a meeting, facts about our company were revealed, it would have been more appropriate for me to be notified in advance of any conversations, even if they are only considered "research."

19.)As a practical and obvious matter, if this company had no value, no person would speak to you about it.

20.)Maybe the amount I offered at first, 40%, led you to believe erroneously that I was enfeebled in regard to business dealings, or that I had no plan of my own, or that I had no possible investors.

21.)In fact, it was your own talents in many areas, which have become apparent to me, that made me value your abilities as a "star" to whom such a large percentage of ownership would be a reasonable cost for the company as it existed only a few weeks ago. Perhaps I was right, inasmuch as the wheels are already turning to bring Incognito to stores and other outlets.

22.)One does not need a Dutch uncle to say before you sell something, you must have it. If you want to sell something you don't have, you are selling a concept. If you are selling a concept which belongs to another, and 40% of the proceeds aren't enough, then you are selling a concept without value.

23.)Those "old records" I carry in my van show a company in very rapid growth, needing only a flow of money to keep going.

24.)If you were to provide between 100 and 200 thousand yourself, we can have a viable corporation servicing thousands of stores by the end of the year – way, way ahead of all competitors. (However, I remind you that I did not ask for that amount, and did not contemplate that amount in our first conversations. These are your amounts.)

25.)If more money were to be raised to provide advertising and publicity, conjointly with the expansion of sales outlets, the growth will be exponential.

26.)There is no mystery in this. By the time you return from your July travels abroad, I anticipate being in the stores owned and operated by GCW, the stores they service in San Diego, and the stores service by the marketing people I talked to today in Woodland Hills. This few stores, a "sampling" of the market, are sufficient to talk to investors here and everywhere.

27.)To say that 40% is not enough for you to perform in this regard, or that the plan to do a pilot program in health food stores as we move in other directions, is to re-define the plan we discussed earlier.

28.)You say we need to re-define our arrangement, which has not yet been ratified or formalized, based on your expectations of a multi-billion dollar company, when we still haven't made the labels for our bags or roasted the Incognito we intend to sell, reminds me of a kind of "deal making" that puts the horse too far ahead of the cart.

29.)Each time you tell a businessman capable of competing with us the story of our coming success, you create a climate for competition. Bill Gates is famous for saying" if you don't want me to take your idea, don't tell it to me."

30.)When you decide to design labels or otherwise alter my product before telling me about it, you are moving ahead of our business relationship. Because I forgive or overlook early overreaching in this regard, means that I believe we can find methods to work smoothly together.

31.)It is my hope that we will readily reach some kind of accord which defines our obligations and intentions. In our first discussions, I said the major mistakes I made in the early company came with listening to "experts" when in fact there

JUNE 26 2001 

are no real experts regarding the soy coffee traded under the name and with the qualities of Incognito. Nothing that has happened to date compels me to revise this opinion.

32.)The same business that I presented to you just six weeks ago is the same business you can present to investors two weeks hence, or two years hence.

33.)You said you would provide me with operating expenses for me of 2 thousand per month, and would provide other operating costs like bags, beans, labels, telephones, etc.

34.)I put no limit, in terms of duration of your contributions or the dollar amount, except for the 2 thousand.

35.)If you don't want to put up any further money, then I will sell shares in Incognito and get some.

36.)That I haven't been selling points in the company, when I have been long in need of funds, is only a factor of my knowledge the company grows in value daily, and I would certainly get much more later on.

37.)However, at this moment, it may be in my best interest, which is the same as Incognito's interest a this point, to sell points or shares so that I am not forced into making a deal with anyone, including you, because of financial need.

38.)As I write this it becomes apparent that I should form a new corporation to reflect all of the above, and when this corporation exists, you may receive shares proportionate to your involvement.

39.)I look forward to working with you in all this, with a resolute, clear and mutually successful conclusion.

Cheers,

Bill

July 2. 2001 (1)

MEMO INCOGNITO
Monday, July 02, 2001

TO: R. Marinaro
J. Dash

FR B. Richert

RE: NOTES ON SATURDAY'S DISCUSSION (June 30) ABOUT THE
COMPANY GROWTH STRATEGY

GENTELEMEN:

Over the years, in the study of various business models and marketing plans, as well as from observations of the rise and decline of dot.coms, ambitious adventurism in film companies, etc. – not to mention my prior experience with our own Incognito, including my awareness that so much depends on what happens at the beginning of any enterprise, herewith:

1.) If we try to make all our costs back from the first sales of our product, the price to the consumer will be much greater than it will be when the business is properly self-funded. We ought as much as possible to charge the lowest possible introductory price, and support the market entry of our product as major companies do.
2.) If we don't capitalize on the low cost of Soybeans, and charge with the other gourmet coffee companies do:
3.) (a.)We will limit our sales to health food stores, where the prices are much higher than supermarkets;
4.) (b.)We will attract competitors, who will reverse-engineer our Incognito and, discovering how cheaply it can be produced in quantity, will undercut our sales and offer mass distribution.
5.) To avoid immediate competition, we ought to introduce our product at the lowest cost possible, and then keep lowering the cost as

July 2 2001 (2)

Incognito costs go down, while we expand our ability to buy and sell in greater and greater bulk

6.) If we need additional outside capital to support our initial low-cost sales, then we should seek it out, rather than hang on to our shares at the cost of the capital needed to seed and control our expansion. To own the whole of something small at the cost of a piece of something infinitely greater, is not sound economically, and will eventually lead to decline.
7.) If we keep both expanding our distribution efforts, and lowering the cost of our product, we can capture the lion's share of the market that we ourselves are creating, and, at the same time, make it unattractive and too expensive for most competitors. As if we were a pharmaceutical company, we can make both the "brand" and the "generic" at the same time, thereby owning our greatest competitor: ourselves.
8.) If we think of INCOGNITO as a new commodity, with an identity that comes from Soybeans but is as well a brand new form of Soybeans, then INCOGNITO may one day be sold in the commodity exchanges through our company and no other, as Diamonds are listed through DeBeers. It ought to be remembered that Microsoft is an upstart compared to the age of IBM, but WINDOWS has become an industry standard.
9.) INCOGNITO can become a standard for a health beverage that is also a food, a cultural and social replacement for hard coffee, and, eventually, a way that millions upon millions can afford organic coffee through 50/50 and 80/20.
10.) INCOGNITO, as well, can become the byword for baby boomers looking for alternate lifestyles and new health habits to better enjoy a prolonged life.
11.) We should offer our product first, and design our campaigns firstly to those who could most benefit from INCOGNITO and have the greatest need to try it: the coffee-fried population, from corporate offices to hospitals and nursing homes, where cup after cup of bad caffeine is fed to oblivious drinkers, making them sick.

July 2 2001 (3)

12.) While INCOGNITO is a pleasure drink, not a medicine, it becomes good medicine when it replaces unhealthy habits.

13.) INCOGNITO can show in its marketing that it is sexy just to be healthy, whatever age. Like coffee, ours is a product for the entertainment of the spirit.

14.) AARP is a great place to start, while we commence distribution to the local markets.

15.) More later.

Cheers,

Bill

Bill

C. July 18 2001

FAX TO JEFFREY DASH

FR BILL RICHERT

PAGES 8

Dear Jeffrey,

Here is some rather lengthy bio stuff taken from Baseline on the Internet (though not up to date with my current BOYLE HEIGHTS or THE LAST MUSKETEERS) which you might want to glance over, since there may be some bit of useful info in it relative to the cause.

Meanwhile I'll write a short paragraph:

WILLIAM RICHERT IS A FILMMAKER AND NOVELIST WHOSE WORKS HAVE APPEARED WORLD WIDE IN THEATERS AND ON TELEVISION. AS A DOCUMENTARY MAKER HE WON THE NEW YORK CRITICS AWARD AND INTERVIEWED THE DAUGHTERS OF TEDDY ROOSEVELT, FRANKLIN ROOSEVELT, LYNDON JOHNSON AND RICHARD NIXON FOR '60 MINUTES. AS A DIRECTOR HE WORKED WITH SUCH LUMINARIES AS JOHN HUSTON, ELIZABETH TAYLOR AND JEFF BRIDGES ALONG WITH RIVER PHONEIX AND MATTHEW PERRY, WHO WAS DISCOVERED BY RICHERT FOR HIS FILM 'A NIGHT IN THE LIFE OF JIMMY REARDON,' DISTRIBUTED BY 20TH CENTURY FOX. AS AN ACTOR HE CO-STARRED WITH KEANU REEVES AND RIVER PHOENIX IN 'MY OWN PRIVATE IDAHO' AND WITH SUSAN SARANDON IN 'THE CLIENT' ALONG WITH TV GUEST STAR APPEARANCES. RECENTLY HE FINISHED THE FIRST FEATURE FILM TO FEATURE ALEXANDRE DUMAS AND THE THREE MUSKETEERS, WHICH HE PRODUCED, DIRECTED AND CO-FINANCED. DURING THE COURSE OF HIS CAREER HE BECAME ACQUAINED WITH MANY PROMINENT FIGURES IN THE CAUSE OF WORLD HEALTH, AND THIS LED HIM TO 'INCOGNITO, THE COFFEE ALTERNATIVE,' AN ENTERPRISE WHICH ENABLES HIM TO USE HIS FILMMAKING AND PUBLIC RELATIONS BACKGROUND (AS A YOUNG MAN HE WAS A PRESS AGENT FOR STEVE ALLEN AND SPEECHWRITER FOR DONALD H. MCGANNON, PRESIDENT OF WESTINGHOUSE BROADCASTING) TO PROMOTE A GLOBAL SWEEP FOR A NEW COFFEE THAT NOT ONLY TASTES GOOD, BUT IS GOOD FOR YOU.

I really don't have a bio up to date and hope this suffices.

Cheers,

Bill

Bill

INCOGNITO

COFFEE... *ONLY BETTER!*

INCOGNITO is a caffeine-free coffee alternative made from pure certified organic soybeans. **INCOGNITO** carefully roasts these organic soybeans, to create a smooth, robust taste that rivals the best specialty coffees in the world, while providing the nutritional benefits of protein, amino acids, Isoflavones, Niacin, Riboflavin, Vitamin C, Calcium and Iron to energize and satisfy. Alkaline in nature, **INCOGNITO** reduces the acidic effects of regular coffee when evenly mixed with coffee. Imagine, delicious coffee taste that's good for you.

INCOGNITO offers two exciting coffee substitutes to invigorate and delight all coffee lovers. The first is **INCOGNITO**, made with only one ingredient, certified organic soybeans. The second choice is **INCOGNITO 50/50**, a blend of certified organic soybeans and certified organic French Roast gourmet coffee that's not only surprisingly good, it's good for you.

Mixing **INCOGNITO** with a favorite coffee, which will take on that coffee's flavor, or brewing the delicious **INCOGNITO 50/50** French Roast blend gives real coffee drinkers the luxury of cutting their coffee consumption in half and NOT GIVING UP A SINGLE CUP! Certified organic roasters use a unique, proprietary method to roast our select soybeans to optimize the taste and keep in all the nutrients. Everyone now has the freedom to have the great taste of coffee all day and all night!

It has been documented that organic soybeans provide powerful, nutritional benefits. However, for years the word "soy" made most folks scrunch their nose thinking they were making a sacrifice to have it in their diet. It's only been in the last two or three years that soy has become a strong, and ever growing presence in our nation's grocery stores and for good reason.

As a result, many consumers want to know that their soy products are safe and unaltered by man. Respectful towards the consumer and consistent with "GENERATION GREEN", **INCOGNITO** and **INCOGNITO 50/50** are certified organic, eco-friendly, vegan, supports sustainable agriculture and is grown in the U.S.A.

Both **INCOGNITO** brands can be brewed like any regular coffee, in a drip coffee maker or a French press. Once brewed, flavor as you would your usual cup of coffee, with cream, soymilk, and/or your sweetener of choice.

INCOGNITO and INCOGNITO 50/50

The ONLY coffee alternative that has both the nutrition that health-minded people insist upon AND the taste that serious coffee drinkers demand.

AUGUST 15, 2001

INCOGNITO

The Coffee Alternative

WHAT IS INCOGNITO? Answer: Pure organic soybeans, carefully roasted using a cutting-edge proprietary method to create a smooth, robust taste that rivals the best specialty coffees in the world.

Each delicious and satisfying cup of INCOGNITO contains protein, amino acids, Isoflavones, Niacin, Riboflavin, Vitamin C, Calcium and Iron. Soybeans are known to provide powerful and documented health benefits, which have brought them to the forefront of today's nutritional frontier.

INCOGNITO is caffeine-free, for those trying to cut down on too much caffeine.

INCOGNITO is alkaline, which helps to reduce the acidic effects of too much regular coffee.

MILLIONS OF COFFEE LOVERS can now mix their regular brand with INCOGNITO and cut coffee consumption without giving up a single cup! Try our 50/50 Brand for the best Gourmet Coffee available roasted to perfection and blended with pure INCOGNITO.

GENERATION GREEN: INCOGNITO is organic, eco-friendly, vegan, supports sustainable agriculture and is grown in the U.S.A.

####

FROM : FAX NO. : Aug. 20 2001 09:37AM P4
Label Corrections (3)
ADVERTISES ONLY SOY COFFEE
NOT OUR SPECIAL KIND
TOO SMALL TO MATTER
incognito
roasted
soy
coffee
The coffee alternative
50% organic coffee
50% organic soybeans
Where is company name
roasted
soy
coffee
The coffee alternative
caffeine
free
100% organic
soybeans
ADVERTISE GENERI BRAN
TOO SMALL
ROASTED SPECIA
THE NAME "INCOGNITO" IS FRAGMENTED + BROKEN + DIVIDED INTO ASIAN SEGMENTS
LITTLE MAN IS "SERVANT" IN CLASSLESS SOCIETY. NOT empowering or given to free choice
*THESE LOGOS CANNOT BE FAXED. BUT FAX + COPY IS CRUCIAL.

FROM : FAX NO. : Aug. 29 2001 09:36AM P3

NOT A "DESIGNER" FOOD! Label Corrections ②

"DESIGNER" FOODS ARE SUSPECT.

incognito

The coffee alternative

WHAT IS INCOGNITO? INCOGNITO consists of pure organic soybeans, carefully roasted using a proprietary cutting-edge method to create a smooth, robust taste that rivals the best specialty coffees in the world.

It has been documented that organic soybeans provide powerful, nutritional benefits and you'll find them in every delicious cup of INCOGNITO. Designed to fortify and satisfy, INCOGNITO contains protein, amino acids, Isoflavones, Niacin, Riboflaven, Vitamin C, Calcium and Iron.

BREWING INSTRUCTIONS: Using your regular drip coffee maker, add two heaping tablespoons of Incognito per cup, preferably with filtered water. We think Incognito tastes better when it's dark and strong. Flavor as you would your usual cup of coffee, with cream, soy milk, or sweetener of choice.

FOR REAL COFFEE LOVERS: Try our INCOGNITO 50/50; a blend of organic soybeans and organic coffee. INCOGNITO is caffeine-free and alkaline (which helps to reduce the acidic effects of regular coffee). Now you can enjoy the great taste of coffee all day and night!

GENERATION GREEN: Grown in the U.S.A., Incognito's soybean is organic, eco-friendly, vegan and supports sustainable agriculture.

INCOGNITO IS ONLY COFFEE ALTERNATIVE THAT HAS BOTH NUTRITION FOR THE HEALTH-MINDED AND THE TASTE THAT REAL COFFEE LOVERS DEMAND.

MADE IN U.S.A. Studio City, CA www.incognitocoffee.com
Call us toll free at 866-769-2333

NET WT. 1 LB.

incognito

The coffee alternative

WHAT IS INCOGNITO 50/50? Imagine enjoying stimulating coffee withless caffeine, less acid and all the health benefits of soy. INCOGNITO 50/50 is a blend of certified organic soybeans and certified organic coffee. Carefully roasted using a proprietary cutting-edge method, INCOGNITO 50/50 creates a smooth, robust taste that rivals the best specialty coffees in the world.

It has been documented that organic soybeans provide powerful, nutritional benefits and you'll find them in every delicious cup of INCOGNITO 50/50. Designed to fortify and satisfy, INCOGNITO contains protein, amino acids, Isoflavones, Niacin, Riboflaven, Vitamin C, Calcium and Iron.

CAN'T DRINK COFFEE?: Try our other INCOGNITO brands, they are all caffeine-free, alkaline, made from 100% organic soy and brimming with all the health benefits that soy can offer. Either way, now you can enjoy the great taste of coffee all day and night!

BREWING INSTRUCTIONS: Using your regular drip coffee maker, add two heaping tablespoons of INCOGNITO 50/50 per cup, preferably with filtered water. We think INCOGNITO 50/50 tastes better when it's dark and strong. Flavor as you would your usual cup of coffee, with cream, soy milk, or sweetener of choice.

GENERATION GREEN: Grown in the U.S.A., Incognito's soybean is organic, eco-friendly, vegan and supports sustainable agriculture.

INCOGNITO IS ONLY COFFEE ALTERNATIVE, THAT HAS BOTH NUTRITION FOR THE HEALTH-MINDED AND THE TASTE THAT REAL COFFEE LOVERS DEMAND.

MADE IN U.S.A. Studio City, CA www.incognitocoffee.com
Call us toll free at 866-769-2333

NET WT. 1 LB.

ARE NOT ALL COFFEE LOVERS "REAL"?

BORING! BORING!

BOTH GOOD FOR YOU + GOOD TASTING.

PUTTING ON COFFEE LABEL IS OPPOSITE OF INTENT. Remove

MEMO INCOGNITO

September 18, 2001

To Dr. RON MARINARO
THE PAIN RELIEF CENTER
STUDIO CITY, CALIFORNIA
FAX 818 505 8623

Fr WILLIAM RICHERT
INCOGNITO COFFEE ALTERNATIVE
1423 EUCLID STREET
SANTA MONICA, CA 90404
TEL 310 394 7308 FAX 310 394 6028

RE: 'CEASE AND DESIST'

Dear Ron,

Yesterday you told me that one of the reasons you would not honor the verbal agreement we made the last week of June, 2001, regarding my company INCOGNITO COFFEE ALTERNATIVE, is that you were presently spending the funds you promised to me on attorneys and legal fees.

I don't know what attorneys or legal fees you are referring to, or why you have hired attorneys regarding my company without informing me, but I would like to point out to you and Jeffrey Dash that whatever you are presently paying attorneys or anybody else will be a fraction of what it will cost you and others if I must defend my rights and ownership in INCOGNITO, as well as the rights of others who invested $175,000 US ten years ago – along with my own $300,000 -- and who have steadfastly stood with me and INCOGNITO all this time, without compromising the formula and without selling INCOGNITO without my consent or permission.

During the past few days, you and Jeffrey Dash have suddenly begun telling me that INCOGNITO has no commercial value whatever, since it is based on a "recipe" which everybody knows. You know this is not true, even though there are hundreds of uses for soybeans, and it is widely known that Henry Ford made soybean coffee for the 1929 Worlds Fair.

There are, as we know, thousands more recipes for chocolate chip cookies than there are for soybean coffee, but Famous Amos and Nabisco have made fortunes nonetheless for making and selling chocolate chip cookies.

The reason you give for the sudden declaration that INCOGNITO is in the "public domain" is that such information was discovered by attorneys and investment bankers hired or involved in INCOGNITO by Jeffrey Dash.

Sept 18, 2001 (2)

You tell me that the "Due Diligence" performed by Jeffrey's bankers and attorneys "uncovered" the recipe for INCOGNITO. Since I know of only one recipe for INCOGITO, and that formula has been held in trust by employees or investors until now, there can be no other "recipe" except the recipe which has been in BACK TO EDEN since the 1930's as well as other cookbooks and health books, a "recipe" which involves ovens totally unlike those used by INCOTNITO.

To suggest that another "recipe" has been discovered similar to INCOGNITO means that some person other than those I have informed of the formula, such as you and Jeffrey Dash, have been informed of how to make INCOGNITO.

I was not told that Jeffrey Dash was speaking to attorneys or Investment Bankers of any kind, and I was certainly not informed that Jeffrey Dash would divulge the method of making INCOGNITO, which is its central value at present, so "Due Diligence" might be performed.

Jeffrey Dash is not an employee of INCOGNITO. Jeffrey Dash is someone I met with at your request to help negotiate the contract between you and INCOGNITO in order to defer legal costs. I was told categorically by you that I could trust him as much in counsel as I trusted you as my Doctor.

To reveal my formula or recipe or process without my permission, to a society not noted for their ability to keep a secret of any kind, and to tell me, as you did, that "somebody is writing about this for Wall Street" -- is not the behavior of a partner.

I must have the names and all correspondence, e-mail and records from Jeffrey Dash relating to bankers, lawyers or investors other than you. He was not given authorization from me to raise money this way.

If Jeffrey Dash has revealed to any person or persons the method I use to make INCOGNITO I shall become very angry.

Then also:

a.) I would like you to forward a copy of the other recipe you are referring to, since I know of only one or two which are in print and neither of them use my process. If there is one which does use my process, you ought not to withhold this information.

b.) I informed you long before I presented you with the first bag of INCOGNITO that I was well aware that soybean coffee has been made for 5,000 years. However, until I developed my secret process in 1991, nobody had ever made INCOGNITO.

c.) I revealed to you my "recipe" in confidence, based on a verbal agreement that you would tell no person without my permission or without my presence. If, along with Jeffrey Dash, you are comparing my "recipe" with others, and therefore revealing the process, you are violating the legal rights of my intellectual property. I demand you immediately cease telling any person or company the source or formula for INCOGNITO.

d.) If you think that my "recipe" has no value, then why are you involved in my business at all? There is not a single fact you know now that you did not know months ago, when I revealed the story behind INCOGNITO in your office, in total confidence.

PLF 00109

Sept 18, 2001 ③

e.) Finally, in this regard, I ask you to read earlier correspondence between us and Jeffrey Dash when I stated that we would certainly have competitors, dozens of them, when our formula was "reverse engineered" by major food companies, which must be the case in any kind of success.

For you, or Jeffrey Dash, to expose my formula and process and methods to the commercial marketplace, without fundamental agreements or contracts, may forever injure my ability to sell INCOGNITO, resulting in a total loss of all research and development costs, as well as a future loss of income.

I believe you have already assessed the future income of INCOGNITO in your contacts with Jeffrey, and that such projections exist. If you have such projections of revenue for INCOGNITO, they will indicate to you the losses I may incur by your actions. I have begun to make my own projections of the success of INCOGNITO, using statistical methods of the motion picture industry. My indicators, based on the orders from COOKES MARKET and the beans Richard Karno is already roasting, is that damages to me could be in the millions, solely as the result of the activities of you and Jeffrey Dash.

As an example of my recent discovery of your conduct, I offer the following example:

Yesterday (September 17) I stopped by the Gourmet Coffee Roasters to get the labels requested by your associate, Mike Moss. It turned out the labels were being used to prepare re-orders for COOKES MARKETS and new orders for other places unkown to me.

I asked Richard Karno why he decided not to distribute INCOGNITO to his 3,000 – plus Specialty Coffee Stores. He told me that in a meeting with you, which I was not invited to attend, you and Mike Moss asked him to cease distributing to any stores, because this would interfere with "your" methods and "your" other distributors.

If you have methods for distribution, or distributors other than those I know about, who are they? Why did you cancel a sure-fire way to establish the INCOGNITO brand name among hard core coffee drinkers, many of whom are not served by health food stores or supermarkets. Surely, an alternate to coffee like INCOGNITO, placed among the devoted coffee market, would be a success unrivaled by any other company.

To go against my hopes and wishes for INCOGNITO behind my back, when I have told you that you are in breach of our verbal agreement, is not in the interest of any kind of "partnership."

Richard Karno also provided me with manufacturing cost estimates he gave to you, which you did not provide to me, although you promised that you would.

I have been working with Gourmet Coffee Roasters and Richard Karno for more than a year. He has vowed to not to compete with INCOGNITO or to reveal to anybody the "recipe" or process for INCOGNITO.

PLF 00110

Sept. 18. 2001 (4)

If you involve my chief roaster in conversations with yourself and others without informing me, thereby signaling him that I am no longer a partner/owner of INCOGNITO, you are undermining the basis of my credibility with him, and thereby weakening or destroying the basis and structure of my confidentiality with him. This could create an atmosphere of conspiracy that might result in his rejecting all prior agreements with me and ultimately, INCOGNITO.

Recipes for cola and sugar drinks existed for hundreds of years before the "recipe" for Coca-Cola. The special soybean roasting techniques revealed to Richard Karno by me alone, with instructions from me alone, are available nowhere else on earth – except from you, as I revealed the special recipe to you and your entire family, believing and trusting that we had a verbal agreement.

Sadly, you now say things have "changed" and our verbal agreement is no longer in effect. This has caused me grief, for I must now seek ways to protect myself and the integrity of my company.

In addition, you are placing the reputation of INCOGNITO in possible legal jeopardy in the highly visible community of Malibu.

I was distressed to see the stickers you have placed on the INCOGNITO in COOKES MARKET. You had told me that "Barry", a person employed by COOKES MARKETS, told you that stickers were "lost" on their customers. I disagreed with you, but you insisted there would be no stickers.

Then, to my surprise, I visited the store and discovered that you put a sticker on INCOGNITO stating that our 100 per cent is CERTIFIED ORGANIC. Not only does this negate what you said earlier; it puts INCOGNITO under legal suspicion.

As you are aware, INCOGNITO is organic but not "Certified Organic." Thus, this advertising is false and misleading. While it is true this is perhaps a minor infraction or mistake, it must be corrected at once, for it creates a dangerous precedent for a company which intends to become a public corporation.

If these "mistakes" are not corrected immediately, I will notify the Corporate Officers at Cookes that the product must be removed from the shelves.

Not only that, I have repeatedly stated that the prime reason the large baby boomer market wants INCOGNITO is because it is CAFFEINE FREE. This is Issue # 1 in their purchase of the product. I had placed this information on earlier stickers, which you choose to ignore.

In addition, placing FRENCH ROAST in the forefront on my FIFTY FIFTY brand of INCOGNITO is reductive and off-putting to customers who do not like FRENCH ROAST. In fact, as you ought to know, our "French Roast" is not roasted to the specifications of the usual "French Roast" at all, but is roasted at a slightly different temperature. Moreover, when combined with INCOGNITO it is per se not "French Roast" at all but something entirely different.

Customers who like COLUMBIAN or ITALIAN will not buy our FRENCH ROAST. Therefore, INCOGNITO loses buyers it might otherwise include.

PLF 00111

Sept. 18 2001 (5)

If you and your colleagues intend to rush forward with ill-considered methods and schemes, then there is no hope for long term success with INCOGNITO no matter how much money you throw at it, or whomever else that you involve. Stocks issued to a failed company have no value.

I am disappointed that I am now in the position of seeking legal advice which could inflict months of difficulty on me and INCOGNITO, as well as mounting debt. It would be catastrophic to INCOGNITO if lawyers are immediately engaged to protect my rights and the rights of all those who have known and kept the secrets of INCOGNITO for more than a decade. All my friends and prior investors have kept the secrets of our process in the belief that one day they might benefit us all. Now you and Jeffrey Dash are telling strangers how we make this very special coffee.

You said that if I must, I should send you a "Cease And Desist" letter. If this is the only way to bring your attention to my distress, and the distress of others, then such a letter will be forthcoming.

If you and Jeffrey Dash decide that my requests for disclosure and fairness are excessive, and want to "get out" of the deal, this option is immediately available to you, and the sooner you sign off the better.

It was not my intention to commence a partnership that would involve only dispute and shame and recriminations.

Therefore, if you decide to leave this field of dreams, I will not follow you. I will stay with INCOGNITO. However, you will be engaging your own best interests by not leaving a scorched earth where my INCOGNITO stood, or inciting others to develop a property not owned, conceived or invented by them. Great effort has been expended in the formation of this company. Although it was in a quiet state of rest when we began our discussions last Spring, it was never abandoned or forgotten.

When you first showed your interest in INCOGNITO, you were aware that Barry Lawrence was meant to become a member of the Company. He has written to you about various aspects of the company, but you have not responded to him, although you have been in contact with many others, and Jeffrey Dash has written about INCOGNITO to many others, and not informed me of his contacts. You cannot decide to work only with your side, and not with associates of mine.

We need all copies of any correspondence or documents between you and Jeffrey Dash, and Jeffrey Dash and others, which have not been presented to me.

It is my earnest hope that some kind of agreement can be reached between us before any pain-laden and costly legal measures become absolutely necessary.

Many companies and productions go through internal turmoil and dispute, yet they continue on to success and wealth. Perhaps this will occur in this case. I truly hope so.

PLF 00112

Sept 18, 2001 (6)

However, nothing endures without mutual respect and trust.

Sincerely,

William Richert
Founder, President, Owner and CEO of INCOGNITO
THE COFFEE ALTERNATIVE

Cc H. Roy Matlen
Jeffrey Dash

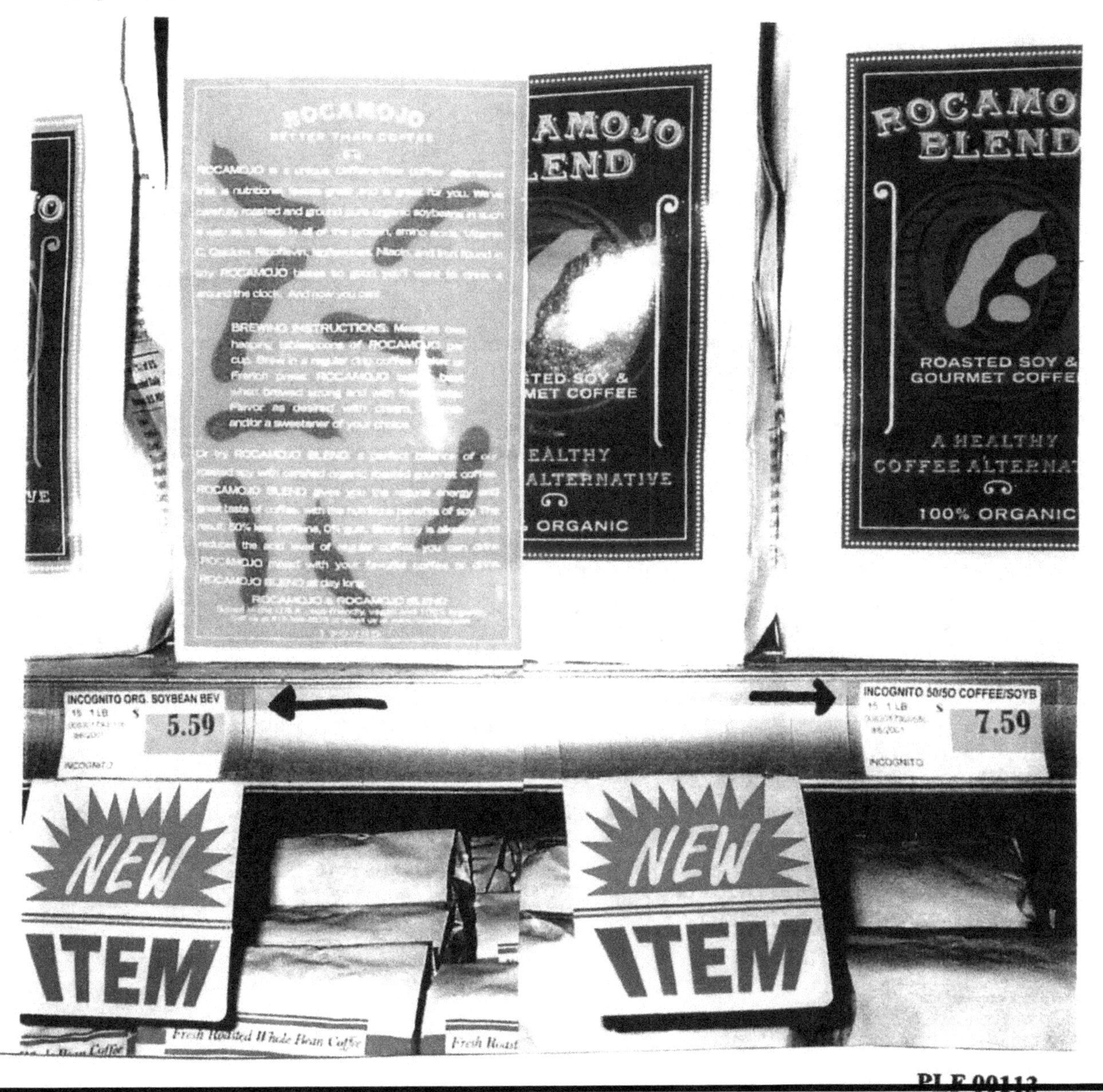

PLF 00113

Fax From Incognito

September 23, 2001

TO: Mr. Michael Moss
THE PAIN RELIEF CENTER
12215 Ventura Blvd.
Suite 208
Studio City, California 91604
FAX 818 505 8623

RE: Cease and Desist/Gourmet Coffee Roasters
Fraud
Breach of Contract
Conversion of Intellectual Property
Conspiracy
Misappropriation of Copyright
Misappropriation of Funds

Dear Mr. Moss:

You are hereby notified to cease and desist all contact of any kind between you and Richard Karen of Gourmet Coffee Roasters.

You are hereby notified to cease and desist all revelatory conversations about the proprietary formula for the making of INCOGNITO with any person or entity.

You are hereby notified to cease and desist all sales and marketing activities regarding INCOGNITO and persons at SONY; WHOLE FOODS; KIRKLAND OF SEATTLE; COSTCO; 'BEN' and 'BARRY THE DELI MANAGER' at COOKES MARKET, MALIBU; MIKE OSTERMAN OF PACIFIC GREENS, MALIBU AS WELL AS OTHERS TO BE DISCOVERED AT TRADER JOES OR ANY PERSON PRESENTLY EMPLOYED AT PARAMOUNT PICTURES.

You may be aware that at approximately 10:18 Friday, September 21 I met with Dr. Ron Marinaro in his office at THE PAIN RELIEF CENTER in Studio City, California.

You may be aware I informed Dr. Marinaro that unless he provided copies of all our agreements as promised, I was breaking off all business relations with THE PAIN RELIEF CENTER and removing all INCOGNITO materials from the premises of THE PAIN RELIEF CENTER. He refused to provide any kind record of our previous agreements. I told him he therefore had no contract with me. He agreed.

I took the giant flag of INCOGNITO from the walls. I was told THE PAIN RELIEF CENTER would send me my files the following week.

If you were not aware that INCOGNITO stopped doing business with Dr. Marinaro and THE PAIN RELIEF CENTER on Friday morning, you were prompted by some other personal or business motive when you telephoned our Proprietary Roaster and asked him to begin roasting INCOGNITO under a new brand next week, promising him "big bucks."

There are many ways of saying fraud, or theft, or misappropriation of Intellectual Property, or theft of process or theft of trademark or theft of copyright or conspiracy, and there are many ways of saying "shame on you."

SUBSTANCE OF COMPLAINT AGAINST MICHAEL MOSS
OF THE PAIN RELIEF CENTER

You were employed by Dr. Ron Marinaro and THE PAIN RELIEF CENTER to work on INCOGNITO THE COFFEE ALTERNATIVE. It was my understanding that part of your salary was paid by you had to THE PAIN RELIEF CENTER, as was the debt of two other patients of Dr. Marinaro, along with Elizabeth R The entire network of patients involved in Dr. Marinaro's business experiments with INCOGNITO were informed and understood the gravity of any knowledge of how INCOGNITO is formulated and made.

Each and all of Dr. Marinaro's patients report to you in your office in THE PAIN RELIEF CENTER. I understand you have communications in writing and e-mail with some of these patients. I ask that you provide me with copies of all correspondence relating to the foregoing as well as all correspondence relating to the sales and marketing and retail outlets, as well as any distribution proposals for INCOGNITO, along with a copy of the $98.00 check Dr. Marinaro told me he had received from COOKES MARKETS.

I also need to know if Dr. Marinaro has opened a bank account in the name of INCONITO, and who signs on this account. It is illegal to open a bank account for a wholly owned company or to deposit or withdraw funds from any such account without consent of the company owners. Individuals who have done what you are doing now have gone to jail.

SOME FACTS

On Friday, September 21, Dr. Marinaro told me that he and I had no longer any deal regarding any investment by him in INCOGNITO. We agreed to discontinue our association. He told me he would give me my files back next week. I removed the gigantic Company flag from the wall near your desk, which you could not have failed to notice.

3

Michael Moss, you have known and have at all times been aware that all facts regarding the making, marketing and distribution of the products of the 18 year old company are trade secrets, and that by agreeing to perform services for INCOGNITO you agree to keep and hold those secrets and to tell no other person or entity.

I have information and belief that you have violated this policy of trust and agreement. I have information and belief that you called the Proprietary Brand Roaster of Incognito and requested that his company join with you in exposing the trade secrets of Incognito to Third Parties, as yet to be named, but whose names you know.

In addition, I have information and belief that you and Dr. Marinaro and THE PAIN RELIEF CENTER have received money from the sale of our product, INCOGNITO, but have not reported this to us and may have deposited these funds in an account which is not accessible to the true owners of INCOGNITO.

Conspiracy and conspiracy to commit fraud, in addition to misappropriation of funds, are offenses which can be prosecuted in civil and criminal courts, either or both.

By asking my Proprietary Roaster to make my secret recipe for your new brand name you are attempting to enlist into a conspiracy a trustworthy man, a professional Roaster who holds my INCOGNITO formula in confidence, a specialist whose livelihood depends on clients whose livelihood, in turn, depends on his keeping their secrets.

By asking the INCOGNITO PROPRIETARY ROASTER to conspire with you, you invite him to participate in unlawful activity, and you intice him to perjur himself. Further, you ask him to manufacture counterfeit goods, goods made from soybeans which were meant to bring health to people, not temptation to criminal acts.

You are to CEASE AND DESIST all work on my company, INCOGNITO, and provide us immediately with any and all correspondence signed by you relative to our company.

We need to know immediately whether you acted on your own, without instructions, or as an employee of THE PAIN RELIEF CENTER and Dr. Ron Marinaro.

Inasmuch as the future of INCOGNITO depends on entering the national and global markets before competitors, we need all documents in your possession immediately.

You have told me that all INCOGNITO files are recorded and available from your office computer located on the second floor of THE PAIN RELIEF CENER.

If we do not receive the contents of the hard disc in the IBM computer assigned to INCOGNITO by THE PAIN REIEF CENTER on or before close of business Wednesday September 26, we shall report your activities, along with a copy of this letter, to appropriate law enforcement as well as Officers/Employees of COOKES MARKETS, PACIFIC COAST GREENS, WHOLE FOODS, COSTCO, TRADER JOES, KIRKLAND and SONY.

4

We shall have no choice but to inform them that if they purchase any kind of soybean coffee from you or THE PAIN RELIEF CENTER, or engage in any other soybean coffee dealings with you or Dr. Ron Mariner or other patients/employees of THE PAIN RELIEF CENTER, they will be dealing in stolen or counterfeit property, and they will be liable for damages caused to our reputation and our ability to do business.

Michael Moss: I hope you understand the seriousness of the facts contained in this letter.

I suggest you contact me at once to provide for delivery of all materials requested, as you will otherwise most certainly receive a request from a Judge at a future date, when your admission of refusal or delay could prove even more costly and damaging to you.

Sincerely,

William Richert
Owner/Inventor
INCOGNITO THE COFFEE ALTERNATIVE

Cc H. Roy Matlen, Dr. Ron Marinaro & THE PAIN RELIEF CENTER, Jeffrey Dash & THE DASH GROUP, Max Esq., Daniel J. Esq., R. Karno, H. Phoenix, J. Phoenix, R. Phoenix, W. Hayden, D. Hayden, L. Meserole, K. Morris, James C. Esq.E. Tauscher

FR WILLIAM RICHERT
INCOGNITO THE COFFEE ALTERNATIVE
FAX 310 394 7308

September 25, 2001

TO: DR. RON MARINARO
THE PAIN RELIEF CENTER
STUDIO CITY
FAX 818 505 8623

Dear Ron,

Boy, you and Mike Moss sure freaked out Richard Karno yesterday, telling him how much money you had behind you and how many lawyers and how quickly he would be sued by you if he didn't comply with your demands to stop roasting for me, and start roasting for you and Michael Moss and Jeffrey Dash.

Calling from THE PAIN RELIEF CENTER, you freaked him out so much mainly because he built his business by sweat, as I have done, not by inheritance. You were so successful in frightening him with your money and your lawsuits that he says he will not roast for INCOGNITO any longer. He also says you owe him $1,000. I hope you pay him right away.

You frightened Richard because he built his company over years, starting at the same time I started INCOGNITO, and he cannot afford courts and lawyers and the time they take from his productive enterprise.

You frightened Richard by saying you and Michael Moss were the true owners of INCOGNITO and that you were going to use another brand name henceforth, and that you were already in discussions with another Roaster, so there would be no hurry to pay him his $1,000 for his work, as you would be done with him if he continued to work for Richert and INCOGNITO.

Justice delayed is justice denied goes the saying. In fact, justice ought to be an ongoing enterprise, just like the building of a business is ongoing, and indissolubley connected to the healthy growth and direction of a business. Along with Accounting, Receipts and Marketing there ought to be Justice, Ethics, Decency and Conscience.

But, Ron, all you know is money. All you want from INCOGNITO, you told me, is a large and quick cash return.

In fact, I do not think a start-up company, particularly in the food industry, can succeed in this "quickie" way. I know you might turn around a clothing line in a few months for a quick buck, but food products work a whole 'nother way.

2

You and Jeffrey Dash talk about a "shell company" and you talk about IPO's and Loans and INVESTMENT BANKERS but I do not hear from you a true understanding of the rate a small company can safely accumulate debt, no matter how ambitious and global its goals.

During the many hours I spent explaining my direction and goals for INCOGNITO, again and again I said I didn't want bank loans for INCOGNITO, that I wanted private investment because banks require the kinds of "Security" for their loans that would expose the formula for INCOGNITO to public view, and expose the formula to a bank takeover in the event of default. The formula for INCOGNITO, you are aware, has never been written down. It is disclosed orally, in sworn secrecy, as historic recipes of old.

You have always known that since 1985, when I first tasted soybean coffee and began experimenting to improve the flavor and consistency of my formula, no person has ever publicly revealed any secrets of INCOGNITO – except, now, you and your wife Catherine and Tony and his wife are openly discussing my secrets and methods, along with Michael Moss and, apparently, others from Paramount Pictures, Sony Corp., Kirkland Corp. and Cosco Corp.

You got a big mouth, Ron.

You may have, as you say, several millions behind you, and you may have millions in the your bank, and in the bank accounts of THE PAIN RELIEF CENTER, but you lack depth and you lack the ability to tell a consistent tale. Maybe that is because you are so busy with your Chiropractic business. However, while you can "crack backs" you cannot crack the spirit of true enterprise, or break the back of Bill Richert.

Since you threatened Richard Karno with a lawsuit if he continued to roast INCOGNITO, declaring that the process and idea was owned by you, and since he's not roasting for me now, and since you have found a new roaster, I suggest you begin roasting INCOGNITO immediately so that I can satisfy my re-orders at COOKE'S MARKET and PACIFIC COAST GREENS.

If I must remove my product from the shelves of these two hot supermarkets, in one of the most publicity craving spots in America, because you have threatened my Proprietary Roaster, then the months of work I've just completed presenting INCOGNITO to the marketplace will be for naught, and the name INCOGNITO will be tarnished.

By squeezing out my roaster, and attempting to intimidate me out of business, you employ tactics of the kind that sent James Hoffa to jail.

Many doctors have gone to jail, Ron.

When your wife screamed at me in public in the presence of Barry Lawrence, who has written of the event, she revealed that her intention with INCOGNITO was to make a splash with a public company and then sell out. Barry remembers how quite clearly I replied "Maybe you would like to sell out quick, Catherine, but I want to build a company that lasts and has real value over a long long time." After declaiming about how she had started Urban Outfitters and other companies which were highly successful, Catherine said she wanted to have nothing more to do with the company.

But did she mean it? I guess when you tell me Catherine is meeting with reporters from the Malibu papers, I can conclude she has continued to involve herself with INCOGNITO.

I think that if you can meet with the Malibu papers, I can meet with the L.A. TIMES and THE WALL STREET JOURNAL (as a feature story, not news) and THE NEW YORK TIMES and CNN. We will not forget my pal BOGEY who is in my corner at CBS.

How about this in VARIETY: "BACK CRACKER CRACKS STAX IN MALIBU MARKETS!"

You can see in the pictures we took on those Sundays on Drive at Your Place in Malibu the cast of characters. Most prominent are Tony and his attractive wife and marvelous children. Also Prominent is Catherine, and your brother, and your cousin (who'd kept a bag of INCOGNITO in his fridge for ten years) and then there's the psychic and the guy from Lebanon and of course Rose, your mother, and TJ, your father.

All of them were witness to the days I was telling the tale of the birth and growth of INCOGNITO, from the time I first tasted cooked soybeans at County Line to the years with River Phoenix, when he sang songs about the stuff with his guitar.

Will Tony perjure himself for you, if, as you say you will, you succeed in suing me in court over the theft of my own creation? Will your father? Your mother? Your wife? Your children? The fellow who tends your vines? The reporter for the local paper? The manager of the deli at COOKE'S, Barry S

Will Jeffrey Dash lie on the courtroom seat in front of a Judge and Jury? Will his employees? Will yours?

I am not waiting around to find out. Part of your plan appears to involve promising me expenses while I wait for Jeffrey Dash to put our handshake agreement on paper, and then failing to deliver, and causing me financial hardship, so that, perhaps, I will be forced by hardship to relent and accede to your ever changing demands, ever increasing percentages, ever rising "other" "Board Members."

Another part of your plan was the use of free Chiropractic services as a Doctor in treatments with my trusting wife. In effect, you used her and her sessions with you as a tool in the conspiracy to take over INCOGNITO. This is a perversion of a good tool for an evil purpose.

It will not be too hard for me to e-mail every Paramount Executive in Hollywood, or Merv on his boat (Merv would not like the way you have betrayed me, he's a self-made man) as well as all of those involved at COSCO and KIRKLAND etc. I will e-mail a copy of my label, as it appeared on the bags Merv's Chef prepared for Merv. Don't you have pictures from this trip? I'll bet, if you don't, your fellow traveler Tony will.

4

Merv   cannot have forgotten his son's best friend, or his son's best friend's business proposition, INCOGNITO.

In fact, Ron, I fully intend to follow my own path here, using the united resources of truth and common sense. I will not be ground down by your version of the "legal system" which moves slowly and ponderously, smothering almost as many innocents as it liberates. This letter, and the others I am writing and sending, are woven together with facts and truths. Our lives depend, we know, on promises which are kept.

Today my salvation lies in plain sight. While you plot and scheme, Doctor, I will sing and shout about the marvels of INCOGNITO and the weakness of those who attempt to destroy it.

In this morning's letter, I am not focusing on the litany of facts about my relationship with you as a patient/doctor, or recounting the long journal of my wife's suffering, as a result of your actions, because I am separately pursuing the injuries with legal specialists in the field of malpractice and health services.

The charges I am filing against you involving medical ethics will not falter or fail until they are nesting in a Court of Law.

During the hours I spoke to you about INCOGNITO being a company with a "conscience," I referred to breaches of justice I experienced early in my career as a writer and director. We talked at length about ways we might avoid such troubles forever with INCOGNITO.

For some specifics about "ethics," I provided you with a copy of the Barbara Maltby article for THE AMERICAN SCHOLAR. Apparently, you did not read it. Ms. Maltby is a teacher of Medical Ethics, and her husband is Dean of the School of Journalism at Northwestern University. Both of them may have professional interest in the synergy inherent in the multiple breach of trust you have perpetrated regarding my health and the health of my company, INCOGNITO. (Ms. Maltby was first given INCOGNITO by her then-boss Robert Redford in 1991.)

While you might employ "rag" trade tactics in an attempt to take my company unlawfully, I remind you once again that the "rag" trade, which made your wife so rich, does no physical harm or injury to the combatants, while the medical skills of a health practitioner are historically different, and can be more injurious and even fatal, subject to a greater scrutiny by courts and Judges.

Your behavior as a Chiropractor with unsuspecting folks like us is a kind of sickness itself, a disease not described in the philosophic writings Hippocrates, but in the law books of Justice Oliver W. Holmes, and therein lies my remedy.

Sincerely,

William Richert
Owner/Inventor INCOGNITO THE COFFEE ALTERNATIVE

FAX TO JEFFREY 'THE RODENT' DASH
THE DASH GROUP

September 26, 2001

RE: RECENT LETTER TO RON MARINARO 'THE SNATCHER' D.C.

Dear Jeffrey:

I apparently sent you the earlier draft of a letter to Ron Marinaro D.C.in yesterday's morning faxes. Here is the latest. As I improve the taste of INCOGNITO over time, I will improve the quality of my letters.

Letters are an underused weapon these days, weapon in the sense that "the pen is mightier than the sword." Ferdinand and Isabella and of course Elizabeth and Victoria – Churchill, of course, and in show biz D.O. Selznick (didn't we discuss him once?) were all letter writers.

Thomas Paine, writing about COMMON SENSE, required fewer pages than I have already written about you and Ron Marinaro D.C. to inspire the Colonists to break their contract with King George.

You will notice I have not focused much on your involvement with INCOGNITO because, after all, Ron Marinaro D.C. needs constant examination right now. If he had only chosen to abscond with one bag of my marvelous soybean coffee, I might be able to call the cops and they could follow by helicopter as he ran from backyard to backyard, jumping over fences or evading bulldogs. At night, the shot is spectacular.

But Ron Marinaro D.C., and perhaps his wife Catherine Marinaro, who seems to be more and more involved in this than we know, as she met more times than she said with various store owners, and of course you, Jeffrey Dash, have chosen to take my whole company.

Since you and Ron Marinaro D.C. have named over a dozen folks involved with INCOGNITO in various ways, and since you have maintained that INCOGNITO belongs to you in statements to my Roaster and store owners, and since each of those you have spoken to, like distributors or investors – Tony and his father Merv come to mind – and especially experts in marketing working for major food chains —since you are, in effect, blabbing to all and sundry about a formula I and others have held all but sacred – I have to blab even louder, so that the bankers or lawyers or investors you talk to will hear my story, and the story of INCOGNITO which began so long ago, and these people, across the country and even overseas, may come to understand that what you and Ron Marinaro D.C. are apparently saying, even to my business manager (Ron Marinaro D.C. says my business manager is not acting in my interests, a belief he got from you) – and as their awareness of my involvement increases, and they are given corroborating evidence from pictures, letters, diaries, bank statements etc., I believe they will want nothing to do with you and your counterfeit of my invention and marketing ideas, and that upon realizing you have lied to them, they will break all relations and trust with you, and that nevermore will you or Ron

Marinaro D.C. be able to manipulate friend or foe, or hurt a small business, or a trusting human being.

Once there were two Popes.

If you calculate the number of people Ron Marinaro D.C. talked to about INCOGNITO and the number Catherine Marinaro talked to about INCOGNITO and add the number of people Jeffrey Dash and Michael Moss talked to about my creation, invention, concept, trade secret etc. – and then factor in all the names of these people and the names of those in the offices or stores around them, you begin to get some idea of the multiples of people exposed unlawfully to my treasured INCOGNITO COFFEE ALTERNATIVE, and you begin to see why it is that I must speak faster and louder, so everybody knows what's what, and who's who, and where they came from.

Because I must proceed apace, I will not be able to spend the time editing my letters to you and my earlier partners, or decide which piece of evidence has more pertinence than another. I've got to send everything about you and Ron Marinaro D.C., and do it right away.

Please prepare your fax machine for extra duty on Thursday, September 27, as I will be getting my first draft "boilerplate" complaints now being prepared by young law clerks for the New York District Courts, where one of my $50,000. (Fifty thousand-dollar) investors currently resides. As you know, investors of certain amounts have certain rights.

I have decided, you may have noticed, that you and Ron Marinaro D.C. deserve nicknames, like G. W. Bush gives nicknames. "The Snatcher" comes from INVASION OF THE BODY SNATCHERS. I remember watching the gardeners up at Ron Marinaro D.C.'s home in Malibu, watching Catherine Marinaro directing servants to plant rows of ornamental ground cover. The image becomes ominous when I recall recent events and conversations with Ron Marinaro D.C. and Michael Moss and – I gotta say it, Jeff Dash– even you. I won't bother telling where I got your moniker, "The Rodent."

"And tho the fearful Armies March
Be you not much afraid, my friend…
For, In Every Tiny Town and Place
God made the Stars Especially…"
Lord Chesterfield, in letters to his son.

William Richert
Owner/Inventor INCOGNITO THE COFFEE ALTERNATIVE
Cc Ron Marinaro D.C.
THE PAIN RELIEF CENTER
Bcc: list

Not Sent Per Roy's Request

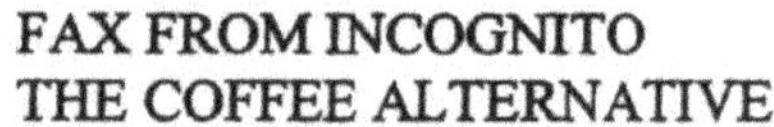
FAX FROM INCOGNITO
THE COFFEE ALTERNATIVE

September 28, 2001

Dear Mr. Godt:

Where you come off sounding like Golt?

If Ron Marinaro "The Snatcher" wasn't my doctor during the times I gave him the formula for INCOGNITO, WHAT WAS HE? Certainly not a partner.

There can be no libel when the truth is told.

The TRUTH often makes people uncomfortable, especially liars, which may be why Ron Marinaro D.C. and Catherine Marinaro, and Tom Marinaro and Michael Moss and Tony and Jeffrey Dash might be worried and concerned.

Michael Moss was the most recent PAIN CENTER EMPLOYEE hired to administer the wishes of Ron "The Snatcher" Marinaro D.C. I spent several hours telling Mr. Moss that INCOGNITO was my scecret and was a trade secret.

You will get future documentation, and firm and concrete documentation, when we are in "discovery" or a court of law and in front of a jury. When one of my cattle is found in a pasture which doesn't belong to me, I don't need a lawyer to call out "rustler!"

You use the psychiatric term "delusional" for my statements of truth. Are you also a psychiatrist? Your clients could certainly benefit from the crossover. Ron Marinaro D.C. understands crossover professions, as several times he said that my labels looked like a "transvestite." Was this a sexual innuendo for some other purpose? Or a criticism? Hmmm.

I cannot wait to face Ron et. al in court on some "actionable" offense.

There will be lots more documents to review at your end shortly and I won't stop writing, ever. I am first a writer, and all my inventions are truly first fiction and inventions, then fact and enterprises, and it was ever thus among creators of any kind.

U are ukcy.

Sincerely,

William Richert

ILLUSTRATION by Riv Sauts

MEMO INCOGNITO

"try it for health...drink it for life!"

October 1, 2001

TO: GODT, ESQ.
FAX 631 847 0910

FR: WILLIAM RICHERT
INCOGNITO THE COFFEE ALTERNATIVE
FAX 310 394 6028

Re: Dr. Ron Marinaro & THE PAIN RELIEF CENTER AND ITS OFFICERS, DIRECTORS, EMPLOYEES, SUCCESSORS AND ASSIGNS INCLUDING TJ MARINARO D.C., ROSE MARINARO, TOM MARINARO D.C., JEFFREY DASH OF THE DASH GROUP AND TONY AND MERV

A BRIEF BUT RELEVANT PASSAGE FROM A LEGAL THEORIST

Interestingly, Professor Gerber *admits* that nominee Thomas lied to the Senators: "it is not unreasonable to suspect that a desire to be confirmed to the most powerful court in the world was the reason . . . . That unfortunate circumstance speaks more to the corruption of the appointment process itself than it does to the veracity of . . . Clarence Thomas." (65) Shame! How can one so easily discount the fabrications of another? When I was very little, my mother used to tell me not to lie: "Not telling the truth leads to thievery, and thievery leads to . . .." In Thomas's case, it led to a lifetime position on the U.S. Supreme Court; not quite the result my mother hammered into me.
Howard Ball is Professor of Political Science and University Scholar at the University of Vermont and an Adjunct Professor of Law at Vermont Law School.

Dear Godt:

2

From your opening statements, I can tell you have the same difficulty I have had regarding Ronald Marinaro; namely, separating "Ron" from "Doctor Ron" from "The Pain Relief Center," a corporation which includes TJ Marinaro D.C. and Tom Marinaro D.C., along with their colleagues and employees, all of whom you represent.

You and I share the same view that all of these characters and entities are in fact financially and professionally connected, linked by practice, purpose and deep family ties.

Also included in the mix is Tony who brought my INCOGNITO to his father as they both were included in Ron Marinaro D.C.'s list of investors. I made up six bags of INCOGNITO expressly and ONLY for the purpose of Tony and Ron's presentation to Merv on his yacht during the week of July 4.

Are you also a criminal lawyer?

At the outset, I feel inclined to comment on your statement that my sense of American Jurisprudence is "warped." My sense of American Jurisprudence was instilled in me by my 12th Grade Civics Teacher at Evanston Township High School in Evanston, Illinois, which is hardly known for a "warped" sense of Jurisprudence and – notably – my teacher was named Best Teacher of the Year! Therefore, while my sense of American Jurisprudence may be rusty, it is not warped.

The Jurist Prudence you refer to in your letter can (I suppose) be deduced as the natural law a Jurist might follow, as a liberal judge might toss ole Ronald in jail, while a conservative judge, acknowledging that Ron's entrepreneurial spirit as pure greed might have "warped" Ron's judgment as a doctor licensed by the State, could in some sense understand Ron's greedy behavior in light of the nature of capitalism itself, and such a judge might let Ron off with just a fine and a slap on the wrist, and a revocation of his license to practice.

However, I think any Jurist with "American" Jurisprudence will nail the sonofabitch.

Secondly, I agree with your statement that I did not bother to read the one-page document presented to me by Jeffrey Dash on September 10, 2001 to form an entity called INCOGNITO COFFEE LLC, as distinct from INCOGNITO THE COFFEE ALTERNATIVE, a California Corporation in which I own more than 800,000 Shares, a company you recognize in your letter as a separate entity from INCOGNITO COFFEE LLC.

As you have pointed out, I signed that document without reading it because both Jeffrey Dash and Ron Marinaro D.C. informed me that by signing this form they called an APPLICATION FOR THE ARTICLES OF ORGANIZATION for INCOGNITO LLC, I was giving up no rights of ownership to my soybean coffee, INCOGNITO, SINCE INCOGNITO WOULD BE CONTRACTED TO THE LLC IN THE OPERATING AGREEMENT OF THE OWNERS, which if course wouldn't happen until the Secretary of State returned the executed Application.

According to Jeffrey Dash and to Ron Marinaro D.C. INCOGNITO COFFEE LLC would be a 50/50 partnership that the Doctor and I define in the Operating Agreement.

Since mid-June of this year, I have agreed to allow Jeffrey Dash to act acting as "our" lawyer to save legal fees. The first and primary purpose of the INCOGNITO COFFEE LLC would be to acquire all my rights and ownership in INCOGNITO COFFEE ALTERNATIVE.

Jeffrey Dash, in his role as de facto legal counsel for both me and Ron Marinaro D.C., insisted that the LLC application meant "nothing" until the new company elected officers, named board members and enacted by-laws. He pointed out that Ron was "Secretary" and I was "President" but that there was in fact no real company whatsoever until the application was returned from the Secretary of State in a complete "kit."

Although Jeffrey Dash declared that there were at least 11 requirements for an LLC to become functional, and the "Application" was only number 2, I have as of this writing received no notifications or documents relating to ANY aspect of the INCOGNITO COFFEE LLC that I discussed with Ron Mariner D.C. and Dash. I have seen no bank account, no financial plan, operating agreement, record keeping system, business insurance, amounts paid for Artist's work on labels, amounts paid to Michael Moss and so on.

I wonder how INCOGNITO COFFEE LLC can exist or, if it exists, how it could summarily withdraw from all knowledge of the "deal" I had with Ronald Marinaro D.C. and his investors Tony , et al, along with ignoring my labor and enterprise and ownership of rights in the formula I have called INCOGNITO since 1991 and CABINO since 1988.

What do you do while you wait to find out if your undocumented "partner" is stealing a life's work and attempting to destroy your marriage

While I wait for the articles of the LLC, I will continue the writing of "DOCTOR RON" THE STORY BEHIND THE MYTH, a true chronicle of shitty skirmishes in a war of petty attrition and perfidy, a war of dreamers and patients Vs harmers and hurters of humans.

When you state that I am sending letters to THIRD PARTIES, whom do you mean? The Marinaros and their best buddies The s? -- Why, I met the when I made the "pitch" about my product to them and even roasted it for them in Ron's garage. I can tell you that the (are certainly not "Third Parties" but Prime Suspects as Associates of Ronald and Catherine Marinaro.

By "Third Parties" do you mean the Press? Do you want silence us, YOU WHO CALL YOURSELF GODT -- lurking way across the country, over there in Melville?

Each person so far to receive my letters is no "Third Party" but a person directly related to Dr. Marinaro and his family and friends, all of whom participated in the aborted LLC for INCOGNITO COFFEE.

When you say I should not tell THIRD PARTIES, DO YOU MEAN THE PRESS AND THE TV AND THE DOCUMENTARIANS? Or the police?

You might shut me up, dear fellow, in New York, but please do not attempt to quiet me in Hollywood. Hollywood understands couples like Ron and Catherine and their Malibu cronies. Their medicine ain't quoted in the New England Journal of Medicine but in LA MAGAZINE and PEOPLE and THE NATIONAL ENQUIRER, a wholly different group of socialites.

ADVICE FROM THE MAN WE CALL 'THE RODENT'

Returning to September 10, the day I went to Jeffrey Dash's Larchmont Office after leaving THE PAIN RELIEF CENTER. While my wife waiting outside in the car, Jeffrey told me in his office that he would immediately "download" my contract with Marinaro, and repeated that I should not worry "don't worry!" -- the new LLC would buy my secret formula and marketing strategies and concepts in return for stock and salary perpetually equal to Ron Marinaro D.C.'s stock and salary, with us as equal partners. "You're PARTNERS! Neither of you can act without the other."

So Jeffrey Dash and Ron Marinaro D.C. told me I was just to sit tight and allow them to help make me a very rich man. Somehow, this was not totally comforting.

Needless to say, in spite of these good promises, I continued to demand what I called "the deal" with Ron Marinaro D.C., since each and every day I performed some service or duty to help get my product in the stores. Ronald Marinaro D.C. said that he was putting his money out "in trust" and that I should trust him as well.

Then on a certain Friday, I got a call from my Roaster that Michael Moss had called and asked if my Roaster would roast for Ron under a different name. Then I get a call from my Roaster saying that Ron and Michael have "worked things out" and they now have investment of 2.2 Million as of Today, October 1, 2001.

This is pretty magical financing.

At the same time, INCOGNITO appears in Cooke's Market and Pacific Coast Greens in Malibu, but I am not notified.

Did these Malibu stores buy product from Ron or Ron's Wife or Michael Moss believing that these people had the legal contractual rights to INCOGNITO? Moss and Marinaro operate out of THE PAIN RELIEF CENTER. Did that entity provide legitimacy and funding for the operation? How many knew about it?

And WHY, you might certainly inquire, did I continue to attempt to do business with folks I was trusting less and less, hearing from less and less, even as the "company" seemed to be expanding more and more, with more and more names on Dash's "cc" list.

5

THE CAUTIONARY TALE:

A BRIEF HISTORY OF PAIN
AT THE PAIN RELIEF CENTER

Less than one hour before I signed the LLC Application at the office of Jeffrey Dash on September 10, I was in the office of INCOGNITO at THE PAIN RELIEF CENTER.

The INCOGNITO office is located in a room which formerly was assigned to a Childlren's Scoliosis Center, but which Ron Marinaro D.C. decided might be more profitable as the headquarters for our soybean coffee company.

At that meeting, I accepted the $1,000 expense/consultation check which had been due me on the First as part of our handshake agreement whereby I would receive $2,000 per month for Consultation and Expenses from the doctor while I rebuilt INCOGNITO into a functioning company, providing the process, beans sources, bean varieties, bean companies, label companies, the label copy, meetings with designers and brokers etc. This was not to be the final dollar amount for my "Consultations," but a kind of advance to live on while the Company grew.

I accepted the $1,000 in good faith and said that, in good faith, I would sign the LLC application in the trust that Ron Marinaro D.C. would finalize the "deal" according to our agreement from June 26. Since one week before Tony and Ron Marinaro & Family left for Merv s Investment Meeting, I had been asking for a "written deal memo" and I was delayed and stalled and am still delayed and stalled this very day. For, while you have much to say in your letter, you say nothing about the quid pro quo between me and Ron, which must be the only reason you could have any reason to contact me all the way from Melville, New York with admonishments about "Jurists Prudence." (Please see the June 26 Deal Memo re: Marinaro, Dash & Incognito.)

Ron Marinaro D.C. and Catherine Marinaro and TJ Marinaro and Rose Marinaro and Tony and Mrs. Tony are all aware of my ownership of INCOGNITO because I presented the soybean coffee to them during two separate Investors Meetings at the house of Ron Marinaro during the month of June, 2001. I went to his house as a meeting of Investors and for no other reason, and my wife went with me. We felt absolute trust in the whole proceedings because we were patients of Dr. Marinaro (on one of these days, Gretchen received a chiropractic adjustment.)

In mid June, anticipating Ron's departure for Merv's yacht, I engaged the Gourmet Coffee Roasters in Venice, California to make INCOGNITO and bag it with my company labels, also written by me, so that Tony and his wife and Ron Marinaro and his wife Catherine could bring the product to Merv on Merv 's yacht the Fourth of July Weekend, 2001. Many discussions took place among all of us, and others, before that Weekend and afterwards, all regarding INCOGNITO.

6

Tom Marinaro D.C., the brother of Ron Marinaro D.C. and a partner in THE PAIN RELIEF CENTER, made digital records of his family, and Tony s family, tasting and experimenting with INCOGNITO at Ron Marinaro D.C.'s house in Malibu.

During this period I had no reason to suspect that:

Ron Marinaro D.C.'s wife began meeting with buyers and executives at COOKE'S MARKET. She enlisted the services of Mr. Barry to help put INCOGNITO on the shelves of COOKE'S MARKETS.

For weeks I met almost every day with Dr. Marinaro in his offices at THE PAIN RELIEF CENTER, where we discussed strategy and planning for INCOGNITO while my wife was on the table being adjusted. Finally she asked that I not be present when she received treatments, because I was staring to argue with Ron about "the deal" and that only increased her mental suffering and physical pain.

We were now almost totally dependent upon Ron Marinaro D.C. because my Writer's Guild Insurance had stopped. I no longer entered the treatment room when he "adjusted" Gretchen. We continued our discussions in the office or the halls or at lunch.

And my wife was getting worse.

Gretchen's pain now lasted almost the entire night, every night. It seemed that *after each adjustment she took longer and longer to recover from her agony.*

On the business front, even as my demands for written documents increased, Ron Marinaro's accessibility decreased. Without my consent or informing me, Ron Marinaro D.C. installed Michael Moss in the office. I was never given a key, although all the boxes of INCOGNITO and all of the files belonged to me.

I was increasingly worried about my wife's health, and fearful that if I had to break the deal with Dr. Marinaro, she would be inconsolabe. Since we talked about everything in our marriage, she could not avoid knowing my concerns about Dr. Marinaro's business dealings with me. Each day she became more and more apprehensive. *HER PAIN WAS INCREASING, WE HAD NO INSURANCE, AND DR. RON MARINARO WAS STARTING TO TELL ME HE COULD NO LONGER 'CARRY ME' WITH HIS PROMISED CHECKS. HE STARTED TO TELL ME THAT 'ANYBODY CAN MAKE SOYBEAN COFFEE.' THESE NEW DEVELOPMENTS RAISED ALARM BELLS LIKE CRAZY*

During treatment in the doctor's office

In Dr. Marinaro's office, I told him that Gretchen was eating at the dinner table kneeling down, because it hurt for her to lift her head. I told him that she spent part of the night unable to put her head down, and that it reminded me of the story of the Elephant Man, who dies in his sleep when he lays his head back to be like a "normal" person.

Dr. Mariner's solution is to go "deeper." He refuses to take money from Gretchen, but offers to move her bill to INCOGNITO, where she can pay it off with office work. I inform him that under no circumstances will my wife be forced into office work.

Privately, not to interfere with her treatment, I ask Gretchen what it means to "go deeper"? How deep can the neck go? But these questions cause Gretchen to go into spasm.

MEANWHILE, IN THE COFFEE BUSINESS

Dr. Marinaro stalls on the next check to me for my expenses, even though I improve the flavor of our 50/50 brand with a new French Roast.

It seems to me imperative that Gretchen see another doctor. She refuses to see anybody at UCLA or Santa Monica Hospital, even though she was born at S.M. Hospital and did her nursing training at UCLA. She will not do anything

I tell Gretchen that the constant pain will surely make her less strong. She says she'd be better off tossed in the river to drown, than to be with such hurt. I wake at 6:AM one morning and pace until finally I am able to make an emergency appointment with Dr. Donna Alderman, a D.O. I insist Gretchen see her, if only to get pain medication. Gretchen will not see Dr. Alderman without first seeing Dr. Marinaro, so I stop by Dr. Marinaro and THE PAIN RELIEF CENTER for Gretchen to get an adjustment.

Dr. Alderman sees that Gretchen is in such pain that she needs help getting up onto the table. She sees that Gretchen is in far more pain than the previous visit, 8 months earlier.

Dr. Marinaro has treated Gretchen from better to worse, in my opinion. Dr. Alderman prescribes painkillers, which Gretchen up until now has refused to take.

At this point in time, Gretchen is able to eat only once a day. She has to stand up until she is too tired to stand any longer to be able to sleep at night.

And Dr. Marinaro is not returning my calls regarding INCOGNITO.

Then, on Sunday, September ---- around two in the afternoon, he telephones me at home to say that he and his investors have discovered that the formula for INCOGNITO is in public domain, but that he is a friend, he is my "only" friend he declares, saying that even my wife has a "problem" with my behavior, and that from here on he'll have to take over the business. He tells me that the investment bankers he and Jeffrey are talking to about INCOGNITO are asking why I should even be kept in the deal. Even his friend Tony thinks I am "baggage."

I remind him that I taught him the recipe in front of all his relatives and friends, and that all his relatives and friends were going to invest in it, and that for five months there was no question that the recipe belong to me. "Things change," said the Doctor. I told him that in that case, there was no deal, for the only way to change our deal was to break it.

My wife, when I told her what happened, and that I thought we could go no further with Dr. Marinaro and his family, became silent and stony, and withdrew into such pain that she could barely speak.

All that night she slept with her head bent over her knees, because it hurt to lie on her back or her sides, and all night long, I swear, I cursed that doctor and I cursed my own helplessness, because it was clear to me that Gretchen felt that only he could help her neck, and she was worried, also, that we had no money to pay anybody else. Neither of us slept.

Grim details

In the morning I received a call from Ron Marinaro D.C. from his cell phone in his silver Mercedes as he headed East on Kanan Road from Malibu. He told me that somebody was getting him the "recipe" for INCOGNITO and that from now on, I would have ten per cent and he would control 90 per cent of the LLC.

He also said that in view of the fact that the recipe was public, he could no longer pay my fees and expenses until all issues regarding the Corporate structure of INCOGNITO were resolved to his complete satisfaction, and the satisfaction of his investors, who he would no longer name to me.

I told him the important thing for me was that my wife continue to receive treatment. He said, "I am a Doctor! I will always treat your wife!" But then his Mercedes entered a dead zone and the cellphone shut off.

TREATMENTS OKAY, SAYS CHIROPRACTOR MARINARO, BUT PATIENT IS NOT

By the following mid-week, Gretchen needed more painkillers than ever, and she was afraid of becoming dependent on them. I had already stopped attending any "treatment meetings" with her and Dr. Marinaro. He talked to her during the sessions about INCOGNITO, and she began to see inconsistencies in all that he was saying to her, versus what she knew he was saying to me on the telephone.

Gretchen realized that her doctor had been pitting her against her husband to gain control of a company. ("Gretchen: The Wife's Story" is being written by Gretchen and will be available soon.)

We soon discovered that Ron Marinaro D.C. had actually succeeded in putting our product in stores without first informing us. We wondered what happened to the meetings he was to set up on behalf of INCOGNITO with executives and buyers at KIRKLAND, COSCO, WHOLE

FOODS, TRADER JOES and others. My broker, Bob Krieger, said he was pumped for information, and then never called again.

When Gretchen found out that Dr. Marinaro and Michael Moss had called her husband's proprietary roaster, asking that he roast for them under a new brand name, Gretchen saw that her Doctor had been using her. Then many other events and conversations she'd had with Marinaro D.C. began to fall into place. The result was not pretty.

More chronology will be circulated later as part of the BOOK OF R.O.N.

THE CRUEL USE OF A WIFE'S INCREASING PAIN VS HER HUSBAND'S RELUCTANCE TO CONTINUE A COMMERCIAL PARTNERSHIP

A MARRIAGE IN CONFLICT OVER A DOCTOR'S TREATMENTS

WHY DOES SHE HURT MORE AFTER EACH ADJUSTMENT?

You have said, Mr. Godt, that my letters might be considered an intentional assault on your client's person.

YOU ARE SENDING A PROCESS SERVER TO THREATEN ME WITH SLANDER SEND HIM HURRY MR. GODT BEFORE YOU HAVE TO SEND TEN THOUSAND AND THEN ONE HUNDRED THOUSAND BECAUSE THERE IS SOMETHING SO ROTTEN HERE THAT ONE HUNDRED THOUSAND...

You will see from what I have only sketchily described in this brief letter, that I belief Ron Marinaro D.C. did in fact, with his hands as well as his words, his skills as a chiropractor as well as his skills as a businessman, intentionally assault the person of my wife and intentionally attempt to alienate her from me, her husband, so that he, Dr. Marinaro, could conspire with others to take my company and my peace of mind.

He has not succeeded in silencing me, and you will not succeed in intimidating me or harassing me with threats of "process." I have seen, in Ron Marinaro and Dash and "The Marinaros" a kind of process from Hell.

In my mind it is a true and urgent question as to whether -- by not informing the police -- I am in compliance with his actions, or a possible accessory after the fact. This is the reason I am sending all these letters to experts in the field of law enforcement. I am indeed seeking counsel to protect myself from association with those who intend to commit harm.

It is not always in the nature of the injured to understand the exact nature of the wound or injury; it is for this reason we go to Doctors. A doctor is the very Principle of Fiduciary.

My discussions about my invention and process and manufacture of INCOGNITO began with my first treatments with Dr. Marinaro, and they ended with my wife's last treatment.

Furthermore, if you say you are advised by your client (THE PAIN RELIEF CENTER, DR. RON MARINARO, DR. TOM MARINARO, ROSE MARINARO, TJ MARINARO, MICHAEL MOSS, JEFFREY DASH, AND THEIR ASSOCIATES AND EMPLOYEES) that I have no known rights regarding INCOGNITO, then how do they explain the six months they spent working with me on it, or the business plans I wrote and Jeffrey Dash says he wrote, or the checks they gave me from THE PAIN RELIEF CENTER. Nobody had a cookbook?

In the 90 plus pages of research on soybean products I sent to Jeffrey Dash and Ron Marinaro and Tony , there was no recipe for soybean coffee which remotely resembled mine.

Are you trying to tell me that your client spent months of research, travel, discussions and thousands of dollars before finding out that his enterprise was common knowledge just as the company was being funded by investors with more than $10,000,000?

Tell it to the judge.

I am the sole owner and inventor of all trademarks, copyrights trade secrets, marketing plans and all intellectual property rights including formulas to INCOGNITO and no research conducted by me or anyone else from 1985 to July 2001 has proved otherwise. I have written copyrighted information about INCOGNITO and sold INCOGNITO COAST TO COAST since 1992. I have only given trade secret information to possible investors, whose names I know by heart.

As you so succinctly state, "The statue of frauds in California requires that for a contract to be binding, it must be in writing, signed by the party to be charged. A handshake at the very most is an expression of an agreement to agree."

Exactly.

Marinaro, Moss, Dash, & Company must get out of my business immediately.

In your September 26 Fedex you mention that I have "allegedly violated..Fiduciary responsibilities to the business…tortuous interference with business relationships and economic benefits..' Do you mean by that that I informed Moss & Marinaro they were guilty of false and misleading advertising on my company bags, which they had placed for public consumption in Cookes? Or that yesterday, after an employee of Pacific Coast Greens Market told me my Incognito tasted "Nasty" I was forced to try a batch and conclude the stuff was undrinkable, as well as labeled "CERTIFIED ORGANIC" which Moss and Marinaro have been told it is not? If they make consumers sick with their rush-to-market, and I interfere, isn't that my duty?

And what about Dr. Marinaro's fiduciary duty to his patients, where it all began?

As for the Paradoxical Pain Healer and Jekyl-Hyde performer Marinaro/MarinaroD.C. (whom I have nicknamed "The Snatcher": He is to be held accountable for both sides of his personality, both sides being guilty, not only in the local Malibu press, which he and his wife Catherine are attempting to manipulate, but in the health community at large, across the Nation, and in the Courts.

Hey, what about Ben Stiller in the mini-series? I ask this because Dr. Marinaro is the "back cracker" for BIG BROTHER 2, a reality show that pales next to the drama in the Doctor's own Life.

Sincerely,

William Richert

OWNER/INVENTOR
INCOGNITO THE COFFEE ALTERNATIVE

Sanli Pastore & Hill, Inc. The Premier Business Valuation, Financial Analysis & Litigation Consulting Firm

VALOREM PRINCIPIA

The Principles of Value Volume 12 Issue 3 November 2004

Jury awards $14.75M

in Fraud, Breach of Fiduciary Duty, and Breach of Contract Case

Richert V. Rocomojo, Marimaro, Dash, et al.

Incognito Coffee Alternative Corporation ("Incognito") was a soy coffee company founded by SP&H client, Mr. William Richert ("Plaintiff"). After founding Incognito, Mr. Richert invited his chiropractor and friend, Dr. Ronald Marinaro, to join Incognito as his partner. Subsequent to learning Mr. Richert's secret formulas and business plans, Dr. Marinaro and his best friend Mr. Jeffrey Dash misappropriated Incognito's identity, strategy, and product and seamlessly transferred them to his own entity called Rocamojo, Inc. ("Rocamojo" or the "Business").

In the process of growing Rocamojo into a multi-million dollar business, Dr. Marinaro discarded Mr. Richert entirely from the Business.

Aided by Johnson & Rishwain LLP ("Johnson & Rishwain"), Mr. Richert charged Dr. Marinaro and Mr. Dash ("Defendants") with Breach of Contract, Breach of Fiduciary Duty, and Fraudulent Concealment, amongst other wrongdoings, and he sought damages for his losses as a result of the acts of Dr. Marinaro and Mr. Dash.

See *$14.75M Award - Page 2*

$14.75 M Award - *From Page 1*

SP&H was retained to:

- Provide expert witness analysis to determine whether, and to what extent, Richert suffered damages as a result of Dr. Marinaro and Mr. Dash's actions;
- Determine the business value and viability of Rocamojo, Inc.;
- Determine a reasonable royalty rate Mr. Richert should receive from sales of Rocamojo product; and
- Determine the net worth of each Defendant as the basis of awarding punitive damages in the event that the court ruled Mr. Richert entitled.

SP&H assembled a team consisting of Mr. Nevin Sanli, ASA, President, and three experienced analysts. SP&H's analysis found inconsistencies between Rocamojo's financial statements and its income and expense ledgers, which highlighted possible fraudulent activity. We also discovered numerous non-operating expenses that were inconsistent with what the Defendant's claimed to be a "failing" business. This analysis proved to be crucial during Mr. Neville Johnson's direct-examination of Mr. Sanli as well as in his cross-examination of the opposing expert.

Ruling

After presenting our findings in court, the jury found that Dr. Marinaro and Mr. Dash had engaged in fraudulent actions and that Dr. Marinaro had breached his fiduciary duty and partnership agreement with Mr. Richert. The judge ruled that the Plaintiff could not seek a 50% interest in Rocamojo and only monetary damages could be awarded. To compensate Mr. Richert, the jury awarded him in excess of $6,500,000 in damages.

Further, as a result of the Defendants' fraudulent activities, the jury found that Mr. Richert was entitled to an award of punitive damages in the amount of $8,000,000 against Dr. Marinaro and $250,000 against Mr. Dash.

DAILY JOURNAL NEWSWIRE ARTICLE

http://www.dailyjournal.com August 26, 2004

ONLY IN L.A. COULD SOY-COFFEE DRINK STARTUP BREW SO MUCH BITTERNESS

By Garry Abrams

A famous young actor, River Phoenix, who died of an infamous overdose at age 23 in 1993; a chiropractor; suspicions of treachery; and a secret recipe for roasting soybeans that supposedly makes the main ingredient of tofu hot dogs taste like coffee.

These are among the elements of a fascinating case in which a Los Angeles Superior Court jury this week awarded very much alive actor-producer-writer William Richert damages totaling nearly $15 million against his former business partners, including his onetime chiropractor Ronald Marinaro.

The jury made the award in compensatory and punitive damages in a dispute in which Richert, who among other things directed Phoenix in the 1987 movie "A Night in the Life of Jimmy Reardon" and acted with Phoenix in the 1992 film "My Own Private Idaho," claimed that Marinaro, co-defendant Jeffrey Dash, described in the complaint as "a celebrity print agent," international currency expert and "long-time friend of Marinaro," and others illicitly squeezed Richert out of a promising startup company.

That company, originally named Incognito but now called Rocamojo, markets two types of soybean-based, coffee-flavored drinks that the company touts as protein-rich and healthful, according to the company's Internet site. (An article from The Chicago Tribune posted on the site said that most tasters of the soy-only coffee substitute didn't like the taste. However, two tasters "who cannot consume caffeine were thrilled with it," the article reported. A half-soy, half-coffee blend also sold by Rocamojo "pleasantly surprised" tasters, The Tribune noted.)

Richert's complaint alleged that in 2001 Marinaro offered to help set up and financially back Richert's dreams of marketing a soy-coffee beverage. The partnership developed while Richert and his wife were being treated by Marinaro.

Later, when the startup was showing signs of success, Richert alleged that Marinaro took over management of the enterprise, contrary to previous oral and written agreements that included Richert in company organization and management.

Until I learned about this case from Richert's attorney, Neville Johnson of Johnson & Rishwain, I never would have guessed that the lowly legume, perhaps best known as a vegetarian substitute for meat and fowl, could be the spark for so much bitterness and contention.

But emotions ran high in the case, particularly for his client Richert, who had invested years of effort and experimentation in developing a method for turning soybeans into a tasty coffee substitute, according to Johnson.

Richert himself told me Wednesday that the case, especially the 11-day trial, had been draining.

But Richert, who said he had never been to a trial before, added the outcome made him a believer in the legal system. He noted that he was impressed with the jury, whose members appeared to pay attention throughout the proceedings.

"These were 12 strangers I had never seen before," Richert said. "But, boy, did they see us."

Not long after the jurors completed deliberations Tuesday, Richert said one member of the panel e-mailed him that he had hummed a patriotic tune on the drive home, so great was the juror's belief that justice had been done.

Not surprisingly, an attorney who represented defendant Dash had a different view of the case.

C. Timothy Smoot, a Redondo Beach sole practitioner, said he was "totally surprised" by the jury's awards.

"I don't think the evidence supports the verdicts," Smoot said, declining to discuss specifics.

Smoot said, however, that in the case's post-trial phase his side would seek to have the awards at least reduced and possibly thrown out.

"It's a long way from being over," Smoot said.

I didn't reach attorney Robert E. Levine of Hanger, Levine & Steinberg in Woodland Hills who represented Marinaro for comment.

Meanwhile, Richert said he may use some proceeds from the verdict to get back into the soy-coffee business himself.

"As soon as we get any money at all, I've got a roaster lined up, and I'm going to compete with Rocamojo," Richert said.

In our telephone conversation, Richert portrayed himself as a moviemaker, screenwriter and actor who had a separate, 20-year career as a proselytizer for the health benefits of soybeans. (Richert said the 1979 movie he directed, "Winter Kills," is due to be re-released later this year.)

Indeed, Richert said that he and Phoenix, who was his principal backer before his untimely death, shared a belief in the power of soybeans not only to taste like coffee but to feed the hungry.

"We had ancillary goals of feeding the world with soybeans," Richert said.

!-- Only in L.A. Could Soy-Coffee Drink Startup Brew So Much Bitterness

Breach of Oral contract against Marinaro $586,000
Breach of Fiduciary Duty against Marinaro economic $3 Million, non-economic
$30,000
Fraud and Breach of Confidence against Marinaro and Dash, $3 Million, non
economic $30,000
Punitive $8 Million against Marinaro
$250,000 in punitive against Dash

There were 11 days of trial, which started August 5 (there were some breaks
due to witness availability)

To: williamrichert@williamrichert.com
Subject: congratulations

Dear Mr. and Mrs. Richert,

My name is W. and I was juror number 2. I'm sorry I couldn't stay and chat with the two of you after the trial today, I was honestly just so moved by the whole thing, I was on the verge of balling, and I did when I got to the parking garage. This experience was really a great one for me. I was humming the song "Proud to be an American" all the way home. It was really so wonderful to see the good guy win and the bad ones get punished. I thought they should also get a public ass kicking too. Jesus, those two are such slimy liars I could just spit in their faces. It was a good feeling when I saw you yesterday, because you looked like you had gotten really good sleep over the weekend. That made me feel good. Can you mention to Mr. Johnson that he has my total respect and admiration. He seems like a very good, honest man to me, and I thought he did a fantastic job.

I think I heard you mention something about a movie you wanted to give everyone. I'd love to see it.
My address is

I hope you and your wife have a wonderful life.

Best wishes,

W.

To: williamrichert@williamrichert.com
Subject: Congrats from Juror #1

2 unnamed **text/html 2.78 KB**

Bill,

As juror #1, I just wanted to send congrats on…not being screwed. You seem like a nice man and certainly deserve a fair shake. That's what I think you got. I'm sorry I didn't get a chance to read the venomous (I gather) letters you sent to the Body Snatcher and the Rodent. I'm sure they were a hoot. Even though they were born of anguish I'm sure they were entertaining, kind of like watching a bad car wreck where no one gets hurt. Please don't think I take the situation lightly – I just know your way of expressing things lends itself to tragic and comedic proportions, sometimes at the same time. I have read Kant, but I'd rather read Woody Allen and I am by no means an intellectual, but I'm certainly not stupid enough to be fooled by what the defense team would have had us believe. And so I am using your method of blowing off steam after a long four-week ordeal– writing a letter and sending it as an indication of closure. My meager imposition doesn't compare with what was your challenge, but it consumed a bit of my life and deserves to be put to rest in the same measure. Good luck with whatever remains and best wishes for the future.

S.

To: williamrichert@williamrichert.com
Subject: hello there
2 unnamed text/html 3.24 KB

Hello there Mr. Richert, my name is C. and i was one of the jurors in your case against.."the rodent" and "the body snatcher"..I got to speak to you after the case was over and i believe i told you that you and your wife Gretchen are both very humble people and you sir are a very talented man. It is good to know that no matter what happens in this crazy society good things can still happen to good people.
It was a privelage to be on this case because not only was it a good experience for me but I got to shake the hand of the man who will become bigger and have more success than what you have already accomplished , as well as shake the hand of the marvelous and strong, supportive wife who has not only been behind you 100 percent on everything but the wife that has been right beside you every time i turned and looked down the hall of the courthouse. I must say that you two are adorable together..
They always say that "what doesn't kill us only makes us stronger" I believe that people live and they learn by every mistake that is made and those two bad guys who thought they were so slick throughout this entire thing got partially what they deserved however you are the one w/ the good ideas so you will progress and your success will be their pity and their downfall.
Well I will leave it at that..congrats on your earnings, you deserved it because after all it was YOUR VISION and i wish you nothing but the best in the future for you and your wife and your new soy coffee. Take care

C

or also known as juror #12

"BEHIND EVERY MAN THERE IS AN EVEN STRONGER WOMAN" that reminds me of you and Gretchen

To: williamrichert@williamrichert.com
Subject: [No Subject]
2 unnamed text/html 3.89 KB

Mr. Richert,

It's M here, Juror #7.

I hope both you and Gretchen are well and relieved from all the stress of the trial. I must admit, it took a lot out of me on 4 other cases, but none of those had affected me like this one. This time I feel a HUGE sense of pride in knowing serving justice. Perhaps because our country is at war, it's election time, and with the Olympics, serving on this case priviledge knowing that our system in the U.S. does work. I thank you for that.

I just read the news section of your website regarding the trial. Great story!

I thought I'd give you a few days before writing to you to take you up on that offer of a copy of A Dancer's Life. I can My address is below along with my direct phone number at Warner Bros. Please feel free to call me if you need anyt Not that you don't already have contacts in the movie business, but feel free to add me to that list.

I wish you and Gretchen all the best now and in the future of your case.

Best,

M

CAPITALISM SUCKS

Had lewis and clark been lawyers there's no doubt that after reaching California they'd've gone for Hawaii, and claim it even if they only got the Channel Islands, where they got shipwrecked and lost their bouillon and bracelets. The problem with the profit motive as motif is that it eventually bottoms out, or we'd all be working for the Hudson Bay Company.

This lawsuit, Richert vs Marinaro, which got a sweet judgment and sweet publicity, is now on a profit-seeking track without resources, near as I can tell. So far, we've spent more than we've gotten, and that's anti-good business practice.

In addition, the more Johnson and Rishwain is paid, when I am not equally paid, the more liable I am to various other liens or lawsuits, as your timely letters to seek outside counsel remind me.

To say that J&R has spent 305K plus and yet remains in debt to this litigation is both surprising and predictable, one only need read about legal behaviorism and law firm economics and one instantly knows that Johnson and Rishwain acts by definition in its own regard.

It is your relentless pursuit of legal victory that has cost me all of my profit and share in the lawsuit as we originally agreed. I amended our agreement so that you could righteously collect some of the damages against Marinaro. What I didn't realize was that once Johnson and Rishwain were no longer acting as my contingency lawyers, that you were now receiving fifty percent of your fees as well as fifty percent of the profits and one hundred per cent of the expenses – when the foregoing became apparent the "aha" also burst forth into light which showed a horizon blank with any monetary return for me and for Gretchen, who spent as many thousands of hours on this case as I did.

No regrets in signing the amended agreement, and only praise for your litigating talent skills, yet there is the knowledge that the new amended agreement forges a new economic model for payments accruing from this lawsuit to Johnson and Rishwain , a revised and transformed allocation of present and future resources which does what capitalism nearly always paradoxically does: destroy capital.

"I have no further resources or time to devote to a case that will only benefit the lawyers, if anyone at all. The varmit has been named and shot at and that's enough for me."

SHOULD GRATITUDE A SHMUCK MAKE?

I am thankful that you gave me advances in the amount of 20k. However, the thousands of hours of detail work we did here during the many months and years of depos and meetings and accountings, and the high hopes that came with a 14.75 million settlement led to higher expectations, especially when 305. 000 came in the door. It doesn't take much effort to calculate that with ongoing fees and expenses, and the ineptitude of

Marinaro and the lack of relative strength of his "bad faith" claim – after all Marinaro was proven in court to be a liar, why would his lawyers be immune and why would the insurance company pay out to Marinaro more than Marinaro has paid out to us – it isn't hard to do the math and see that future prospects of a payout to the client in this case – me that is – is a long shot at best and at worse an ongoing crisis of "relative destitution."

The Richert vs Marinaro lawsuit continues to generate less income than the amount billed and paid to Johnson and Johnson. Following an imaginary path to the outcome of Marinaro's bad faith litigation, and including the amounts your law firm charges against future earnings, I foresee a lot of difficult and painful effort on my part – since this theft will always be an emotionally charged issue with me -- and only you guys reaping any significant rewards. This is due to your smart negotiations with me, and who would expect you to be otherwise than self-interested? I perfectly well understand your business decisions.

When the guy who gets the money from a deal controls how the money is got and how it is spent then the guy in business with that guy can expect to see very little money. This is not genius thinking. You told me when, we re-wrote our original contract and agreed you could start collecting fees in addition to your percentage and your costs, that I should seek the advice of another attorney. I did not fear the outcome of such a revision, and so I signed it. Even today, I am not complaining. Instead, I am reviewing a deal that cost me the profits on the money taken in so far. You will agree that if I made a bad deal I should either change it or get out of it if at all possible, and as quickly as possible.

I am discovering that since the lawsuit itself now accumulates debt and obligations it may not be able to pay that If I act on my own behalf, as I am certainly obligated to do, then I have every incentive to get out of the lawsuit as quickly as possible. It's true there may be some areas you may still liquidate from Marinaro's accounts and real estate, but as evidenced by events up to this minute, the costs eat up all the profit – from my end, not from yours. Although I think you're doing something about Marinaro's time shares, I've not seen any documents about that.

RELATIVE DESTITUTION

Adam Smith talks about the

Now that you are no longer partners with me, but are paid lawyers working on the appeal for Richert vs. Marinaro,

Dear Brian,

Since our last accounting, where we were almost at the break-even point, I see that you added $216,734 in "collection" fees and an additional $340,000 in other fees to my bill.

It is clear to me, and should be to anyone looking at the matter in its entirety, that this "accounting" happened after I sent you notice that I was withdrawing from the WGA lawsuit. I know how you enjoy revenge, and I conclude that this is your way of punishing me, since these lawsuits are now commingled.

Charging almost $700,000 in fees before splitting with me on a contingency agreement is egregious and greedy and not at all what Jim Ryan was telling me would happen, nor what I understood from the promises and optimism that we would be fairly treated conveyed by you in your emails. I was certainly omitted in the intent of the agreement amendments, which I signed after assurances it was all "okay" and which I will collect and forward to you and anyone else willing to look at them and help in this matter, concerning amounts approaching one million dollars.

I regard this as vengeful bait and switch, and the wrongful use of one lawsuit against another.

People should know how you treat your clients, so that this won't happen to others, and as long as the 1st Amendment is in force, they will know.

This accounting will no doubt shock Judge Minning and the jurors. They could not have imagined that all their efforts on our behalf would benefit you alone, making a mockery of justice and the law, in my opinion.

I hope you are not going to employ similar "accounting" practices against the writers in the foreign levy case.

I contest this bill and the methods you used to arrive at it.

Sincerely,

William Richert

Gentlemen:

I reject your accounting. It is self-serving and contrived and violates our basic agreement and trust.

You saw me in your offices almost daily for 8 months before the trial, you saw me and Gretchen search through 10,000 documents, you read the volumes research I provided, you listened to my arguments about why you should prosecute the case, you saw me and my wife rise at dawn for four weeks and sit through a difficult trial with my hip requiring constant pain attention, you listened to the moving voices of the jurors who said they were disgusted by the doctor's greed, and when they awarded me (not Brian Rishwain) 14.5 million dollars you read the headlines in the newspaper and the law journal and you crowed about your success to your colleagues, and then – and then – after an additional year in which claimed you were spending thousands of dollars on other lawyers as experts – when you did not spend any such money – during a time we said we absolutely trusted you and would not as well as could not seek outside counsel on your expenditures, apparently giving you a green light to pay yourself whatever you like, a trust from clients that is not uncommon when the lawyer pretends to be fair – and then you took every single penny that came in, $331,000 – and now you are demanding the next $340,000 that may come in, and another 64,000 for who-knows-what, thus assuring that I be put into debt after three years of hard labor on the lawsuit, all designed to redress the wrong of a doctor stealing my company; this is worse than the doctor's theft, because he never pretended to offer me truthful "counsel" or kept me up night after night working on legal briefs to help my case and cause. If I am twice a victim, what does that make you?

Re-reading our original agreement, it leaps to my understanding that it is a template for abuse, if the lawyer so chooses. Those little notices after various paragraphs telling the client to consult a lawyer if they are not understood – how genuine are these black-label warnings, when one is already consulting a lawyer?

Because this is your profession, you knew three years ago how you would be able to manipulate all the incoming funds if you wanted to grab and control the whole lawsuit for your benefit; you knew that the contract was riddled with paragraphs that could end up cutting me out of all the money the court intended me to have, but you withheld information about the huge amounts you were billing all these long months, while you had me sign one new agreement after another, each one based on some new promise that we were "doing great" and each one putting more money into your pocket.

I repeat: I reject your accounting, and I question the reasons you gave to get me to sign the amendments that you did.

To say that I am angry that you took three years from my still-productive life as a writer and filmmaker is to minimize terribly the personal cost of all this time and energy.

We know from the world around us that even the strong and smart can be duped by the ingratiating and cunning. It is a constant, universal irony that honest and trusting folks are almost always the ones most harmed by those in a position of power. Just because you took all the money, doesn't make you smarter or better than me, or mean you will prevail forever.

By any fair reckoning: you and Neville Johnson are allowed to recoup your expenses only; all other amounts collected are to be split 50/50. Had you ever, even once, told me anything different during the years I spent on this case, I would have been given the right to make an informed decision. By not divulging your fees an entire year, until this accounting was delivered by email, you denied my opportunity to save $340,000.

I agreed to adjustments in our agreement based on your statement that a $40,000 payment urgently needed to be paid to attorney Quisenberry. Since this amount apparently was not paid to Quisenberry, I conclude you provided this information to induce me to sign a statement not in my interest.

Even if you did paid this money to Quisenberry, , it would provide another example of how you have created billing opportunities which only pay yourselves, based on the long time line and the helter-skelter list of these costs. The result is that you subvert the court's award and avoid sharing the proceeds of the jury judgment with your client.

By keeping me off-balance with each new attempt to "collect," you have been using my case over time as a private bank, with you the only beneficiary. This was not the intent of our agreement, this was not the verdict of the twelve folks who gave days and weeks of their lives to achieve justice in the courtroom, and it certainly cannot have been the intent of the ruling of the Honorable Judge Minning. I refer you to the letters from the jurors.

They did not put their lives on hold for an entire month in the courtroom to enrich Neville Johnson and Brian Rishwain, lawyers who are seeing to it that the plaintiff, their client, will never receive a nickel or a penny.

This is the opposite of zealous representation, it is zealous rip-off; it makes a mockery of the trial in front the Honorable Juge Minning, and it ignores the entire intent of the jury's verdict.

I will be sending you the juror's letters, to remind you of their desire for justice; this is more than a dreamy concept, as you should know.

By my calculation, based on our agreements and understandings over the past several years, ignoring any realistic monetary compensation for my years of work on the case, along with the help of my wife, you owe me $107,220.50 which is $331,948 minus your expenses of $117,507. Of course I recognize some expenses as necessary and legitimate. Other expenses appear to have been incurred by you in expensive forays that were nothing more than "fishing" expeditions designed to maximize your fees, as borne out by consistent and total failure in almost every instance

You have had more than one calendar year to prepare the hourly accounts I asked for. You still have not provided them, as called for in our agreement.

I also see a direct link from this stunning accounting to your anger about my asking for full and honest disclosure to union members in the case of RICHERT vs. THE WGA. Is this is your idea of revenge? (More about this issue in the letters and articles to follow.)

Please remit $107,220.50. It is long past due. Out of this money, I will repay all loans you made to me during the three years I worked on the case. I will pick up the check in person, as soon as May lets me know it is at the front desk. Look forward to seeing you then.

Naturally, I find all of this extremely depressing.

Sincerely, Bill Richert

Sept 1

~~August 30~~, 2006

RE: 3 WEEKS AFTER JOHNSON & RISHWAIN LLP QUITS RICHERT V. MARINARO, STILL NO INFORMATION PROVIDED

RE: URGENT REQUEST FOR CRUCIAL DOCUMENTS

Dear Brian,

You state in your email of August 8, 2006, "the relationship between us is completely broken down" and "we cannot continue to act as your lawyers."

Although you resigned three weeks ago, you still you have not given me any of the information vital to the protection of my rights and property in the case of RICHERT V. MARINARO.

It is especially important that I have all communications relating to what you refer to as "a global mediation being set up now" between all parties. You state this even as you refuse to provide me, the Plaintiff, with any knowledge of the settlement.

There must be some statute regarding lawyers who quit a case and then refuse to provide the client with documents relating to a settlement when they are available. This is obviously very damaging to my case.

Not only that: In addition to the global mediation you only revealed last week, you say about my stocks: "As every matter has deadlines you should seek the advice of an attorney immediately about this so that these deadlines do not pass or that your rights are not jeopardized."

Apparently it is you and your firm who are jeopardizing my rights in the letter of resignation you wrote after I questioned your accounting and procedures, stating you have dropped my case and showing how I will suffer because of it; how you would, in effect, punish me.

It was only after one full year of repeated requests that you finally provided me with information about your skyrocketing costs and fees. To injure me further, at the same time you present me with your stunning accounting you inform me of a "global mediation" taking place "now'" and tell me that "your stocks may be worthless" – facts which put tremendous pressure on me to do what you want.

And then, when I disagree with your methods, you tell me to get another lawyer, knowing that I have no means to do so – since you took all the money; – further, you suggest that no matter what, I might already have lost out: unless I accede to your costs and wishes.

This kind of putting-the-squeeze-on-the-Contingency Plaintiff-who-is-not-a-lawyer, like the surgeon waking the patient from anesthesia to discuss additions to his bill, has got to have some legal prophylactic, some preventive means, as well as a special legal adjudication for a lawyer who writes to frighten a client in a way that only helps the lawyer get more money.

Your accounting "**IN ALL MATTERS**" given in April 2005 totaled roughly $150,000 in fees and expenses. Your new bill of August 2006 claims the astronomical sum of $1,120,000. That is an increase of nearly 1,000% -- in the space of one calendar year.

Thus the resignation of Johnson & Rishwain from RICHERT V. MARINARO puts at grave risk the remaining possibilities for any return after 4 years of work on this case and a jury award of $14.75 million.

It was just amazing, Brian, to see where you charged more than 3x the hours of Jim Ryan when your email reveals: "I have been out of the loop, but Jim is keeping me informed."

Your accounting methods insure that while you are "on the case," I will get nothing but debt, while you are already $331,000 richer.

Robert "Bob" Levine of Hanger, Levine & Steinberg may well remember Neville Johnson telling him during the trial in August, 2004, that your firm was into the case for $200,000 including expenses, as a basis for settlement. Astonishingly, two years later, according to your email statements and accounting, that amount balloons to $600,000 "at the time" and then almost doubles again to $1,120,000.

Then when challenged, you quit in a snit.

Since you told me not to contact Judge David Minning, I need to know what communications you've had with the Judge, if any, regarding your resigning the case, and what notification/communications you've had with Marinaro's lawyer and any other lawyers representing the insurance company or others.

You've withheld information that allowed my 16 million shares of Rocamojo Inc. stock to be put in jeopardy, perhaps even become "worthless" as you have stated; you have withheld increases of $900,000 in your bills, and you have withheld information about a "global mediation" of my lawsuit.

This imperils my status as a litigant and my standing in the court and may harm my ability to settle the case fairly.

I ask that you immediately provide me the names and numbers of all parties to the "global mediation" you wrote about, including all documents/correspondence relating to it, before you cause me even greater financial damage and emotional distress.

I will send you an invoice for the amount I am due from money you have already received. Since your website declares you've gotten 75 million in the past three years, it will not be hard for you to pay what you owe me.

Sincerely,

Bill Richert

Dear Brian,

I am sorry I feel the way I do as well. The astronomical amounts you listed in your letter today in fees and costs were not evident to me from any of our conversations, or in the email you sent on September 10 (seen below) which was after all the work leading up to a trial and after the trial itself.

Now you stay it cost you $600,000 and more at the time of trial.

Also, suddenly, in this new letter you introduce the amount of $967,000. In addition, for the first time, you talk about the need for a yet new lawsuit in an attempt to recover my company stock.

This and other information was not given to me over the past two long years. Whether these financial figures were withheld from me on purpose or by oversight, either way they prove equally damaging. Your letter is evidence of that.

Please don't be offended by my requests or my being extremely upset. I did not say you were a crook. These astronomical amounts are only becoming public to me now, from the letter you've just written, and the bill you just sent.

That your July 2006 bill came as a total surprise to me, instead of part of a continuing disclosure of costs and fees and the possible future danger to my income and ability to support myself, is the basis for my complaint against your conduct and your bill, which was only provided after one year of asking.

As for telling everybody and his brother about this dispute -- the recipients copied on my email are those who've been part of this from the very beginning. They have a stake in this long lawsuit as I do. I also need to seek additional counsel, as you state in your letter.

Yes, it is unfortunate the way things are turning out. I certainly did say that you and Neville and Jim were brilliant at the trial, and before and during the trial; more than brilliant, I'd say, was the way Neville illuminated the wrongs of Marinaro to the jury, and the way he and Jim Ryan worked together as a team. It was thrilling to watch, and resulted in a historically high award.

But that "shock and awe" has been followed by long and expensive -- to me -- legal machinations that leave me with nothing, and now, apparently, not even the stock in my company, which formed the reason for the fight in the first place.

If you read your letter from my point of view, I think you'll understand why I continue to be disturbed and unhappy and very worried about the situation.

You must not be allowed to succeed. Neville's vow of fairness must be executed fairly, for the sake of judge and jury and court and the pursuit of justice, who may be blind, but is not stupid.

Collected Richert Papers

The Justice Letters

Volume II

III. Sampler:

- -CRP The River Phoenix Letters
- -CRP The Presidents Daughters/
  The President Elopes Letters
- -CRP The Richert VS. WGA Letters

There are people among us who can take our breath away with their character and style, with qualities of goodness and generosity which make us blink to be sure we are seeing correctly; they are rare, and so beautiful. River Phoenix was such a person.

Angels were not restricted to Heaven until the Dark Ages. Before that, they were thought to walk among the living, ever-present benefactors and spiritual guides. River was like that; no one who ever met him can deny it, nor can anyone explain it. For me he was a bright, unexpected crack of glowing light in the universe, and I mean that literally; when he died, a kind of fog and gloom settled in which I feel even now.

River was aptly named; he was a gusher of talent, of curiosity and wonder. His temperament was to go to the very edges of life, and with his humanness and the tentacles of his talent, to feel around, and to probe with that mischievous, cat-like smile on his face, extending himself in empathy and generosity.

He was always asking questions. When I last saw him, he had all sorts of questions about how I was living my life, and about subjects multifarious. Nobody close to River could escape his scrutiny (or his sly teasing wit) and I, perhaps, represented an "Older Person's Point of View." We were in my funky apartment on the ocean side of the Pacific Coast Highway in Malibu. Still full of energy at 2 A.M., he asked if he could play his guitar on the deck when I said I had to sleep. I said, "Sure," and left him looking out over the ocean and playing. I told him he could lock up after himself.

In fact, River was still there in the morning; he was sleeping on the floor with his guitar, lying on pillows he had taken off the couch. He had slept in the clothes he was wearing the night before. I woke him making coffee. Getting up sleepily, he thanked me for waking him, and drove into town to the set of the motion picture in which he was starring. From his clothes, from his very simplicity, you'd have thought he was homeless. Maybe he was.

Maybe he's home now.

Often I think about the image of River lying on the pavement toward the end of My Own Private Idaho, and about the image of our real-life River lying on the sidewalk in front of the Viper Room on Halloween; I wonder if the first was a prophecy and the second a destiny.

All of us who knew River miss him. For a while we decided in unspoken agreement that we would stop speaking about him to reporters or writers because so many of us had been misquoted. That was a mistake, I think now, because it left those who knew River less well, or almost not at all, to speak on his behalf, and misrepresentations crept into the stories that were written.

Barry Lawrence said he lived in a house on a mountaintop, that he was a vintner, and that he wanted to write every true thing he could discover about River Phoenix. He was persistent and thorough, and seemed hungry for every detail of River's life. His devotion and research have been extraordinary. I think this book will be of great value to the memory of River, and helpful to all those who want to know more about him.

On his last night I know River had been on a six-week vegan's diet of artichokes and corn, that he'd been working until late to help the film crew of the production he was starring in, and that the responsibilities he'd taken on with his work, his friends and family were bearing down on him. Among his own he was the breadwinner, and he worked tirelessly at his craft. When River started a film, he not only knew his own lines but the lines of all the other actors as well, and he could recite the stage directions to boot.

On the night he died, he had come to L.A. for R&R like any hard-working guy. He drank a fatal potion given to him by a person he trusted, and it killed him. I think his body was too pure for the common weekend-night assault that far less healthy eaters and drinkers could handle. However, I also think he wanted to touch danger, too, and that the artist he was felt he could handle death, perhaps even collaborate with it and play out a scene or two. This time, however, he opened the one door from which he could never return. He was locked out . . . or we were. The bit of Heaven he brought to earth he took away with him.

Nevertheless, he could not take away our memories and illuminations, and we have Mr. Lawrence to thank for helping us to keep them.

— William Richert

With the permission of author Barry C. Lawrence, William Richert's Foreword for this book has been reprinted as a eulogy for River Phoenix in the newly-released 2003 book edited by Cyrus M. Copeland: Farewell, Godspeed/The Greatest Eulogies of Our Time [ISBN 1-4000-4946-6]. As reprinted in the book, it is entitled "River Phoenix: Eulogy by William Richert", and it is acknowledged as being "in commemoration". William Richert is credited as being River Phoenix's "Director" and "Confidant".

RIVER FIRST FACEBOOK POST

This was one of the first posts I made on Facebook years ago. I joined FB mainly to fight against the bullshit about how River died, outright lies of omission promoted by his own family and those 'friends' who were too scared to speak up for him for fear of being implicated in murder or manslaughter.
It's been a long while now since I first wrote this, naively thinking somebody among River's 'friends' might read it and mention John Frusuciante, which never happened -- and I am finally inching forward on my documentary/memory of him; and I should add that my meeting with Samantha Mathis back then was not 'hearsay' but 'testimony' from a witness who was present and watched John Frusciante hold up the draught to River which killed him. River, trusting this 'friend,' had no idea what was in the drink -- and this guitar player never made or conveyed another brew that killed anybody; he was a 'professional' drug user and knew not to kill himself -- the guitarist is still alive and has been welcomed back into the 'family' -- but somehow this killed River.
There is more on all this, boy is there ever, but this has just arisen on my "Jimmy Reardon" page and I thought I'd post it again, thanks to Sharon '
William Richert
May 28, 2012
Fie on the Phoenixes who would deny a single frame of River's work to be buried like his scarred body in a vault hidden by deceit and blood bonds like the mafia, holding back the truth with a kind of insidious untruth conceived with unctuous self-love among a cultish Jim Jones or David Berg "Children of God" kind of family, a remake with movie stars. Oh let me tell ya folks that reading that the actor's "family" won't help the director of River's last movie brings me back to the long-ago late morning in my old Malibu pad when I asked his mother Arlen ("I changed my name to Heart," she said with a huge toothy smile and wink at the obvious boy toy she brought with her) -- when she was going to reveal what happened that night, and she said no, they weren't going to file any charges or talk about it publicly. Oh let me say here that River did not die as the "family" has led us all to believe. For 20 years I've waited for one of them to say it, to say what River drank the moments before he started his death spasm, what the draught was and who made it, and how River came to be in the Viper room and why they waited half an hour to call 911 and oh -- they should tell who it was Johnny Depp was meeting with on the memorial day we all held hands for River in Ione's back yard, bowed our heads and so sorely wept for our young friend. River played the part of me in a movie I made, him being the same age I was in the tragic-comic satire of my teenaged self. We became long time friends, and I remember his phone message 3 days before his death, saying "I'm just trying to keep my head above water in this crazy business". Although my movie luckily was finished, not subject to his family's wish that all "bad" language be cut, his mother would not allow him to promote the

film because she thought at the time it was bad for his young teen fans to see; she called it a "sex comedy" and her boycott then reminds me of the boycott now over another director's movie, a man I met in Amsterdam not long after River died and who told me that on location River was helping the crew pack up at the end of a day's shoot, wanting to be a part of all aspects of filmmaking, wanting to help the exhausted crew on overtime, such was his energy and passion for moviemaking on location. Samantha Mathis told me in horrific detail about the black event that took place that night at the Viper room – which I will not be the one to speak about, which I demand Arlen and Samantha and Joaquin and Rain speak about, and speak out they will you shall see. The face of Joaquin in his new film is the face of a man who has betrayed his brother, and who will live to tell about it, and come at last to peace within himself. I'm willing to tell about it, but it is not my place, as it could be declared "hearsay" coming from me but ask Joaquin what was in the paper cup handed that night to River with enough drugs to kill a horse presented with the words "Riv – drink this. It'll make you feel FABULOUS". Joaquin will have to tell the rest. About how they left their hotel room with River being one way, and how instantly he became "jelly" after consuming something at his table he did not make for himself. What this was and who gave it is known to many. As for my long-restrained fury and outrage and helpless feeling of despair for River's long-distorted legacy – well, that's partly in respect to River's own love for his family, as when I criticized his mother to him River always shook his head which silently said "please, she's my Mom." But I know a thing or two about Riv's mom and how she raised her kids and where she came from and why she felt self-promotion for herself and her surviving children was more important than defending her no-longer-productive son. I know about cover-ups, and how a large number of people can keep quiet about huge lies for years and years. For almost ten years I've been basically single-handedly fighting the cover-ups at the WGA DGA and SAG where billions of artist's foreign royalties have been stolen or 'disappeared." Last week in LA Superior court I told the new Judge on our case, Judge Wiley, that the lawyers for the unions represented a "labyrinth of insanity." This is morally and ethically and fiscally true, though my lawyers are still willing to settle for breaches and cover-ups; but the new Judge says he will not let me speak any longer in court, after all the years Judge West allowed me to speak directly to him in open court on the record. The new Judge says he will not hear my declarations for my class of 20,000 writers, even though I told him my class action lawyer, Neville Johnson, does not really represent my class. How is this connected to River? Well, it's just ole Bill against the "system" one more time, some folks would say, casting doubt on my veracity. Bunk. I say years of across-the-media press silence about a rip off of tens of thousands of actors, writers and directors – with nobody writing about it (heard from Nikki on this?) - just shows again how large numbers of people can be duped or scared into silence by great lies for long periods. Now the information newscasters we depend on are members of SAG. The WGA blatantly lies on its website about the settlement and my role in it. But we know that facts have lives of their own, and they will be heard eventually. Lies are not the only festering offspring of deceit, truth bursts forth from long suppressive entropy – like the Phoenix, and for me there is only One. The big bang began with truth. I have worried on my behalf that talking about River would only make it worse, bring up hard memories and another long time bout of mourning. Not only that, as Lead Plaintiff in RICHERT VS. WGAW et. al., Unwanted By Both Sides, maybe the WGA bosses and my lawyers would use my defense of River against my Writer's Guild Class, as if I were only stirring up controversy, when I've waited since 1993 for one of the family to come forward. Talking about River is still hard and I have tried to avoid it, wondering who might benefit from the truth being told after all this time. Then I read all the loving letters to River on the internet, and realize that he'd be loved even more if the truth were told: that he wasn't killed by "addiction" but by deadly intervention from Another. Not long ago Van Gogh's death was revised with the revelation he was shot not by his own hand, not a suicide, but killed by two local teenagers. In his selflessness, Vincent died not wanting to implicate them or send them to jail. It is overwhelmingly significant that Van Gogh was not suicidal or crazy in the way he's been portrayed, but a compassionate artist in control of his work not his destiny. It is crucial society know their pure artists from their addicts and suicides, even if some are both. River was not an addict/suicide. Van Gogh was not a suicide either, and was not committed to an institution, he put himself there, to paint and structure his wandering wits. River accepted a drink from a friend, off guard, among those he trusted with his life, like a dreamer killed while he was sleeping. He overdosed not of his own knowing or doing, in front of his co-star and brother and sister, lifting the cup to his lips like it was just any other drink on Sunset Boulevard. For years I couldn't look easily at a photo of River or even read about him, even regarding our own movie. But just weeks ago I read articles written at the time of his death where his mother seemed to say River was destined to die early, seeming to accept that he overdosed by himself as part of an addiction while omitting the deadly intervention that was described to me by his co-star Samantha who was at River's table that night. Now I read that the "family" wants to impede River's work on DARK BLOOD (irony) from being seen – it's led me to pen this letter quickly, before I think about it too much, and get too sad again to write about it for a while again. My friend River deserves his truth and I intend to see the record is set straight. – William Richert

36
Theresa James and 34 others
18 Comments
4 Shares

Like

RIVER PHOENIX'S FAMILY ABANDONED HIM TO LIES; JOHN BELUSHI'S FAMILY SOUGHT THE TRUTH

I was living at the Chateau Marmont in LA and from my terrace window I watched the activity in John Belushi's bungalow on the hillside several stories below as the police put yellow ribbon across the pathway.

Belushi was dead. River Phoenix was 12 years old at that time.

I used to see John when he arrived at the Imperial Gardens restaurant on Sunset Boulevard which was sort of the cafeteria for the Chateau, which only had a little coffee spot next to the front desk but nobody ever went there. Belushi used to trip on the top step every time he came into the eatery like he was going to fall backwards and we laughed every time. Finally of course he fell farther.

The woman who killed him by injection overdose was known to him.

The police had little trouble discovering that Cathy Smith gave Belushi his injection — John Belushi's family demanded justice, allowed police to investigate, and the woman who gave him the drug that killed him went to prison sentenced for 15 years.

Tyler Skagg's death by overdose has triggered a high-stakes legal battle as his family refuses to accept anything less than full disclosure of who provided the drug.

My friend Carroll O'Conner would not stop looking for the dealer who gave his son that fatal dose.

Contrast this with the way River was treated.

River Phoenix also died of an overdose - not by injection or from snorting - but from a drink given to him by person he knew and trusted, but the purveyor of the dixie cup contents that killed him, John Frusciante, got none of the investigation or attention demanded by the Belushi family even though there was a Viper room table of girlfriend and siblings who knew exactly what happened.

Instead of caring in such a way that the brother and sister and Mother would demand a hearing, "Heart"(less) Arlyn Phoenix, River's Mother, directed her lawyer that very night to call off detectives starting to investigate — her lawyer also being the lawyer for the Chili Peppers and Johnny Depp, owner of the Viper Room — .

Telling the cops no charges would be filed against anybody, Mother Phoenix flew Joaquin and Rain directly to Florida, cremated her son River, and then refused to say a word about who gave River his poison in all these years, recently prodding Samantha Mathis, who was promoting her last movie with River, to tell the phony story that River took drugs in the crowded men's room at the Viper Room — even though Ms. Mathis knew Frusciante gave River the fatal drink because she told me face to face that he did in awful detail and I've repeated this for almost 30 years and I'm not the only one who knows these facts.

When asked, Rivers mother basically says River was meant to die, that she even dreamed he would only be on earth a short while, as if she were in charge of that; and worse, as decades pass with not telling the truth she and her surviving children perpetuate her cruel lies by silence that River was a junkie and did this to himself.

In the autopsy she's quoted saying River used multiple drugs yet he had just finished months of shooting in the desert living on artichokes and corn.

I met George Sluizer in Amsterdam and when I asked the director of Dark Blood if he ever saw the actor on any kind of drugs he said absolutely no, not never, not once, even though he said otherwise in a later interview. Maybe by doing Mother Phoenix's bidding he was hoping River's mother and brother would help him release his movie, but they fought that, preferring DARK BLOOD was never to be seen by audiences, even if it was River's last film. Joaquin refused to help even with narration.

And the River stories changed after River could no longer defend himself.

When Samantha Mathis told me who killed him, she also told me how River tried to get several of his friends into addiction help, especially Frusciante. Shortly before River's murder, River had dropped the highly intoxicated guitar player John Frusciante off at one such rehab center on the way to "The Thing Called Love" location in Tennessee, telling Frusciante he'd get the help he needed. Then, as River drove off, Frusciante ran after him stumbling and screaming "I will kill you for this River! I will kill you!"

Josh [illegible], who grew up in River's circle and was almost a brother and who played the drums in River's band Aleka's Attic, gave me an interview of what actually happened that night after Frusciante realized he was being submitted to an "intervention." Considering the family involved, it took guts for Josh to do this.

"Sky Phoenix" was a witness and participant in this event, but has never come forward to acknowledge Frusciante's murderous threats; he has, however, attempted to block showings of River's last movie in Miami, and taken down tons of River youtube videos. His role and conduct in all of this is fascinating, and remains to be deeply examined.

Soon after the intervention, Frusciante showed up at the Viper Room and really did kill River, who trusted this faithless friend enough to drink a Dixie cup filled with poison, no doubt thinking it would be okay. After all, he'd done drugs with the guitar player before, and this was a rare night on the town after months of rigorous shooting for the 23 year old artist.

As for the bogus claim he 'speedballed' in his nose or veins: the autopsy shows no evidence whatsoever that River snorted or injected the cocktail that killed him; it was in his stomach. He drank it. Read the autopsy, and note that the top-listed expert was a detective Mike Lee from "homicide" — but nothing was investigated.

FROM WIKIPEDIA: "Homicide is the act of one human being killing another. A homicide requires only a volitional act by another person that results in death, and thus a homicide may result from accidental, reckless, or negligent acts even if there is no intent to cause harm."

This news of a threat to murder from Frusciante corroborates with what Mathis told me, and is part of a pattern of contradictions and deceit about a homicide that remains to be investigated in the matter of River's death, even after all these years; I for one, won't give up.

But the job is no longer mine as a loner, as it was for many years.

Today there are many people looking into the lies his family and 'friends' told by staying silent. Newly discovered facts and remembrances are all over the internet.

Recently Samantha Mathis, an actress who is also an executive at the Screen Actor's Guild, revealed something new to many of River's fans but not new to me: when he died, River thought he was almost broke.

FROM A RECENT ARTICLE QUOTING MATHIS:

"He lead the family into vegetarianism and even during his final years, he was only thinking of making films to put his siblings through college. "River said to me in that last year: 'I just have to make one more movie to put away enough money so my youngest sister can go to college'," actor Samantha Mathis recalled. "I don't know if that was true, but I remember him saying that."

This film that River meant to send his sisters to college with was my version of THE MAN IN THE IRON MASK, which we worked on while I was acting in THE CLIENT.

This was in fact the “one more movie” Samantha Mathis was talking about in the Far Out Magazine article. Mathis was going to play River’s love interest Valliere.

River was my co-producer and was going to direct the scenes I finally wound up performing as ARAMIS, since he was the one who got me into acting.

It was to be River’s birth as a director.

THE MAN IN THE IRON MASK with River as the star was part of a "package" which was being worked on in 1992-93 at MGM with Frank Mancuso, who ran the studio, and we had extended conversations about schedule and budget etc.

Jeff Bridges had agreed to play D'Artagnan and sometimes he left messages on my answering machine practicing his accent.

There were many 'names' that River and I were talking about, and I had stars of my own in mind to play the roles that wound up being played by lesser names. We hoped to bring together the same kind of star-studded cast I’d had in WINTER KILLS.

In fact, Leonardo DiCaprio met Axel Vendel in Paris at Regine's and told him he knew River was going to do that film we'd been working on and that he felt honored to be in River's footsteps -- he also mentioned another movie River was going to do that he starred in -- the TITANIC.

So when River was murdered, which he was, whether the perpetrator was in his right mind or not, I lost my close and dearest friend along with my co-producer, soybean coffee company partner, and movie star.

The world lost a guiding light. (Although he has since been seen by a lot of folks.)

I cast my son in the role of the dual kings because in real life he had some of River’s qualities, including being a vegan at that time; and he sounded a bit like River too.

When River died MGM decided to make their own version of Dumas' book without me, directed by someone else and starring DiCaprio. In fact, in an extraordinary conversation, Frank Mancuso also discussed releasing both films at MGM since I had originated the whole idea of doing the movie with River; of course, that didn’t happen.

Our last face to face meeting was at St. James club on Sunset, just before he left for location on Dark Blood.

River was angry in ways I’d never seen him before, saying he wasn’t able to make his next investment in our soy coffee company INCOGNITO because his mother had spent all his money, and besides that, he'd given 250 thousand to his father for land in Costa Rica.

He told me that the MASK script we'd been working on, which was to be our first film together since "Jimmy Reardon", a movie that provided his first leading role and the family's first big paycheck, would be the last movie he would make as an actor.

He was telling other people too, that he was giving up acting. I'm not sure he really told them why.

His new angry decision contradicted what he'd said just a few months before, in a meeting where he brought Samantha to my house, when he'd talked about how he was working with three other directors too on various films.

People don't realize River was as ambitious as he as talented. He really wanted to change the world. Like. Really.

I told him quitting acting was ridiculous, he was an actor and would always be an actor, and what he should do about his 'family' was get his own lawyer along with a new agent and press agent. I reminded him he wasn't a kid any more, and he should take care of himself as he took care of others.

I believe that the agitation his 'family' talks about when 'remembering him' that fatal weekend when he came to LA from the Dark Blood location to shoot studio scenes in Hollywood — this agitation was due to his frustration and fury about what had happened to his money, which his mother had always been handling for him.

We were going to meet that Halloween week to read our screenplay. Instead I met with Samantha Mathis to hear how he died.

Not long ago I got help from to find somebody to help create a 'deep fake' which puts River into the Iron Mask scene we'd been reading together on the phone. I'm attaching it here in its first incarnation.

So River and I made his first leading role film as an actor and are now making his first film after death. This is not so far fetched according to the many who say they are visited by River these days.

If I actually do manage to do an entire 'deep fake' movie with River, concluding our last work together, you can imagine how River's fans would react to seeing the conflict between two brothers which is the basis of the Dumas story; one kind and innocent, the other cruel and deceitful. This could easily be seen as relating to River and The Joker.

River's siblings Joaquin and Rain and his mother and her foundation are profiting mightily from the devotion and affection and money from those who love River, along with many who sense his presence here on earth even to this hour.

Now Joaquin has named his newborn son River. Maybe the boy will grow up and ask about his dead uncle. Joaquin has laid a heavy trip upon this child; almost like a new blood line in the "Heart" (less) Children of God cult. Maybe it was her idea. It almost is a marketing ploy; exculpatory from Joaquin's haunted guilt. It is a helluva burden to follow for the kid. Almost cruel.

I cannot imagine River returning to infancy in the custody of a brother who denied him, and a grandmother who exposed him to abuse as his mother, who is now friends with his killer again.

My job here is almost done. With new help and information I will soon be released from my examination of this joker family and the true crimes surrounding my friend's death. I'll move on; but not just yet.

There are still a lot of threads to be knitted together in an ever tightening noose of undeniable realities.

Before he died John Bottoms Phoenix said if he ever came across John Frusciante "I will kill him."

Well I certainly don't want anybody killed, or even jailed, for events in this tragedy.

But I do want the facts to be known, so River's soul can be at rest at last— along with the many other restless souls who know in their hearts that something about all this is terribly wrong.

Over the many years I've got communications from a lot of people — most notable being Samantha Mathis, whose searing description of River dying in front of her after trustingly gulping the Dixie Cup in one grand slurp is indelible in my mind; but she is only one of those during these years who offer revelations and then simply refuse to speak again or change their stories. There are such things as the Unforgivable, and what the 'family' and 'best friends' allows to be said about River since they all know what happened entombs my ability to forgive.

Thus, as I am old and disappearing as we all do into the next dimension, I want to make sure that the footprints I leave can be cast in iron later on.

River's memorial has got to be rewritten right now with all the fame and greatness and meanness of its living cast and characters in subordination to the amazing truth about him. He once left a message on my answering machine calling himself a "Magnificent what the ‘family’ and ‘best friends’ allows to be said about River since they all know what happened entombs my ability to forgive.

Thus, as I am old and disappearing as we all do into the next dimension, I want to make sure that the footprints I leave can be cast in iron later on.

River’s memorial has got to be rewritten right now with all the fame and greatness and meanness of its living cast and characters in subordination to the amazing truth about him. He once left a message on my answering machine calling himself a “Magnificent Failure” after being unable to change the focus of a scene he was doing in the BoGdanovich film, where he protested the direction by behaving slightly off.

His strategy didn’t work; the director didn’t listen; but even if he called himself a failure, and the scene stayed in the picture, River made his protest. And he didn’t compromise, either.

Like he did not compromise his trust in his friend by examining the drink that killed him. River is magnificent now, without qualifiers.

River should get the kind of respect given to John Belushi and Tyler Skaggs. Although he is a man, the child he was deserves his own.

DRAFT LETTER TO THE NEW YORK TIMES 'COUNTERPUNCH' FROM WILLIAM RICHERT, SCREENWRITER

The WGA union members Lawton and Schiff have both got it wrong in the union's role in credit "arbitrations." Along with my original writing partner on "The President Elopes," the screenplay which begat THE AMERICAN PRESIDENT and the version of my script which was the basis for THE WEST WING, I have first hand experience with the WGA Arbitration process, which is as arbitrary and arcane as a blind Ayatollah in its decision making. The process, which gave Aaron Sorkin sole credit on THE AMERICAN PRESIDENT without what nearly all Americans would call "Due Process," is conducted entirely in secret. Kyle Morris and I are presently suing Mr. Sorkin and the WGA and Castle Rock Entertainment and Alan Horn in the U.S. Federal Court in Manhattan. Our position is that because Castle Rock paid five million U.S. dollars for the rights to our screenplay to Redford's company Wildwood and Universal Pictures, we were denied by the WGA Arbitration process the right to sue Aaron Sorkin for plagiarism. We believe that any court in the land would see the overwhelming evidence that Sorkin lifted the plot, structure, characters and dialogue from various drafts of my screenplays – written for Robdert Redford over a decade-long development process – but the WGA arbitration denied us the right to review Sorkin's statement to the arbitration board, and denied us the right to know which scripts the board read of ours, and because Aaron Sorkin wrote a letter to the board saying he had originated his story/characters/structure "separately" from our scripts, the arbitration review board – composed entirely of televison writers, which is another kind of work altogether from original screenwriting – gave Sorkin sole credit. Sorkin was simply more famous and had bigger clout than I did, or Mr. Morris did, for this can be the only explanation for the WGA's decision. Since that time I have not worked as a writer in Hollywood and will not work as a screenwriter in the studio system which takes the copyright from the original author, gives it to the studio for "the Universe" and "in perpetuity," and then allows hacks in the WGA to take away credit in spite of its own rules. The WGA is a studio creation in its Arbitrary Arbitration process, for if the public had been allowed access to my screenplays in court, Sorkin would have been seen for the thief that he is. The WGA strikes, which have so burnt the role of true original writing in television, are threatened by the results of votes of as few as three dozen guild members, affecting tens of thousands. We can see the suffering in today's economy of the WGA sponsored defacto strike of two years ago. Less visible are the actions of the WGA arbitration board, but they are no less devestating. It is my hope that our lawsuit will offer a new way to return the copyrights to the true authors of screenplays, so that liars and plagiarists like Sorkin can be sued and brought to justice. William Richert

The American President Cold Case

The Aaron Sorkin WGAw Scam....

https://usac16strong.wixsite.com/-aaron-sorkin-scam

RE: RE-DO OF WGA ARBITRATION THAT NEVER HAPPENED ON 'THE AMERICAN PRESIDENT'
UPON NEW DISCOVERY OF WEST WING PILOT SOURCE WILLIAM RICHERT DEMANDS WGA ARBITRATION THAT NEVER HAPPENED AND RE-DO OF AARON SORKIN'S PHONY CREDIT FOR 'THE AMERICAN PRESIDENT' – WRITER ASKS UNPAID VOLUNTEER SCREENWRITER-PRODUCERS ON BOARD OF DIRECTORS TO READ THE ACTUAL SCRIPTS IN RARE UNUSUAL REQUEST – WRITER-DIRECTOR WILLIAM RICHERT ACCUSES ADMITTED 'CRACK WRITER LIAR' AARON SORKIN OF LYING IN 1995 LETTER FROM DRUG REHAB CENTER - BOARD MEMBER KATHERINE FUGATE ONLY WGAW MEMBER WITH COURAGE TO ASK REASON FOR FIRST SCREENWRITERS LONG-TIME ANGER AT CREDIT AWARD TO SORKIN – VOLUNTEER BOARD PROTECTION BY TONY SEGALL AND DAVID YOUNG GONE ASUNDER

MEMO TO:
KYLE MORRIS,
CO-WRITER ORIGINAL SCREENPLAY 'THE PRESIDENT ELOPES AKA THE AMERICAN PRESIDENT;

CC WGAw ALL-VOLUNTEER BOARD MEMBERS AND CREDIT EXECUTIVES:

Katherine Fugate, Stephen Schiff, Carl Gottlieb, Patric Verrone, Chris Keyser, Scott Alexander Howard A. Rodman, Alfredo Barrios, Jr. Marjorie David, Carleton Eastlake, Jonathan Fernandez, Karen Harris, Chip Johannessen, Peter Lefcourt, Aaron Mendelsohn, Michael Oates Palmer, Billy Ray, Ari B. Rubin, Shawn Ryan, Thania St. John et.al.

FROM: WILLIAM RICHERT

July 4, 2015

Dear Kyle,

In Hollywood I discovered that I was one of the chosen people. Not of tribe, but of talent, which has a tribe of its own. If the 400 know each other, so do the talented. No secret handshake or password required. The talented people know each other and recognize each other from afar.

Now, Aaron Sorkin is certainly among the talented people we know in the instant. So am I and so are you. We each contain talents of different atmospheres, like the planets circling the sun, of patrons, fame and "success" (the title of one of my favorite movies of mine) , but nonetheless we are spinning in the same space, chasing or subject to the same rules.

That is why when one of the talent tribe swings way out of orbit, almost to defy gravity and throw off the solar system of the light prisms of talent into shit, we have to restore order to the system of gravity, however elliptical our orbits.

Continual striving for greatness is not for the feint hearted. The use of the screenplay form is equal to the use of the novel form or the poetry form or the forms you fill out to get into college, though I didn't go to college, that institutionalized leveler of boundless youth, another system like the Writers Guild of America that may have gone awry.

The Writers' Guild ought really to be seen for what it is: an exclusionary group of "writers and video game creators" (talent not required to join, just a pay stub) who control how a "writer" gets paid in Hollywood by the studios with secret contracts; WGAw "protection" from "enemy" studios is like the payouts to mobsters; and anyhow "studio" has itself become an inclusionary term for the interlocking systems formerly centered geographically in Southern California. (What constitutes a "studio" any more? One of 7 major corporations? Something in your garage? Who is that artist formerly known as "Prince." Anybody remember?)

The writers guild was begun by Lillian Hellman, among other "scribes" who eventually created that original "black list" in the 50's which has been converted by the WGA into a new "black list" but this time a praise and accolade for scripts, the same kind up upside-down gymnastic linguistics that allowed them to award Aaron Sorkin sole credit.

WGA founder Lillian was both a convincing playwright and plagiarist about whom Mary McCarthy famously said: "Every word she says is a lie, including 'and' and 'but,'" and the whole of the WGA has come to be like that.

Not long ago John Wells, maybe to cover up his treatment of our own script, awarded Dalton Trumbo his writing credit on "Roman Holiday" — after 59 years, and after Wells had run the union for ten years in various capacities. This is rather longer than the fast track for sainthood given that South American dude by Pope Francis.

[Click following link to Eric Hughes' websie to see how far back the WGAw has been collaborating with the studios against the true rights of authors who choose screenwriting as an art form and ignore WGA dictates; back then they called them commies: http://www.screenrights.net/creditsescapeclause.html]

20 years ago, on November 16, 1995, the WGA gave Aaron Sorkin sole "written by" credit on his draft being the last in a series of drafts starting in 1982 with the sale of my original story to Walt Disney Company.

By this time I'd already spent an earlier 20 years doing re-writes for Redford's producers and other executives, thinking my director contract would be honored. It was originally set for me to direct: as a writer-director, that was my whole reason for the long trek.

During this time, the project was very well known, often in the press, and VARIETY announced in 1993 that Sorkin was doing a revision of our script to make it more political, or something.

It was always in rewrites, it seemed. In a letter he wrote to me that Alan Horn copied to the WGA Directors and Robert Redford the Disney CEO referred to our original as "Your much re-written screenplay."

Alan Horn should know. He knows how much he paid for re-writes, and all scripts attached to each other in a time line back to '82, like the chain letters you've recently written the WGAw Board Members. The fact that Alan Horn paid 5 million dollars for the right to take our script off the market (?!) makes it the largest script sale in modern times, but we didn't get credit for that either. Nor did we get any of the money, even after all the free-writes I did for Bob, a very conservative reader. Finally I refused to give him any scripts until I read them to him first, after he called me to say he was in the office. Maybe he gave Sorkin the credit because he didn't like to listen to me, "another actor," he called me once.

At the time of the Writer's Guild "arbitration" in 1995 -- an arbitration which we know today never occurred -- Wildwood executive Sarah Black told the LA TIMES: "THE AMERICAN PRESIDENT" belongs to Bill Richert the way France belonged to DeGaulle."

Of course this is hyperbolic; France never belonged to DeGaulle. But neither was he written out of his own history as I have been written out of mine by Sorkin and the WGA.

I thought it was kind of hysterical, in the old female psychology sense, that Sorkin called me a "Hack" in 2010 in THE DAILY BEAST or somewhere. I'm nothing like a script factory, just the opposite. I'm a beat poet making movies as a sideline for the fun of it, and my output is very slim. Actually, I've written only a dozen or so scripts in the past 50 years, a few of which I'm still working on, while Mr. Sorkin wrote over 86 "teleplays" for our uncredited series THE WEST WING even though he never really got the original point of it, and damaged the reputations of some pot smokers.

Michael Douglas would have been miscast in our original THE PRESIDENT ELOPES along with THE EXECUTIVE WING/WEST WING; Douglas tends to Borcsh Belt when being satirically philosophical, while I was after a President more in line with a Roussaeu-enlightened Ronald Regan, if we can dare imagine such a persona.

You might have thought Michael Sheean would fill those shoes, if his President weren't a secret drug user, like Sorkin, with perpetually sweating feet.

Sorkin did a fair job of mimicking my long "walk and talk" dialogue passages he claims he invented (forgetting Shakespeare) — which I started in my own venues way back in WINTER KILLS, a movie I found out he used as part of his "research" — and Sorkin also sparked to and copied my President-Speechifying Moment of ripping into a long monologue to the astonishment of his staff, like Pavarotti bursting into THE HILLS ARE ALIVE.

AS an aside, to show how scripts can influence society if made into movies, I quote myself in a recent letter to Jeff Bridges, who is presently reading WHAT GENRALS DO AT NIGHT, a film I'm producing. I include it here because it relates to the vast reach of movies, and the results of deceit:l

[Dear Jeff, Many years ago I sent you the first draft of THE PRESIDENT ELOPES which you said "Sorry Billy it doesn't float my boat", a line that still makes me smile a little, but that led to Robert Redford optioning the screenplay and 20 years of re-writes for various studios until production when Redford so hated Rob Reiner and Sorkin's revisions that he quit the picture, while this picture became the basis for THE WEST WING which led to the revulsion of the "evangelists" towards Democrats because the President in the series used drugs, and that led to the election of George W. Bush, which led to Iraq and the present conflagrations of humanity everywhere. Not to say because you declined a role we now have the crummy state of the planet earth, but I gotta say if you'd been in that movie, we would quite possibly be living in a very different kind of nation with a different recent history on a way more peaceful planet…however, we can make up for lost time…etc…]

If the "iconography" of actors is part of the design, you see why I would not have chosen Michael Douglas for the movie, and neither would Redford; it was Sorkin's choice.

AS FOR MY DIALOGUE FOR PRESIDENT SAM ANDERSON, THE CHARACTER BEFORE SORKIN'S 1994 NAME
CHANGE/TRANSFORMATION INTO 'PRESIDENT ANDREW SHEPARD'

(NOTE: HOW THE NAMES ARE ALMOST SCRABBLE VERSIONS OF EACH OTHER; TRICKY AND NEAT BUT NOT NICE - nor original to him.)

TV critics made much of these long monologues. If you think of Jeff Bridges in the role of Andrew Shepard/Sam Anderson, you get the idea of what it might have been had I directed the movie, from my script, as intended. For better or worser, Here is the original of those long Aaron Sorkin speeches, as written by the author; pls think of Jeff Bridges doing the lines, and then how Sorkin might re-write into his own image:

EXCERPT FROM 1991 'THE EXECUTIVE WING/WEST WING' DRAFT SCREENPLAY by WILLIAM RICHERT:

SOLVANG (CONT)
-- If you were to reach her, propose to her, and be rejected •••

HOVERMANN
It would be a knife in the heart of your Presidency.

PRESIDENT SAM ANDERSON
Is that why you're asking? Not occurring to you the effect her saying no might have on my ••.
Sam trails off.

CYRUS
-- All benefits which might accrue from your bold, romantic and adventuresome move would reverse themselves to liabilities.

SOLVANG
The polls would kill you.

HOVERMANN
Think of the headline: President turned down, caught out of the White House with his pants down, so to speak, and -- •

Sam turns to his son Peter.

PRESIDENT SAM ANDERSON
Peter, this concludes White House Politics 101. I want you to go to your room like we said __
(looks over at the Men) while I tell these three gentlemen just where to sit when they ride on these upcoming poles.

PETER

Okay.
He crosses to the door. Sam is about to speak once more when Peter turns back.

PETER
Will I have to call her Mom?

PRESIDENT SAM ANDERSON
Well, her given name is Catherine. I'm sure the two of you can work that out together. If we get the chance.

Giving him a "thumbs up," Peter leaves.
Sam looks at the others.

PRESIDENT SAM ANDERSON
Amazing. The four of us have faced some tough situations since my inauguration, but I've never seen any of you this scared. Do I appear to be a dangerous person to you? Some kind of threat, or obstacle?

THE THREE: Stare at him.

PRESIDENT SAM ANDERSON
Then why do you look at me as if I'm Abul Nabul? Am I merely a political being? If so, I'm a walking historical artifact __ nothing more -- certainly not an evolving, evolutionary, biological being -- No wait, I'm not going off the deep end here __ •
He crosses to a pile of books at the base of the couch, where he's been doing "research." The three observe the President of the United States rummaging through pages like a graduate student.

PRESIDENT SAM ANDERSON
(opens book, reads)
"Our happiness is not an ordinary matter of young lovers; it is, for me, a matter of efficiency.
I am absolutely dependent on intimate love for the right and free and most effective use of
my powers. Love, personal love, is the one thing a man's heart cannot do without."

CYRUS
President Woodrow Wilson's love letters. Great.

PRESIDENT SAM ANDERSON
-- At the height of the bloodiest war in all history. We men do need our women from time to time, do we not?

SOLVANG
Forgive me, but I gave up a very lucrative position in the private sector thinking you intended to both be and stay the President, sir.

PRESIDENT SAM ANDERSON
What?

SOLVANG
I do not think this is a win-win situation.

PRESIDENT SAM ANDERSON
Good God, if I am denied because of questionable theories or possibilities or press reaction the ability to be all that I am, or who I am, as a human, feeling being, then how can I possibly represent the human feelings of tens of millions of beings? Don't you see, the best I can do for my country is equal to the best I can do for myself? If the goal is greatness, for me and you and this administration -- which is only a blink in the long list of forward-moving administrations - then I've got to strive for the heights -- I've got to at least prepare myself for the possibility that I -- like you, Cyrus, or you Ben, or you, Reggie -- that I could be the hundredth monkey!

Now he's done it. He can tell by the looks on their faces they're not au courant on the hundredth monkey theories. He can tell explaining it would be to lengthy and probably counter-productive. He can tell that they probably think he's lost it. But what really frightens him: he doesn't care.

PRESIDENT SAM ANDERSON
(a little patiently)
The hundredth monkey is not a-creature. It's just the theory that we can learn from each other in simultaneously evolutionary ways, as opposed to legislating laws alone or -- or --
•

He turns to the desk, starts collecting a pile of small volumes into his briefcase, as if preparing to end the meeting.

HOVERMANN
We'll not abandon you, Mister President.

PRESIDENT SAM ANDERSON
I expect you won't.

I might add that Sorkin mentions Harding's love poems in one of his scripts too, but doesn't bother to quote them; I wonder how he found out about them. I first heard them when they were read to me by Alice Longworth Roosevelt as we drank copious scotch together in the tea room at the house of Katherine Graham while i was interviewing Nixon's daughters in the White House. Sorkin can mention Harding, but he don't know Harding like I do.

Even in the original plot of our first version of the 1982 THE PRESIDENT ELOPES/AKA/AMERICAN PRESIDENT, there is still the central element of a widowed father with an only child living in the white house, courting a woman who is unsuitable.

Scientists win Nobel prizes with one sentence formulas. Ours would be Widowed President + Only Child + politically unsuitable woman + courtship from within whitehouse to impress + a scene where they dance + a scene where they romance in the White House + a break up + a get togetherwiththe unsuitable Woman with the American President.

That's the formula followed by Aaron Sorkin which originated with us, scientifically and factually. There is no other formula fitting any other scripts in history, besides our versions and Sorkin's version. Our DNA is all over the movie and the Series Sorkin stole from my last draft, and DNA will out.

(Few know there is an original King Lear with long bits directly sounding like Shakespeare, so that the original writer Raphael Holinshed would have surely gotten a credit from the WGA just like us, and if alive he'd be angry still, just like us. We are on the side of the original Lear.)

INSIDE JOB AT WGAW

In the early 90's John Wells is volunteer Secretary Treasurer.

Carl Gottlieb was WGAw Vice President, and he brags that during that time he was setting up the illegal foreign levy scheme with Brian Walton along with Universal Picture's Robert Hadl. Universal owned rights in THE AMERICAN PRESIDENT and in the copyright.

John Wells and Carl Gottlieb are still at the WGA as a volunteers with Gottlieb back for a second time as secretary treasurer. Not long ago Carl wrote a check to me for foreign royalties, then took it back. I consider that an act of retaliation for my efforts for the Sorkin arbitration overturn, and for demanding the court enforcement of RICHERT VS. WGAW INC. settlement, a related issue of Board oversight failure.

BOARD MEMBERS MUST ACT LAWFULLY AND REVEAL THE FACTS ACCORDING TO CIVIL CODE

"Activities which are unlawful must be made known to the Board of Directors if the Executives are acting in a criminal manner, AND THE BOARD MUST RESPOND." FYI

It is ironic that the screenplay the producers didn't want anybody to see — Sorkin being a Producer who cannot say he didn't see Sorkin-the-writer's material— is the screenplay that will bring them all down, the rats and cats in he same dumpster, the script entitled THE EXECUTIVE WING/WEST WING which was written in 1991 for Redford and director Fred Schepsi. Both of whom told me the script could be the basis of a TV series after being a movie. They were correct. A series was even in my Universal contract.

The key thing is that there never could have been any kind of legit arbitration at the WGA because the prime scripts and contracts were not given in evidence; were, in fact, willfully withheld.

But not skillfully withheld, or we wouldn't have been able to figure this out, albeit 20 years later (the title of a Musketeer book; my film THE MAN IN THE IRON MASK INDIE VERSION has been gathering foreign royalties for 15 years, collected by the WGAw but not given to me; another story, but involving the same characters like Tony Segall, etc.)

In his deceitful letter written to Sally Burmester at the WGAw 1995 purportedly written from NYC but actually mailed from Hazelden where Sorkin was incarcerated for his addiction (Burmester still works there, but is an employee and therefore exempt for personal lawsuits, unlike the volunteer WGA board members Wells and Gottleib and the ones we must put on notice.)

Aaron Sorkin claimed he'd been hired separately Rob Reiner -- the co-producer with Redford! -- to write a script entitled "untitled Washington project" but we know from Eric Hughes that his was a "blind script" deal and he began no writing until working for Redford's production company and Universal -- on his re-write of our script.

In 1995 Sorkin copyrighted THE AMERICAN PRESIDENT Draft 3, dated 11/11/94. We don't know what was in the first drafts. The one I read was 350 pages + and had large chunks of dialogue from earlier versions of mine and other writers of THE PRESIDENT ELOPES so that reading it I wondered why he bothered to re-write for the worse and more pedestrian dialogue.

Other drafts existed before Sorkin started writing for Reiner and Redford and it is those he used as the basis for his characters and dialogue and story. He omitted the charms of my "Sleeping Beauty" aspects in the 1986 version for Universal, and his President Shepard didn't sneak out of the White House as my President Anderson did -- who started out as President McCormick in our 1981 original, with my grandfather's surname. So the names change as these drafts are rewritten by the likes of Ron Bass an Alice Arlen among others. But they are the same men, the difference between Shepard and Anderson being a re-write by Sorkin. That's how it is in "development." Aaron Sorkin simply aborted the credit system with a lie the system wanted to accept for reasons of money and status.

But the crux of it all, and the reason a new arbitration and script comparison is required, is that THE EXECUTIVE WING/WEST WING draft I wrote in NYC was totally omitted from the WGAw decision process and arbitration, as was my contract with Universal/Wildwood to write the screenplay.

Your letters to Stephen Schiff and the credits committee and Board of Directors over the past few years are now part of a chain of information that shall bind them, since they cannot say they didn't know you thought they were covering up criminal behavior — and as lifetime WGA credits expert Eric Hughes wrote, there was no way we could have known until now how they did what they did — it was a coverup!

What is germane and the source of this gravitas for courts is that the this key bit of evidence shows overwhelmingly that we were not liars when we said that Sorkin took his script from the source of ours.

We had to sit for years in front of the teleplay Taj Mahal that Aaron built, knowing we were the true architects. No more waiting. In a literary spin, It's not hard to see the ghost of the meal in the cannibal Sorkin's brain; it shows up in print and on the screen, and that is where we must direct the attention of the West Wing fan hoard:

When it becomes known that the Writers guild never compared the William Richert/Kyle Morris original and early drafts with Sorkin's rewrite -- as Disney executive and then Castle Rock CEO Alan Horn wrote in a long lying letter to me at the time -- and Tony Segall declared to the Judge — when the basis of all this is examined and finally includes "my last draft for Redford" - namely the eponymous THE EXECUTIVE WING script — it will become a clamorous clarion call for credit redux, in our favor, at last.

In your chain letter you have thus far provided a running demand for justice from Stephen Schiff and Katherine Fugate and the board of directors, without any real response.

A man, a writer, a member Emeritus of a guild – like you -- is due proper respect. Neither you nor I signed on to the WGA as collective bargainers leaving our individual rights behind, especially the right to due process.

We should adhere to the "principles" Aaron Sorkin put down in his August 1995 letter to Sally Burmester, addressed from NYC but written by Sorkin from Hazelden rehab for crack addiction:

QUOTING AARON SORKIN'S LETTER: "In closing, I note that the 'Guiding Principle' of the WGA's system of credit determination is that the 'writing credit should be a true and accurate statement of authorship'. Let the credit arbitrators, therefor, make their determination solely based on reading the scripts in front of them. Their judgments should not be restricted or predetermined by an artificial minimum 'irreducible story credit' to any writer other than me. This would be a gross and fundamental misapplication of the Guild's own guiding principles."

But they did not have all the scripts, and didn't compare ANY of the scripts by reading them -- so how could they possibly decide who gets the credit?

Sorkin seems to say the Guild's guiding principles apply only to him, or otherwise be grossly misapplied. As the WGAw's prime public mouthpiece, he might consider other phrases, or put his principles where his mouth was.

In other words, the WGA should have been given THE EXECUTIVE WING/WEST WING screenplay, but they never saw it.

The WGA and its Board of Directors has thus far denied us the right of due process, as they must do to be given credence in a court of law, and their willful negligence in excluding the last draft in the PRESIDENT series of rewrites is our prime exhibit in a new case against volunteers with duty that can be filed both in the courts and in the social media, where the interested people or West Wing scholars can read for themselves what we are talking about.

While we re-examine the blatant con that went on with the phony "Pre Arbitration Special Committee" held in secret etc., we will also look at the reality show playing out in '95 at the Bev Hills Peninsula Hotel, where Rob Reiner and Julia Bingham and Alan Horn are desperately looking for a place to put Aaron Sorkin as he was, he says, under a 2K a day crack habit, his per diems up in smoke, while trying to finish his rewrite of THE PRESIDENT ELOPES AKA THE AMERICAN PRESIDENT, which he admits he doesn't completely remember writing, grasping at dialogue from the stack of drafts from other writers.

IN the world of celebrities, where Aaron resides, it is nearly impossible to miss wedding photos and announcements etc. — to the varmint gossip collectors it will be a true Holmesian insight that the person who benefited the most from this fraud, after John Wells, is the former Castle Rock attorney, VP of Business Affairs, and personal advisor to Aaron Sorkin: Julia Bingham, that rare lawyer who marries a crack head.

We can be allowed cracks about how the one who benefitted the most was Aaron's lawyer at Castle Rock, where he was a long-term employee. The Rangers always get their man, and lawyers always get his/her fee.

Sorkin was a screenwriter literally in bed with the studio. After they started their romance, Julia stopped memos on Castle Rock stationery that began: THE PRESIDENT ELOPES AKA THE AMERICAN PRESIDENT.

We should not cease our the "original creator" demands and the "irreducible story by" credit promised in the WGA MBA, that is the minimum.

This is a great, rousing campaign for rightful credit to all, and we have assembled the Braveherts among us, ready for auld ang sine. We can do the Sorkin/Zukenberg thing to Sorkin/Bingham/Horn/Reiner to the tune of "Guys and Dolls."

That's another copyright worth owning.

ONWARD

BILL

CARL GOTTLIEB

HOWARD A. RODMAN

CHRIS KEYSER
Katherine Fugate
The Executive Wing aka The West Wing PDF.
SCRIPT NEVER SHOWN TO THE JUDGES AT THE WGAw
Sorkin Theft lettter From England
Producer Barbra Maltby Tells the History of The American President "the American Scolar"

WilliamRichert.Com
AARON SORKIN

Y U
Violators
Richert vs.
WGA
Jury
Trial
Demanded
Alas, we-the-pumlers
R-pummelled
10,000 writers wronged

Grand Theft Hollywood

HOW THE UNIONS AND STUDIOS CONSPIRED TO TAKE MILLIONS IN FOREIGN ROYALTIES FROM ACTORS, WRITERS AND DIRECTORS

THE FOLLOWING CONTRACT IS AN EXCERPT FROM A GROUP OF EXHIBITS IN A CLASS ACTION LAWSUIT REGARDING 1.8 BILLION DOLARS OF FOREIGN ROYALTIES EUROPE SENT FOR AMERICAN ARTISTS OVER A PERIOD OF DECADES -- MONEY THE ACTORS, WRITERS AND DIRECTORS HAVE NEVER RECEIVED.

USUALLY FOLKS FIND OUT ABOUT THESE CLASS ACTION LAWSUITS AFTER THEY ARE SETTLED OR SEALED. THAT COULD BE HAPPENING IN THIS INSTANCE, TOO.

AS A SAG MEMBER, WERE YOU EVER ASKED, OR WAS ANYONE YOU KNEW ASKED, TO AGREE TO A DOCUMENT LIKE THE ONE ROBERT PISANO SIGNED IN 2002? ONE WHICH ALLOWS THE COLLECTIVE BARGAINING AGREEMENTS TO BE IGNORED TO MAKE A DEAL WITH THE STUDIOS GIVING THEM UPWARDS OF 92.5 PERCENT OF THE ACTOR'S ROYALTIES?

The WGA is preparing to settle the RICHERT V. WGA et. al. case, which is similar to SAG's but SAG lost much more money over the years, simmplay because there are more actors and they get bigger paychecks.

The WGA has so far admitted takingin 97 million since 1990, and have only begun to pay out this money since the Richert lawsuit was filed in 2005. And that amount, being roughly 7%, means the whole amount was close to one billion dollars for WGA -- and non-WGA -- writers, as the union collected whether writers were union or not.

SAG actors could be owed much much more.

-- W. R.

Your Hoor should be informed that there is a trial going on in your courtoom but it has no judge or jury, only the a mob is just another name for group, or gang, or gathering, or union.

at times

while pondering the most recent statement by thw WGA regarding our settlement in the foreign levy class action case RICHERT V. WGAw et. al. I have done some investigation and made a starling discovery that I believe points a lazer-like beam to the center of the lawsuit, revealing a scam, a scheme, a hoax and a fraud in the heart of the case.

Congray to your admonishing from the bench that WGA Exeuctive Director David Young (not named) aginst using the WGA website to claim that the settlement absolved the WGA of any wrongdoing, and gave legal cover to any kind of embezzelemnt of writer's funds in the past decades.

David Young and Emma Leheny are fond of compaing their roles with the Writer's Guild as union protagonists furthering the rights of writers as they wuld further the rights of laundry workers. Well, some writers may do their own laundry, but they are not launderers.

If you squint just one eye and look at the whole thing stretching back from checks given to named Plaintiff's in thi very case dating from 1947, the scope of the theft of billions of "foreign roylaties" that reached their final destination in studio=union secret splits, the sope of the firieng levy swindle is breathtaking, and at this moment, even during this moment, they continue to get agway with it.

It has been six months (time flies) since I sat in your courtroom and listend to Tony Segall vow that the WGA was near=desperate in its desire to fulfill its obligations) obligations it gave itself) to send the millions owed to writers union and non union.

Your honor, also be advised that I do not think that the distortion of my role in this lawsuit is the intent of the false information the WGA. Bill Richert the lone writer is surely unworthy of the massive collusive mendacious effort within the hall's walls lhat led to a distortion on the official WGA website, where Richert learned, as writers sometimes discover in Stalinist states, that his role has been "downgraded."

SCARE THE WRITERS, KILL THE CULTURE

I'ts not me John Wells wants to frighten, it's the others in the union who might oppose his policiesand the policys of David Young which led to a tinycadre of unin leaders to corral an entire industry within their own controlable circle, no mater how many thousands of others were shut out.

Pretending to work for the fragile free-lance writers -- which most writers are, union or not -- while disrupting the flow of production funds giving only the largest entities --

hundred million plus producers like John Wells and studios like those run by Alan Horn -- makes the rich richer.

Presently I fugrue the WGA has absconded irht or divert to their "general fund" or the studios as much as a hundred thousandd dollars. The amount SAG has withheld from its members is staggering, and apparently, there never even was an actual foreign levies account, as signed by Robert Pisano in 2005.

Millions of dollars meant for actors have gone into the same wormhole as the millions meant for writers, although according to whistle blower Teri Mial, the WGA kept better records.

The role of Lead Plaintiff in a class actin lawsuit, as I understand by reading the text of the 105th Congress, and knowing how a layman's reading of legal lingo is often not well taken in court, it is still plain to me that a Lead Plaintiff's investigative duty remains in force until the settlement, if any, is fulfilled in all its terms.

Your honor, I ask that the settlement RICHERT VS. WGAw et. al. be set aside, and that truly independent auditors -- taht is, chosen neighter by the lawyers for the Plaitiff or the Lawyers for the Defendants, who I have alwfays said are in come kind of cahoots with each other -- be chosen by the court.

How many lies make a liar? How many years of stonewalling before union accountants and bank statements readers tell what's up with foreign royalties for US authors and screenwriters.

In a sense, there is nothing less mysterious than a leger. There are ghost writers but not ghost checks that can be cashed.

The WGA knows the names of the writers these moneys were intended for and they knowthe amounts and causing a 7 year lawsuit based on willful misreprestnation of facts about class plaintiffs union standing so as to first mislead the courts and second to disparage the settlement of this lawsuit to resemble the disgrutnled demands of a "hack" as described by Aaron Sorkin in a manner to suggest mediocrity, not the determination of a writer to hack his way to the truth, the source of all good writing.

I ask that thesettlment RICHERT VS. WGAw et. al. because of an ongoing organized publicised campaign to discredit the lead plaintiff, William Richert, by either calling him a "former member" in their current revisionst official publication, or by calling William Richert a "non member" by firtue of his calling John Wells, Carl Gotlieb, Sally Burmester and others "bums" in 1995.

The present union officers and accountants and their minions have shown themselves incorribale, and, in a phrase Aaron Sorkin copied from a naval courtroom transcript, they "can't handle the truth." Sorkin seems especially jealous professionally of my near-perfect role as a total outsider-insider .

Your honor, the truth, at least part of it with more to me, is seeking protection and vocalaztion and outright payment due within the walls of lyour courtroom.

It would be bad for the people, we the people, if the source of so much wisdom and enlightening entertainment as listed in the now-secret rosters at the WGA should remain in thrall to mean spritied and collusive individuals, willing to use vast resources to hide facts and disparageone of their own -- me -- though I am not really one of them in almost any essential way.

I am however lead Plaintiff and Class Champion, and I am in hot pursuit of my duties.

September 26 2006

YOU ASKED FOR MY COMMENTS

Dear Neville,

We know each other too well for me to withhold my frank opinion on the settlement of Richert v. WGA.

It reads like a sell out, not a settlement. We started out a year ago, in September 2005, accusing executives and accountants at the WGA union hall of 5 continuing crimes, including fraud, and now we're offering to settle by helping them adjust their accounting procedures.

Who benefits from such an agreement?

In fact, more than one person at the WGA refused to distribute fifty-per cent (50%) of the money due to writers from foreign levies and they did this for a period of many years, in secret, and even now in this settlement the WGA does not intend to reveal where this money went, the amount of this money, and whether current guild leadership, like Patric Verrone, who signed checks during this time frame, was part of any scheme to keep foreign levies from infirm writers not able to trace what was due to them, or the widows and children of dead writers.

DEAD WRITERS DON'T PAY DUES

Our lawsuit was begun almost one year ago to this very day, and yet you've written to me via email several times that "nothing was written" during this entire year.

Now you send a settlement offer. How can you possibly settle the charge of accounting fraud without an accounting?

How can you let go free executives involved in fraudulent accounting without identifying them, and their positions? We knew Lay and Skilling, how about investigating Varrone and Tony Segal? That's what class action lawsuits are for: seeking justice.

This isn't a settlement; it's a cover up.

It was publicly reported in Variety that there was a witness to the foreign levy fraud. Why haven't we deposed this witness? I have heard that she was fired by Tony Segal at the WGA for threatening to murder her assistant. This seventy year old loyal employee has information she says is vital to our case, but nobody has questioned her. Why not?

Maybe you've tried to save the union money by avoiding depositions, which are expensive. But Tony Segal admits the WGA did not pay at least $20,000,000 to its deserving members and their heirs out of $40,000,000 it claims to have collected for them.

Twenty million to hungry writers is a lot of dough. Who kept it from them? Don't we all deserve to know?

Also, how much is this lawsuit costing Guild members? Are we paying union lawyer Tony Segal to withhold information from membership and protect corrupt executives? Will guild money be used to pay your fees and court expenses, thus damaging us even more?

How much is this lawsuit costing writers? Who at the top at the Guild is involved in this Federal case, and what actions have they taken to save themselves at the expense of truth and to avoid jail time?

There are no persons at the Guild who have been asked these questions. There "is nothing written," you say.

More potently: I have been informed that this $20m amount is just the tip of the huge sums concealed and diverted to the wrong people. Hundreds of millions may have been collected for US writers during decades of showing their films overseas, as mandated by laws abroad to protect authors and writers. And I am not the only one informed of this. It was in the papers! -- Yet no questions were asked in writing?

Without informing membership, executives at the WGA dispersed this huge amount of cash to others, using secret Guild agreements between studios and collecting agencies. Records were trashed or burned.

Now Neville, if I know about this, in my limited circle of friends and acquaintances, and if it's been in Variety, why is it not part of our lawsuit?

During the course of an entire year, how it is possible that you did not depose a single person or employee at the WGA regarding these questions, or any issue at all?

And why are you settling with WGA President Patric Varrone's lead attorney, Tony Segal, so as to join with him in some new "dispute resolution process"? Apparently you would set this up in partnership with the WGA, who we're suing for Fraud & Unjust Enrichment -- and with Tony Segal's WGA Officers agreeing -- magnanimously, apparently -- not to keep any interest in moneys collected.

Like the burglars agreeing not to keep the Rolex.

If money was collected by the WGA outside its mandate and outside the law, they damn well ought to pay it back to the WGA members they hid it from, and they don't need three years to do it, they should dedicate a laptop computer and do it today. And they damn well ought to be held accountable for each and every dollar, and the names of those executives or employees of the WGA who withheld 50% or ONE-HALF of all the member's money should be made known immediately to union members, who have legal rights to this information and knowledge, not to mention the money that belongs to them.

The stated purpose of our class action lawsuit was to reveal, not conceal. In this settlement the WGA will retain all its records and all its information; we will never know what happened or who did it, and so the perpetrators will continue in power.

Guilty or not, Patric Varrone is running around passing out blood red t-shirts and disrupting the flow of business to working writers; using incendiary threatening teamster-style organization tactics, hoping to sign up the non-writers who took the original WGA writer's jobs, while Varrone was an officer at the union.

Patric Varrone was Secretary-Treasurer of the Guild for four years. I'll bet he knows where the money went. He signed the checks. Why has he not been deposed? Shouldn't he be first?

If he also uses the old crony-style accounting methods, protected by mob-style lawyers, with secret agreements and bank accounts, then any settlement has to be a true correct and lawful settlement, with penalties and full public disclosure, and investigation of participants in court depositions, with their identities revealed.

This was the point of our lawsuit for: (1) Conversion (2) Unjust enrichment (3) Accounting (4) Fraud (5) Violation of Business and Professions code.

If these charges are false, should not Segal and Varrone and the Guild be suing us? And if a single count of our accusations is true, why is there no mention or admission of it in the settlement? No list of those involved. Are there no humans in the WGA headquarters with a name or title?

It is as if the reason we went to court has been erased, like footprints in the sand. Were we just kidding the WGA? Were we just trying to torment or bait our Union Leaders and their mouthpiece, Tony Segal?

On the whole, I think that writers have good memories, even when the evidence is washed away. Writers want the whole story, when available. And this story is available.

Remember, the same Varrone who signed the checks at the WGA is now the president of the union. He is accountable for the actions of his underlings, and first in accountability to dues-paying members.

Patric Varrone -- Tony Segal's boss -- has a sworn obligation to the membership in regard to protection of authorship rights and money.

If through concealment or conspiracy or gross ineptitude, writers living or dead were denied rights to their earnings by any person at the guild, this must be made known to the entire membership. It means that union leaders have not protected the writers, they have betrayed them.

If any officers of the Guild have attempted to conceal information, intimidate witnesses or make false accusations, then their activities are also of concern to the Department of Labor, as reported in Variety, among other government enforcement agencies.

I cannot believe that you have spent one year on this case, as voluble and articulate as you are, in face to face meetings and telephone conversations with your opposite Tony Segal, along with his assistants and your assistants, and yet when I've asked to see accountings or documents you say that "nothing is written."

This is a preposterous admission, and while it may not be against the law, it seems to break the natural law of lawyers in negotiations over millions of dollars during hundreds of years of recorded legal history.

RICHERT V. WGA, a year-long case involving thousands of writers, computers full of numbers, union officials with knowledge and accountability for decades of money collected for members and not disbursed; a case with industry wide interest and import, affecting widows and orphans, which has been conducted in a Federal class action lawsuit but "nothing is written."

In politics, when "nothing is written" it usually means plenty is hidden.

As lead Plaintiff in RICHERT V. WGA, it seems to me that this very settlement, offered by Tony Segal and proposed by you, is itself evidence of fraud; a pox on the writers of the WGA from their own executive leadership and, a sell-out of the rights of the Plaintiffs should the Plaintiffs agree to it.

Therefore, there can be no settlement as yet.

Sincerely,

William Richert
Lead Plaintiff, Richert v. WGA

W.G.A.
The Levity of
Sir William
with
pen and
sword

www.ingramcontent.com/pod-product-compliance
Lightning Source LLC
LaVergne TN
LVHW080320110826
845155LV00026B/166
* 9 7 8 1 9 5 1 0 3 6 5 2 2 *